ROUTLEDGE LIBRARY EDITIONS: BRITISH SOCIOLOGICAL ASSOCIATION

Volume 17

RETHINKING SOCIAL INEQUALITY

RETHINKING SOCIAL INEQUALITY

Edited by
DAVID ROBBINS
with
LESLEY CALDWELL, GRAHAM DAY,
KAREN JONES AND HILARY ROSE

LONDON AND NEW YORK

First published in 1982 by Gower Publishing Company Limited

This edition first published in 2018
by Routledge
2 Park Square, Milton Park, Abingdon, Oxon OX14 4RN

and by Routledge
711 Third Avenue, New York, NY 10017

Routledge is an imprint of the Taylor & Francis Group, an informa business

© 1982 British Sociological Association

All rights reserved. No part of this book may be reprinted or reproduced or utilised in any form or by any electronic, mechanical, or other means, now known or hereafter invented, including photocopying and recording, or in any information storage or retrieval system, without permission in writing from the publishers.

Trademark notice: Product or corporate names may be trademarks or registered trademarks, and are used only for identification and explanation without intent to infringe.

British Library Cataloguing in Publication Data
A catalogue record for this book is available from the British Library

ISBN: 978-1-138-49942-3 (Set)
ISBN: 978-1-351-01463-2 (Set) (ebk)
ISBN: 978-1-138-47731-5 (Volume 17) (hbk)
ISBN: 978-1-138-47734-6 (Volume 17) (pbk)
ISBN: 978-1-351-10508-8 (Volume 17) (ebk)

Publisher's Note
The publisher has gone to great lengths to ensure the quality of this reprint but points out that some imperfections in the original copies may be apparent.

Disclaimer
The publisher has made every effort to trace copyright holders and would welcome correspondence from those they have been unable to trace.

Rethinking Social Inequality

Edited by
DAVID ROBBINS
The University College of Wales, Aberystwyth
with
LESLEY CALDWELL, GRAHAM DAY,
KAREN JONES and HILARY ROSE

Gower

© British Sociological Association, 1982

All rights reserved. No part of this publication may be reproduced, stored in a retrieval system or transmitted in any form or by any means, electronic, mechanical, photocopying, recording, or otherwise, without the prior permission of Gower Publishing Company Limited.

Published by
Gower Publishing Company Limited,
Gower House, Croft Road, Aldershot, Hampshire, England

British Library Cataloguing in Publication Data

Rethinking social inequality
  1. Equality
  I. Robbins, David
  305 (expanded)   HM146

  ISBN 0-566-00557-3

Printed and Bound in Great Britain by
Robert Hartnoll Limited, Bodmin, Cornwall.

Contents

Acknowledgements	vii
1. Introduction: Rethinking Inequality	1
2. White Sociology, Black Struggle Val Amos, Paul Gilroy and Errol Lawrence	15

3. Female Manual Workers, Fatalism and
   the Reinforcement of Inequalities
   Kate Purcell
	43

4. The Generation Game: Playing by the Rules John Fitz and John Hood-Williams	65

5. Aging and Inequality: Consumer Culture
   and the New Middle Age
   Mike Featherstone and Mike Hepworth
	97

6. Egalitarianism and Social Inequality in Scotland
   David McCrone, Frank Bechhofer and
   Stephen Kendrick
	127

7. Inequality of Access to Political Television:
   The Case of the General Election of 1979
   Alan Clarke, Ian Taylor and Justin Wren-Lewis
	149

8. Classes, Class Fractions and Monetarism Kevin Bonnett	185
9. Moral Economy and the Welfare State Roger A. Cloward and Frances Fox Piven	213

10. Towards a Celebration of Difference(s): Notes
    for a sociology of a possible everyday future
    Philip Corrigan
	241

Acknowledgements

We would like to acknowledge the enormous assistance given to us by Anne Dix and Mike Milotte in the preparation of this volume and in the organisation of the BSA 1981 Conference on Inequality which gave rise to it. We would also like to thank all those who contributed to the conference and those students at the University College of Wales, Aberystwyth who helped to run it. Finally, we would like to thank Adrienne Lee and Jane Watts for their good-humoured and efficient efforts in typing barely readable manuscripts, often at short notice.

Lesley Caldwell
Graham Day
Karen Jones
David Robbins
Hilary Rose

March 1982

1 Introduction: Rethinking Inequality

The study of inequality has been a central project of sociological enquiry, past and present, to the extent that it does not so much constitute an area or specialty within sociology as the very stuff of the subject itself. In British sociology this engagement with the issue of inequality has taken a particular form. The investigations of late-nineteenth century poverty by Rowntree and Booth established a research tradition whose influence has persisted until the present day (Booth, 1903; Rowntree, 1901). The periodic rediscovery of poverty and deprivation in welfare state Britain (Titmuss, 1958, 1960; Coates and Silburn, 1973; Townsend, 1979; Field, 1978, 1980) builds on the tradition of the nineteenth century pioneers.

Given that the political contexts in which the tradition emerged and developed were characterised by class conflict and compromise, it is hardly surprising that it focussed primarily on the inequalities of class and that the deprivations of the working class were its most characteristic object of study. The emphasis on class did not, however, exclude a concern with the position of other disadvantaged groups: women, children and the old (Land, 1969; Piachaud, 1979; Townsend, 1963; Wedderburn, 1968).

It was not so much its subject matter which distinguished research in this tradition as the way in which inequality was conceptualised and studied. The style of the research was characterised by certain distinctive features which must be understood in relation to its methodological orientation and the political contexts in which it developed.

In the first place the 'British tradition' has been predominantly concerned with particular aspects of inequality; those of income, educational achievement and, to a lesser extent, wealth. This can be partly explained in terms of a political concern to monitor the workings of a welfare state established to contain the mobilisation of radical sentiment prior to and during the Second World War. The post-war political context was predominantly social democratic, in that the redistribution of income and wealth by the welfare state was seen as the remedy for class inequality. This was consistent with a sociological tendency to define 'classes' as clusters of manual and nonmanual occupations distinguished primarily by the extent to which they possessed these resources. A related political emphasis saw increased social mobility through educational reform as an important means of breaking down 'the barriers of class' in British society (Fenwick, 1976; CCCS, 1981). In both cases there was a congruence between prevailing political concerns and the aspects of inequality highlighted by contemporary sociology.

Important as these influences were, it seems likely that the focus on income and educational achievement was also the result of the methodological orientation of mainstream British sociology. Positivist orthodoxy required that social life be described in terms of sets of variables that could be operationalised and measured empirically. The distribution of income and educational achievement fitted this methodological bill to perfection. In contrast, aspects of inequality which were not readily amenable to quantitative measurement tended to disappear from view. The perspective was, by its nature, silent on the distribution of economic and political power and on issues of cultural and legal domination and subordination.

The distinctive character of the 'British tradition' is not confined to its concentration on particular aspects of inequality but extends to the way in which these inequalities are conceptualised in <u>distributional</u> terms. The empiricist inclinations of the studies implied not only the focus on empirically measurable types of inequality but also the operational definition of the categories across which such inequality varied. Social classes disappeared behind the terminology of 'income brackets' and 'quartiles', or at best, were treated as aggregates of occupations. As a result inequality was conceptualised as the differential distribution of desirable goods (e.g. money, educational qualifications) between more or less arbitrarily defined categories. There was a tendency to lose sight of the fact that inequality is inherently <u>relational</u>: the deprivation and powerlessness of one group following as the necessary consequence of the endowment and power of another. Also lost was an appreciation of the extent to which these relations of inequality are the axes of continuing conflict and change.

These shortcomings are reflected even in that work in the 'British tradition' which recognises that inequality is the expression of a social relation as well as a pattern of distribution. Townsend's thesis that poverty is both socially relative and objectively definable (Townsend, 1979, 1981) is instructive in this respect. He argues that the minimum requirements of normal social life are consensually defined in a society at a particular time and that the poor are those members of society who possess insufficient resources to maintain this minimum level of social commitment. Critics have questioned whether a clear-cut definition of 'normal social life' exists and, if it does, whether participation in it is abruptly terminated below a given level of resources (Piachaud, 1981). More fundamentally, however, Townsend's reliance on social consensus precludes any sustained consideration of poverty and inequality as the outcome of relations between social groups: relations characterised by conflicts of interests and the unequal distribution of economic and political power. Townsend's victims are poor in relation to 'society's standards' rather than in relation to powerful and privileged groups who are able to realise their interests at the expense of those of the poor.

In summary, we suggest that the characteristic features of the 'British tradition', both substantive and conceptual, can be understood in relation to an empiricist methodology and a concern with an essentially social democratic politics of redistribution. This is not to deny the continuing vitality of work in this tradition or the potentially radical implications of its findings. The conclusions of any genuinely empirical study are not predetermined by the theoretical foundations upon which it is constructed. This accounts for the apparently paradoxical consequences of this research, which, through its 'rediscovery' of poverty and the exposure of continuing inequalities in educational achievement, has been crucial in undermining Fabian political strategy and social democratic theorising.

This brief characterisation of an influential tradition of research has been offered in order to provide a background against which the contributions to this volume may be usefully appraised. Their diversity indicates that sociologists are studying new aspects of inequality in new ways. The established tradition is being challenged by new approaches which reflect the changes that sociology has undergone in the last fifteen years - the abandonment of the hegemony of functionalist theory and positivist methodology in favour of a proliferation of 'perspectives' and, crucially, a closer engagement with the continental tradition of Marxist analysis. The work on inequality in this volume also reflects the appearance on the political scene of new and non-class based political movements.

Conceptually, the most obvious theme that unites the papers is the rejection of a distributional notion of inequality in favour of a relational one. The paradigmatic object of study is not the deprived social group but the unequal social relation, manifested in a variety of forms.

The range of subject matter covered by the papers indicates the way in which a long-standing concern with class-based inequality is being complemented by a renewed emphasis on inequalities associated with race, gender and age. This emphasis is represented by Amos, Gilroy and Lawrence's critique of the sociology of race relations, by Purcell's investigation of women workers and by Fitz and Hood-Williams' analysis of the subordination of wives and minors within the family. For all these authors the determinations of class remain crucially important. Given that most of the contributions to this volume reflect, directly or indirectly, the revival of interest in Marxist analysis, it could hardly be otherwise. What does characterise the above contributions, however, is a sensitivity to the way in which the determinations of class are cross-cut, in a complex way, by those of race, age and gender. Indeed these authors are explicitly critical of those accounts in which the determinations of race, age and gender are simply reduced to those of class and, as a result, vanish from sight. This criticism cnn be levelled against recent empirical studies of educational achievement, occupation and social mobility (Halsey, Ridge and Heath, 1980; Goldthorpe, 1980) in which 'methodological' constraints appear to have dictated the exclusion of any consideration of women. As Amos, Gilroy and Lawrence note, this criticism can also be extended to much work in the Marxist tradition in which an overriding concern with class causes the specificity of racial, sexual and familial subordination to be ignored.

This sensitivity to the inequalities associated with race, gender and age reflects political developments in the 1970s. This is exemplified by Amos, Gilroy and Lawrence's critique of the substantial body of sociological literature concerned with the issues of 'integration' and the 'race relations problem' (Zubaida, 1970). One of the consequences of accelerating economic decline has been the precipitation of a crisis of policing in the inner cities. The rhetoric of 'integration' has been replaced by that of 'law and order' as the state has sought to maintain its control over black communities. Out of the escalating confrontation between police and blacks emerged a distinctive politics of black resistance and it is from this perspective that the authors mount their attack on the theoretical and methodological assumptions that underpin much sociological research on race relations. The need for a relational approach to racial inequality is forcefully argued. They insist that the problems of black communities should not be explained in terms of the peculiarities of black cultures and family structures but in terms of the complex of social relations that locks those communities into a position of subordination in capitalist societies characterised by institutionalised racism.

The influence of contemporary political developments is also reflected in the increasing sociological concern with inequalities related to gender. The resurgence of feminism in the 1970s entailed a critique of established forms of both social democratic and socialist politics. Not only had social democratic reform exhausted its repertoire without substantially affecting the continued subordination of women but, it was felt, the politics of the socialist left was organised in such a way as to marginalise the issue and to deny the specificity of women's experience (Rowbotham, Segal and Wainwright, 1979). Consequently there emerged an independent sexual politics which not only subjected social democratic and socialist politics to critical scrutiny but

4

also extended its critique to the academic discourses that underpinned them. Given sociology's extended silence on questions of gender, its sexism was quickly exposed and influentially criticised (Rowbotham, 1973; Jones, 1973). The result was the initiation of work, often by feminists themselves, which sought to write women and gender relations back into the theory and practice of the discipline (Roberts, 1981).

These developments are reflected in Kate Purcell's sensitive ethnographic study of the way in which female manual workers experience inequality. She relates the 'passivity' of these women to a culture of 'fatalism' which provides the medium through which their everyday experience is interpreted. Although the attitudes, beliefs and life-style of the women workers provide the main focus of her study, Purcell makes it clear that their 'fatalism' is grounded in the social relations that define the subordin-ate position of women in both the workplace and the family. It is not the cause of women's subordination but a learned response to it and, as such, can be unlearned.

The impact of the women's movement has also been re-flected in a substantial and continuing revision of received sociological wisdom concerning the family. Despite Engels' early contribution (Engels, 1884) there has, until recently, been a tendency for marxists to neglect the family and familial relations, presumably as a result of an over-riding concern with class relations. (1) Noting this, Fitz and Hood-Williams echo recent feminist work (Barker and Allen, 1976; Beechey, 1979) in insisting that the subordin-ation of wives and minors is not simply a function of the class position of the male family head but is also deter-mined by the patriarchal relations that prevail within the family. They develop this theme through an examination of the disjunction between familial and capitalist production, as witnessed by the diverse legal forms in which property is owned and transmitted within these two spheres. Familial property relations are diachronic, occur between legally (and usually biologically) related groups of agents and are mediated through mechanisms of inheritance and settlement. In contrast, capitalist property relations are synchronic, take place between formally free and substitutable agents, through free alienation via the law of contract. The nature of familial property relations in England at different historical conjunctures is examined through a study of the legal rules of inheritance, which specify the socially approved family form. Although the rules have changed over time and in relation to capitalist development they have, until recently, specified family relations of firmly patri-archal type. The present legal equivalence of husband and wife in the rules governing diachronic transmission merely indicates the increased importance of synchronic trans-mission in the reproduction of patriarchal family relations, a development resulting from the imposition of death duties.

Again the relational nature of inequality is stressed. The

dependency of wives and minors is the necessary consequence of the legally sanctioned dominance of the male family head. This treatment of age relations in the context of the family contrasts starkly with most existing sociological literature, which tends to categorise 'youth' and 'the old' as distinctive groups which constitute 'social problems'. The increasingly violent resistance of working class youth to social control has provoked the attention of sociologists of education, deviance and culture (Willis, 1976; Cohen, 1972; Hall and Jefferson, 1976) while 'the old' have by and large, remained the subject of research oriented to social policy (Townsend, 1963, 1973). Despite the increasing interest in inequalities associated with age, systematic study of age relations remains sparse.

Recent sociological work is not only distinguished by a relational conception of inequality but also by an emphasis on the cultural, ideological and political dimensions of domination and subordination. These are issues upon which the 'British tradition' has been largely silent, except in its tendency, criticised by Amos, Gilroy and Lawrence, to invoke the cultural peculiarities of a group to 'explain' its deprivation. A concern with the cultural dimensions of inequality is exhibited by a number of the contributions and must be viewed in relation to the general movement in recent British sociology towards an engagement with the issue of culture. This movement was given impetus by the writings of E.P. Thompson and Raymond Williams and has been theoretically reinforced by the assimilation of continental work, notably that of Althusser, Gramsci and the Frankfurt School.

Essentially these developments entail a critique of the approach to culture adopted by much marxist analysis and by the 'sociology of knowledge' tradition, in which the focus is upon cultural objects: typically, systems of knowledge and belief, or artistic creations of various types. The characteristics of these cultural artefacts are explained in relation to a social order constituted 'outside' culture, defined in terms of a particular set of economic and political relations. Recently this reductive approach has come under increasing criticism and substantial revisions have been proposed. These involve a shift of emphasis from cultural objects towards the 'cultural practices' or 'cultural production' through which such products are created. Although 'cultural production' refers, in the first instance, to 'artistic and intellectual activities', this definition is extended to include 'all the signifying practices - from language, through the arts and philosophy, to journalism, fashion and advertising' (Williams, 1980, p.13). The materiality of cultural production is also emphasised: cultural production utilises particular means of production to create products which are both material and cultural objects.

Adopting this approach implies that forms of cultural production are not simply derivative of a pre-given social order; rather, they are crucially involved in the constitution of that order. Effectively, all social practices are cultural practices in that 'signifying systems' are implicated in them, providing the means through which a social order is 'communicated, reproduced, experienced and explored' (ibid.). At the same time a distinction is usually retained between social practices in general and practices which are manifestly cultural in that their primary object is the production and distribution of representations: conceptions and images of the world inscribed in 'texts' of all kinds - written, visual and aural (CCCS, 1981, pp.27-8).

This reorientation is the subject of continuing debate and its implications have, as yet, been only partially absorbed into the mainstream of sociological work. Nevertheless, some of the contributions can be usefully read in relation to the general tendencies implied by these innovations: the broadening of the concept of culture to include a whole range of commodities and practices, and the treatment of culture as constitutive of economic and political processes. In Purcell's contribution, for example, 'fatalism' refers to both the beliefs and practices of women workers and both interprets and constitutes the unequal social relations in which they are implicated. It is, however, Featherstone and Hepworth's discussion of 'consumer culture' and the 'new middle age' that most closely mirrors the concerns of the new sociology of culture. The interest of this contribution lies in its emphasis on the role that culture and cultural change plays in the constitution and transformation of inequalities. They argue that the celebration of youthful bodily stereotypes by 'consumer culture' in the advanced capitalist societies opens up new inequalities not just between different age groups, but also between the sexes and between different classes. These stereotypes pose social and psychological problems for the middle aged and are particularly hard on middle aged women. Such problems are compounded for members of the working class who are less likely to have access to the means of maintaining a youthful bodily appearance.

Featherstone and Hepworth's discussion of 'consumerism' and its implications for the imagery of age also exemplifies the broadened conception of culture favoured by recent sociological analysis. 'Consumerism' does not refer to a discrete belief system, but rather to the changing complex of meanings attached to and signified by commodities and their consumption.

In contrast, McCrone, Bechhofer and Kendrick tend towards a more traditional approach to cultural analysis. They are concerned with a particular cultural representation (in their terms 'a myth'): that of the inherent egalitarianism of the Scot. Although this myth is situated historically as the product of specific forms of academic and literary production and although it may be used to legitimate the inequalities that prevail in Scottish society, they emphasise that, of itself, the 'myth' carries no fixed ideological message. In an argument that echoes Barry Barnes' demonstration of the contradictory ideological purposes to which the belief that 'all individuals are born equally endowed with talents and abilities' may be put (Barnes, 1974), they argue that the myth of egalitarianism is cultural raw material that can be worked into a variety of ideological schemes, radical or conservative.

This highlights an issue at the heart of contemporary debates around culture: the relation between the concepts of 'ideology' and 'culture'. In some accounts (Althusser, 1971) the concept of ideology has been extended to the point where, as Williams warns, it is in danger of 'repeating the history of "culture" as a concept' (Williams, op.cit, p.28). McCrone, Bechhofer and Kendrick's contribution indicates the need to restrict the designation 'ideological' to particular cultural representations and their production, in a way which retains the concept's explicitly critical reference (Larrain, 1979). Ideologies, it may be suggested, are systems of representation which are elaborated in such a way as to serve the interests of social groups by legitim- ating, naturalising or rationalising certain social rela- tionships and practices. The concept implies a specifically contextual reference. The ideological significance of representations is not 'fixed' in the representations them- selves but lies in the meaning that they acquire when de- ployed in particular ways in concrete social contexts.

In contrast to the general cultural concerns of the con- tributions discussed above, Bonnett, and Clarke, Taylor and Wren-Lewis, are concerned with ideology in this restricted sense, specifically, that of the new Right in contemporary Britain. The rise of monetarist ideology with its attendant anti-union and 'law and order' themes marks a significant break with the repertoire of consensus, corporatism and technocracy that has been most characteristic of the poli- tics of social democracy in postwar Britain. The emergence of a political ideology which, in the name of 'improving incentives', requires British society to become increasingly unequal calls for a considered and critical response by sociologists.

Clarke, Taylor and Wren-Lewis analyse the coverage of the 1979 British General Election and, in particular, the way in which that coverage aided the ideological offensive of the Conservative Party. They conclude, firstly, that the coverage was organised entirely in terms of Parliamentary politics, to the exclusion of women's issues or the problems of the black community. Secondly, they demonstrate that despite the formal balance maintained between the coverage given to the two main parties, issues were defined and discussed in terms dictated by the Right.

The analysis suggests that the presentation of the election and its issues was mediated through the conventions of a 'discursive formation' predicated upon the cultural and professional practices of television journalism. It is argued that these practices contribute to an inequality in the power to define political issues which systematically disadvantages the minor parties and extra-parliamentary groups and which, at least in 1979, disadvantaged the Labour Party and the Left. In these respects the paper reflects the concerns of contemporary cultural analysis in that it moves some way towards an exploration of the relationship between ideological representations and their mode of production. It also points to ways in which the analysis could be extended and developed by further investigation of the relationship between the conventions of television journalism and the social and technical relations of television production and by an examination of the ways in which these conventions structure the visual as well as the discursive dimensions of political coverage.

Bonnett's contribution usefully complements that of Clarke, Taylor and Wren-Lewis. His discussion is less concerned with the popular presentation of the ideology of the new Right, than with the relationship between the rise of monetarism and the political and economic context of Britain in the 1970s. This implies a more 'conventional' approach to ideological analysis which centres on the relationship between the nature of ideological representations and structurally defined interests of classes, class fractions and other social groups. While acknowledging the typical complexity of such relationships, Bonnett examines the nature and success of monetarist ideology in relation to the interests and political effectiveness of different fractions of British capital. A congruence between monetarism and the interests of finance capital is argued and substantiated through a study of the role of the intellectual representatives of the City in prosecuting the ideological and political campaign for monetarist policies.

This focus on the current situation draws attention to the crucial role that political processes play in the structuring and restructuring of unequal social relations. Prevailing patterns of inequality are not merely the product of economic relations, they are also the consequences of state policies, which, arising out of the temporary resolution of political conflicts, are continually contested. In its engagement with these issues Bonnett's contribution reflects the influence of important debates within the Marxist tradition over the state, political power, and social classes and class fractions (Holloway and Piciotto, 1977; Wright, 1978; Urry, 1981). While some positions in these debates relate state action to a general logic of capitalist development, rendering it necessarily functional for capital, others emphasise the autonomy of the political and the contradictory consequences of state interventions

Bonnett inclines towards the latter view. He notes the difficulties in imputing objectively definable interests to particular fractions of capital (let alone capital-in-general) and questions the capacities of different fractions to frame and promote political programmes that yield results that will actually serve their interests. In the British case the economic position of finance capital may have been a necessary condition for the success of the monetarist campaign but it was not a sufficient one. The political organisation and ideological effectiveness of the representatives of finance capital and their allies were also crucially important. However, the hegemony of monetarism is unlikely to be long continued. The effects of monetarist policies are inimical to the interests of many manufacturing capitals and deepening recession will ultimately threaten important aspects of the City's own activities. In this situation, monetarist ideology and policy is vulnerable to new initiatives.

Similar themes, but in relation to popular struggles, are taken up by Piven and Cloward's analysis of the current situation in the USA. In their discussion of the economic and political consequences of American unemployment benefit programmes they take issue with sociologically functionalist and politically pessimistic arguments that welfare provision unproblematically serves the interests of capital by defusing popular protests and discontents. Although such concessions may serve the interests of political elites by safeguarding electoral majorities, they ultimately act against the interests of capital by decreasing the effectiveness of unemployment as a means of checking workplace militancy and holding down wages, hence the current political and ideological offensive against them. Moreover the consequences of such policies are not confined to the economic level, but include the creation of a new political consensus in which the state is held to be responsible for economic management and the provision of welfare. In this situation campaigns by representatives of capital to reverse welfare policies are likely to encounter popular resistance, opening up new possibilities for the political mobilisation of labour. The state becomes the site of conflict between the contending forces of capital and popular political movements, conflicts whose outcomes cannot be straight-forwardly read off from the economic dominance of capital but also depend on a complex of specifically political factors.

In summary, it is clear that recent work is moving beyond narrowly economic definitions of inequality to examine its legal, cultural, ideological and political determinants and consequences. In doing so it reflects certain well-defined developments in sociological theory and practice over the last decade. These other dimensions of inequality cannot, ultimately, be understood independently of 'economic' inequalities but neither can they be treated as the unmediated consequences of them. Also, as argued earlier, this is accompanied by a related shift from a distributional to a relational conception of inequality which, in ruling out 'blame the victim' strategies, has implications for the explanation of inequality.

At one level, these shifts are the result of the methodological re-orientation that has characterised much recent

10

sociology. The distributional concept of inequality was rooted in the methodology of survey work. In contrast the methodological orientation of work in this volume is significantly related to the influence of conflict theories, which necessarily emphasise the relational nature of inequality. This is particularly true of marxist analysis in which, paradigmatically, the subordinate position of one class or class fraction is the necessary condition of the advantaged position of another.

At another level, the work in the volume reflects the changing political context of the 1970s. As argued earlier, there is a resonance between a distributional conception of inequality in sociology and the concerns of a social democratic politics of redistribution and social mobility. In the same way, there is a correspondence between a relational conception of inequality, with its emphasis on inequalities as axes of conflict and struggle, and the sharpening political conflicts of the 1970s. Similarly, sociological emphasis on the cultural and ideological dimensions of inequality reflects the fact that the new politics of sex, ethnicity and age is pre-eminently a cultural politics.

There is, then, an important sense in which the implications of different conceptions of inequality are not confined to the choice of methodologies for academic work, but reach into the realms of political strategy. The political implications of the work in this volume point in quite other directions than those indicated by the 'British tradition'. A relational conceptualisation of inequality implies that progress towards greater equality entails transforming the complex of economic, cultural, familial, sexual, racial and political relations through which inequalities are constituted.

This question of the political implications of new ways of theorising inequality is addressed in the final paper, Corrigan's discussion of 'differences'. He points to the dangers in the kinds of theorising and political practice which attempt to <u>erase</u> differences, because they can only be conceptualised in terms of disadvantage. If differences constitute the basis of hierarchies an obvious tactic is to minimise or erase them, claiming, for example, that women are 'just as good' as men or that blacks are 'no different from' whites. Subject to this approach the politics of equality becomes the politics of uniformity. Corrigan's plea is for new kinds of analysis which account for differences without conceptualising them as departures from the norm - the metropolitan, the white, the male, the young - and for a politics which sensitively takes account of differences of historical experience, material situation and 'culture', seeing them as a source of strength, not as a problem to be minimised and overcome. It is a plea that speaks directly to the questions raised by a whole range of contemporary political struggles, most obviously those of women, of racial communities in the cities and of culturally distinct groups in the 'peripheral' areas of Europe. As such it

11

clearly demonstrates the political relevance of the
sociological rethinking of inequality exemplified by the
work in this book.

NOTE

(1) For an important exception see Dennis, Henriques and
Slaughter, 1976.

REFERENCES

Althusser, L, (tr. 1971), Lenin and Philosophy, New Left Books.
Barker, D. and Allen, S, (1976), Sexual Divisions and Society, Tavistock.
Barnes, B, (1974), Scientific Knowledge and Sociolgical Theory, RKP.
Beechey, V, (1979), 'On Patriarchy', Feminist Review, 3.
Booth, C, (1903), Life and Labour of the People in London, (17 volumes), Macmillan.
Centre for Contemporary Cultural Studies, (1981), Unpopular Education: Schooling and Social Democracy in England since 1944, CCCS/Hutchinson.
Coates, K. and Silburn, R, (1973), Poverty: The Forgotten Englishmen, Pelican.
Cohen, S, (1972), Folk Devils and Moral Panics, MacGibbon and Kee.
Dennis, N, Henriques, F. and Slaughter, C, (1956), Coal is Our Life, Eyre and Spottiswoode.
Engels, F, (1884), The Origin of the Family, Private Property and the State, (tr.) Foreign Languages Publishing House, Moscow.
Fenwick, I.G.K, (1976), The Comprehensive School 1944-1970: The Politics of Secondary School Reorganisation, Methuen.
Field, F, (1978), 'The Comeback of Poverty', New Statesman, 29 September.
Field, F, (1980), Inequality in Britain: Freedom, Welfare and the State, Fontana.
Goldthorpe, J. with C. Llewellyn and C. Payne, (1980), Social Mobility and Class Structure in Modern Britain, OUP.
Hall, S. and Jefferson, T, (1976), Resistance through Rituals: Youth Sub-Cultures in Great Britain, Hutchinson.
Halsey, A.H, Heath, A.F. and Ridge, J.M, Origins and Destinations, OUP.
Holloway, J. and Piciotto, S, (1977), 'Capital, Crisis and the State', Capital and Class, 2, 76-101.
Jones, K, (1973), Education, Economy and Society, Open University, Unit E352.
Land, H, (1969), Large Families in Britain, Bell.
Larrain, J, (1979), The Concept of Ideology, Hutchinson.
Piachaud, D, (1979), The Cost of a Child, CPAG.
Piachaud, D, (1981), 'Peter Townsend and the Holy Grail', New Society, 10 September.
Roberts, H, (ed.) (1981), Doing Feminist Research, RKP.
Rowbotham, S, (1973), Hidden from History, Pluto.
Rowbotham, S, Segal, L. and Wainwright, H, (1979), Beyond the Fragments: Feminism and the Making of Socialism, Merlin Press.
Titmuss, R, (1958), Essays on the Welfare State, Allen and Unwin.
Titmuss, R, (1960), The Irresponsible Society, Fabian Society.
Townsend, P, (1963), The Family Life of Old People, Penguin.
Townsend, P, (1973), 'The Four Generation Family', in The Social Minority, Penguin.

Townsend, P, (1979), <u>Poverty in the United Kingdom: A Study of Household Resources and Standards of Living</u>, Penguin.
Townsend, P, (1981), 'Peter Townsend Replies', <u>New Society</u>, 17 September, pp.477-8.
Wedderburn, D, (1968), in E. Shanes <u>et al</u>, <u>Old People in Three Industrial Societies</u>, RKP.
Williams, R, (1981), <u>Culture</u>, Fontana.
Willis, P, (1976), <u>Learning to Labour</u>, Saxon House.
Wright, E.O, (1978), <u>Class, Crisis and the State</u>, Verso.
Urry, J, (1981), <u>The Anatomy of Capitalist Societies: The Economy, Civil Society and the State</u>, Macmillan.
Zubaida, S, (1970), <u>Race and Racialism</u>, Tavistock.

2 White Sociology, Black Struggle
VAL AMOS, PAUL GILROY AND ERROL LAWRENCE

INTRODUCTION

Sociology fails in its attempt to construct an adequate understanding of race relations, it remains irrelevant to the black experience. The sociology of race relations has constructed a 'pathology of black life' which informs not only the policy makers but also 'common sense' understandings of 'race'. (1)

The period after the Second World War saw large scale migration to Britain from the Caribbean and Asia and this sparked off an interest in 'black' people themselves as well as their 'effect' on the British public. It is ironic that the first sociological studies undertaken in the late forties and fifties looked at black communities in the dock areas of Cardiff and Liverpool, areas of long standing settlement, (2) rather than at the newly-arrived pools of labour power, ready to serve the needs of Britain's declining and stagnant industries.

But this is not to say that there was no tradition of research to draw on. In addition to the anthropological studies of black people in various regions of the world, there were also a number of studies of black people in the colonial situation, and the ideological concepts utilised in these accounts were wheeled out again once the colonial problem had become Britain's own internal problem. This work highlighted examples of the processes of discrimination and prejudice, the lynch pin of a great deal of sociological literature in the fifties and sixties. In much of this early research racial ideas and feelings of racial superiority (3) were traced back to the colonial period and as such had a history which was worthy of study, but the importance of race as a structuring feature of the British social formation was obscured and went unanalysed. (4) The commitment was to the understanding of racial ideas, and the 'race problem' was perceived as a matter of getting white people to be more tolerant of blacks by making black culture more understandable. This political project became the basis of the 'sociology of race relations'. The very stress on race relations demonstrates the focus on the interpersonal relations between blacks and whites. The job of interpreter

15

required informing the policy makers and opening up Britain's black communities for scrutiny by the 'academic and objective' gaze of the researcher.

In John Rex's terms, blacks wanted to be assimilated and the task of the sociologist was to aid the process. (5) The problem therefore, was one of integration. However, this argument is premised on profound misunderstanding at best, rampant paternalism at worst.

In order to understand the present state of the sociology of race relations we propose to look at the historical development of that sociology and to draw together its various strands. Our starting point is those studies which concentrated on blacks as immigrants and the problems they were said to represent to white society. Sheila Patterson's research in Brixton (6) is one example of a piece of sociological research that is still discussed on sociology courses today, even if her conclusions are viewed with scepticism. She talks of her sense of shock on seeing black people on the streets of Brixton. Given that that was what she had gone to study her surprise is enlightening to say the least. She claimed that the same sense of 'culture shock' experienced by white residents on seeing black people was the reason for the tensions existing between 'immigrant' and 'host' communities. The 'immigrant/host' model employed by Patterson assumes a passive search for acceptance on the part of the immigrant group and a benevolent, though occasionally hostile, reception on the part of the host community upon whose largesse the immigrant group depends.

A factor underlying this type of sociological research is the sociologists' inability to accept their own irrelevance, in the sense that black people don't need researchers to interpret their lives for them or to make them more accessible and acceptable to white society. The existence of black communities, controlled by black people and over which the agents of the state have no control is perceived as a frightening development. 'Radical alternatives are bound to arise. The most threatening will be those which are set up by minorities for minorities'. (7) The autonomous growth of those communities has gone hand in hand with the growth of a revolutionary politics which it is not within the framework of bourgeois sociology to comprehend. Therein lies the problem.

The early work on blacks as immigrants shifted to a concern with them as settlers. The pattern of sixties legislation, increasingly strict immigration controls accompanied by race relations initiatives, became the model for the development of good race relations. (8) The degree of consensus between state strategies and the needs of capital during the period signalled a certain degree of political and economic stability but the honeymoon was shortlived.

The introduction of black labour to Britain was the solution to an economically problematic labour shortage. Without such labour the main bastion of the 'post war settlement', the Welfare State, would not have come into existence in the way that it did. (9) Sociologists, radical and otherwise, were themselves lulled by the settled nature of British politics: struggle as an impetus for change was seen as irrelevant to the reality of life for the majority of the working class. It was in this climate that sociologists studied the effects of Britain's new found prosperity on the working class and produced the 'embourgeoisement' thesis, which postulated the erosion of traditional working class values with the increasing material success of the class. Class struggle was seen as dead, dying, or expressed only in its institutionalised forms.

By the end of the fifties that hegemony was beginning to disintegrate as the contradictions between the economic and social needs of the British social formation became sharper. The liberal phase - the open door policy - was coming to an end but this had little impact on the work of sociologists until the mid-sixties, when they found that they too were endorsing the positive effects of immigration control for internal race relations.

This period has been characterised as 'the highest stage of social democracy' with its emphasis on equal opportunities for all, but the extension of these opportunities to black people required that their numbers be strictly controlled. Restriction would aid their eventual integration. Roy Jenkins defined integration 'not as a flattening process of assimilation but as equal opportunity accompanied by cultural diversity in an atmosphere of mutual tolerance'. It was a vision which dovetailed with the analysis of racism in terms of the effects of discrimination and prejudice on black people. Having identified the 'problem' as one of discrimination and prejudice the next step was to solve it, something easily accomplished by legislative means.

The sociology of race relations took its place with a number of other social work/social problem issues within the social democratic tradition. What underlies this vision of cultural pluralism? What is its definition of racism, of race relations, of culture? The importance of racism as a means through which the developing crisis was perceived and as a framework within which that crisis was to be experienced, was missing. (10) The emphasis was on race relations, but race relations simplified as cultural relations and lacking any political dynamic, that is, a set of relations outside the wider class/power relations obtaining in the society.

The academic centre for work on 'ethnicity' is the Social Science Research Unit on Ethnic Relations established at the University of Bristol in 1971. The Unit's task was to investigate a number of issues within the black community. The ethos of the Unit was not immediately policy-oriented, although the type and nature of their work has ensured its interest to the policy makers. Their concerns on a wider scale involved the consolidation of research in the field of race relations. British society and culture was no longer conceived of in an unproblematic and homogeneous way, it was multi-ethnic. On this basis they set out to study the various 'ethnicities' which coalesced and became 'multi-cultural' Britain. These were defined in a number of different ways ranging from Watson's 'ethnic redefinition' (11) to Catherine Ballard's 'reactive ethnicity'. (12) There are even 'ethnic resources' and 'ethnic interests'. (13) But nowhere is this ethnicity adequately defined despite its persistence in the literature. 'Ethnic relations' become synonymous with cultural relations and in abstracting out culture from its base in a real materialism the authors merely reinforce the conclusions of the earlier studies. (14) Black people themselves are seen as the source of their problems, hence their obsession with terms like 'identity crisis', 'cultural conflict', 'cultural castration', 'generation gap' - the list is endless. Cultural pluralism and studies of 'ethnicity' have become an acceptable frame-work for race analysis and have provided their liberal pro-ponents with a veneer of 'radicalism'.

By the late seventies the State's concern had again shifted. The SSRC Unit changed venue and personnel. It was said that the Unit under Banton did not engage in enough directly policy-oriented research and that it needed to be sensitive to developments within the black community. When the Unit moved to Aston it saw the 'pulse' of that commun-ity during this period as being in Handsworth, Birmingham. It had all the right elements, a history of black youth/ police conflict, high levels of unemployment and a large number of Rastafarians. As Rex and Tomlinson say, 'a place like Handsworth becomes a stage-set for the perpetual drama of the confrontation between West Indian youth and the forces of law and order'. (15) Rex's work has dominated race relations research for a number of years and perhaps it is reflective of the current state of that sociology and its practice that he was chosen to head the Unit. In the recent book on Handsworth, he attempts to juggle the concept of class (his concept of class) with the Weberian concepts of 'ideal types' and 'market situation'. The preoccupation is with the political sphere, political pluralism as opposed to cultural pluralism. This reflects a concern to locate and contain change within the framework of existing state institutions. Thus he advocates an ameliorative pluralist approach which sets 'the politicians' the 'difficult but nevertheless manageable task of bringing about change'. Black struggle for him represents a threat to the estab-lished social order and his recognition of the importance of that struggle stops at 'an appreciation of the conflicts which presently exist'. (16)

Running parallel with the emphasis on black culture was the growth of 'social problem' theories linked to theories of poverty and disadvantage drawn from the American situ-ation. The emphasis within state policy on ways of ameliorating disadvantage was based on a concern with the political response of the working class to particular changes at the level of the state. The mid-seventies may be said to be the period of the collapse of social democracy, crystallised in the defeat of the Heath government. There was a shift towards more authoritarian forms of control and nowhere was this more visible than in relations between black youth and the police. The establishment of poverty programmes, through the Home Office Community Development Projects, the Commission for Racial Equality and the Urban Aid Programme were all attempts to re-establish control over forms of working class resistance, particularly black resistance. As Lee Bridges stated: 'The introduction of the Urban Aid Programme in 1968 was an immediate and ad hoc response to Enoch Powell's "rivers of blood" speech in Birmingham. It was based more on the grounds of political expediency than on any well thought out theory regarding the nature of urban poverty.' (17)

Black resistance had its roots in the historical experience of black people - a history conceived in the struggle against slavery, colonialism, neo-colonialism and forms of capitalist exploitation. It was a resistance which transformed itself from the narrow confines of black nationalist politics to a mass cultural/political movement. As Jenny Bourne states in her essay on the sociology of race relations: 'The Bengalis who sat down in Brick Lane and refused to move in 1977 were not indulging in an Asian or peasant tradition as a means of recreation on a Sunday morning. They were bringing an Asian cultural form of resistance to bear on their British fight against racism.' (18)

The nature and political importance of cultural resistance is happily ignored by the 'sociologists of culture'. It is either dismissed as a 'peculiar cultural deviation' or, as in the case of Rex and Tomlinson's discussion of Rastafari, relegated to the withdrawal end of their typology of political organisations and characterised as representing 'political alienation from British society'. Their categorisation of particular forms of black struggle as 'alienation' points the way for future research and vividly demonstrates the point at which it can be appropriated by the state - blacks need to be incorporated into the working class lest they disrupt the 'manageable system' of capitalist economic and social relations.

At a BSA conference ten years ago Robin Jenkins criticised Rose and Deakin's <u>Colour and Citizenship</u> for being 'not scientific but ideological'. The knowledge contained in it, he argued,

> made the power elite more powerful and the powerless more impotent. He warned blacks not to submit themselves to the scrutiny of white researchers who, in effect, acted as spies for the government. They should, he said, be told to 'fuck off'. (19)

Bourne points out that his critique 'opened up a major

debate as to the whole direction of race relations research and provided a catalyst in the struggle to transform the Institute (of Race Relations) itself'. This struggle was a reflection of the wider struggles of black people against racism. By 1972, when the dispute in the IRR finally came to a head, the debate had shifted beyond Jenkins' initial critique:

> Where the fundamental problem lay was now the issue. It was not black people who should be examined, but white society; it was not a question of educating blacks and whites for integration, but of fighting institutional racism; it was not race relations that was the field for study, but racism. (20)

We find ourselves a decade later weighed down with the knowledge that the vast body of what we loosely refer to as 'race relations research', still constitutes black people, their ethnicity and cultures as the objects to be examined. Racism is still a neglected field of enquiry. The personnel have changed as have the theoretical frameworks but the object of study remains the same. We have Verity Khan, Catherine Ballard, Geoff Driver, Peter Weinreich and Nancy Foner working in and around the framework of 'Ethnicity Studies'; John Rex and Sally Tomlinson working from a 'left Weberian' perspective; as well as the more eclectic and idiosyncratic doctoral researches of Ken Pryce and Ernest Cashmore. During the seventies we have witnessed the growth of the organised Fascist movements, whose attacks on black people range from verbal abuse to physical harassment and murder. We have also witnessed the growth - within the context of an increasingly authoritarian statism - of state racism. This state racism has been sanctioned, legitimated and underpinned at the political and ideological levels by the growth of new and virulent strains of racist ideologies that are both coherent and popular.

Race relations research then seems to have failed even in its own terms. The researchers have not provided any assistance to black people in their struggle against racism; neither do they appear to have headed off the growth of racist ideologies with their many attempts to furnish 'understanding' of blacks for the education of whites. Yet we still find this dogged persistence in attempting to inform policy options. To be sure this is not always on the exalted level of people such as Banton and Rex. The recent 'ethnicity studies' book Minority Families in Britain: Support and Stress (21) seeks the humbler role of 'engaging in a dialogue with the practitioners'. This avowal is strange on at least two counts. Firstly they seek this dialogue even though they are aware that the practitioners themselves may be openly racist. Secondly, although they assert a formal opposition to these structures and practices, they share the same fundamental assumptions. Their view of the problem is that the practitioners don't know enough about black cultural practices and they aim, therefore, to provide the relevant information so that the practitioners can more effectively deal with black people. In this endeavour they are moving in the same direction as the practitioners themselves. A brief examination of the work of practitioners will confirm this trend. (22)

More humbly Cashmore claims that he only wants to help us to understand Rastafarianism and this connection takes every opportunity to speak on the topic, irrespective of the nature of the audience. (23) Pryce, on the other hand, eschews the humble approach. As a West Indian himself, he wants to give us the blacks' view of things, (24) though as Colin Prescod argued, 'Pryce's publication may not be so much a milestone as a millstone' around the necks of the black people he left behind when he went back to take up his position in the University of the West Indies. (25)

METHODOLOGY

The tendency within race relations research has been to study black people rather than white racism. This raises specific problems both in terms of the information the researchers can expect to glean from their respondents and for the interpretation of that data once gathered. While some researchers do actually recognise this problem, their acknowledgement of it is all too often subsequently suppressed. Cashmore's work is a good case in point. (26)

At the beginning of his book, Rastaman, he tells us that his initial attempts to engage rastas in conversation about their 'new perception of reality', met with a chilly response. It was only after reading everything there was to read on Rastafarianism and approaching members of the Ethiopian Orthodox Church, that he was able to effect an entry into the rasta community. His initial difficulties were compounded by what he describes as the 'cultivation' by rastas 'of an idiosyncratic mode of thought' and a 'brand of patois' designed to stake out a 'social gulf between themselves and the rest of society'. (27) An already problematic situation must have been further complicated by the rastas' insistence that their's was not simply another version of reality as he constantly sought to imply. (28) Cashmore does indeed warn us that his account is unavoidably 'coloured by (his) own perception' and that many of the categories and formulations by which he describes Rastafari would be unrecognisable to them. (29) Yet throughout the remainder of his book the problematic nature of his encounter with rastás in particular, and the Afro-Caribbean community in general, is given no theoretical weight and, in fact, gets erased.

Again, Catherine Ballard in her piece on 'Conflict, Continuity and Change: Second Generation Asians' (30) acknowledges that 'the outsider who attempts to help with an intergenerational crisis in an Asian family is faced with serious difficulties'. The outsider may be 'handicapped by a lack of understanding of the complexity of the cultural factors involved' and end up doing more harm than good. Yet she fails to make explicit her own 'handicaps' in this

regard. Foner (31) also mentions that some of the West
Indians she met only let her set foot in their houses
because she had astutely informed them that she had spent
some time in Jamaica. She also felt that her being American
might have been a help here, since she shared with them the
stigma of being 'foreign'. It's not clear why black people
should view a white American with any less reserve than the
white British, given America's rather dismal history of
racism, and she is quick to tell us that her co-researcher,
who hadn't been to Jamaica and who was not American, had few
difficulties. He did, though, have acquaintances in the
black community who could introduce him to prospective respondents. Their entry, then, into the black community was
not unproblematic but what is more important here is that
although the respondents were concerned about racism, Foner
felt that it was sufficient to mention this as another
variable. It does not seem to have caused her to rethink her
research, her categories or her relation to her respondents
some of whom needed to have their suspicions allayed.

Barry Troyna's work (32) is particularly insensitive to
these problems. His engagement with black youth was in the
captive situation of the school classroom. Although he
introduces his essay 'Differential Use of Media Culture by
Black Youths in Britain' with some radical rhetoric about
Britain's poor record in race-relations, he says nothing
about what his own position might be in this structured
racial hierarchy. Where others acknowledge their invidious
position only to subsequently suppress it, Troyna does not
even appear to be aware that there is a problem here.
Neither does he appear to be aware of the extent to which
his own schema is imposed onto the experience of his
respondents.

What we are arguing here is not so much that white
bourgeois sociologists should not study black proletarian
people, though much of what we have read may incline us
towards such a view. The more important point we wish to
make is that none of these researchers actually take into
account the extent to which their relationship to their
respondents may be structured by racism. They fail to
acknowledge the extent to which the replies they get may
actually be determined by their positions as white 'authority figures' in a situation where power relations are reproduced in and through racism. This is not simply a black and
white issue. Dorothy Smith has recently argued that
traditionally sociology has ignored and marginalised women
and moreover, actively reinforces women's subordinate
position. 'Women appear only as they are relevant to a world
governed by male principles and interests'. She goes on to
warn that:

> To the extent that women sociologists accept that per-
> spective, they are alienated from their own personal
> experience. They speak a language, use theories, and
> select methods in which they are excluded or ignored.
> (33)

We can push this critique further, for sociology has not only traditionally operated within a patriarchal paradigm but within a white patriarchal paradigm. It focusses upon traditional white masculine concerns. To accept such a paradigm is to be unable really to distinguish between bad race relations (sociology) and rampant racism. Pryce's work illustrates the problems of black academics:

> ... primed to produce 'outstanding works of empirical sociology' ... a euphemism for work that is low on critical knowledge and wisdom but high on information. Information which cannot be gathered as easily by white researchers. Information organised in categories which reinforce stereotypes. (34)

To ask of his work 'for whom is this written?' or 'to whom will it be useful?' is immediately to expose its political insensitivity and ideological content.

Black researchers such as Pryce face problems of methodology that parallel those of white researchers. As he himself notes, his class position vis-a-vis his respondents introduced certain tensions to begin with. The nature of his relationship with many of his male respondents changed once they found out that he was researching them. Of more concern is his relationship to the few black women who graced his sample. Here the problems of using categories drawn from a white patriarchal paradigm became particularly acute. His other insensitivities are merely compounded by his total ignorance of the determinations of gender.

CULTURE

We turn now to a consideration of substantive arguments, in particular those concerning black cultures. A degree of consensus about the characteristics of Afro-Caribbean and Asian cultures, appears to unite these accounts. All recognise the commonsense truism that Asians have strong cultures while Afro-Caribbeans have weak ones. What is not often perceived is that race relations researchers invariably reproduce such commonsense at the theoretical level. The theorisation is more sophisticated than the commonsense version but it betrays a truncated historical knowledge of Asian and Afro-Caribbean peoples.

AFRO-CARIBBEAN CULTURES

The theoretical lynch pin here is the notion of 'acculturation', which refers to the 'culture-stripping' or 'cultural castration' of Africans during slavery. This entailed the loss of language, religion and family/kinship system, leaving the slaves with no option, but, as Pryce puts it, to learn 'his (sic) master's language and to ape his values and his institutions'. (35) Thus as Rex and Tomlinson argue they were 'forced into accepting British culture along with their servitude'. (36) This experience is thought to provide the basis for a peculiarly Afro-Caribbean (Afro-American) trait - a 'negative self-image'. Not only have they been 'deprived of a culture' (37) they have also internalised a culture which downgrades blackness and which is therefore at odds with their very being. Of interest here is the way in which American commonsense notions about black personality have been theorised, via the aculturation thesis, to produce ideal types which correspond to 'Uncle Tom', 'Sambo' and the 'marauding young buck'. These types have crossed the Atlantic, and in modified form do service for Pryce, Troyna and Rex and Tomlinson among others.

While we would agree that slavery was a brutal and unhappy experience for the slaves, we do not see that a recognition of this requires the construction of a theory that distills this experience into the supposedly maladjusted personalities of the African slaves and their descendants. Nor are we convinced that the attempt to eradicate the African slaves' cultural heritage was entirely successful. As Stuart Hall has already argued:

> ... the culture and institutions of the slave population are rigidly differentiated from that of the 'master' class; and African 'traces' enter into the structure of these institutions. (38)

The preservation of 'Africanisms' and the development of Afro-Caribbean cultural forms took place, it is true, within the context of slave society. Their culture was locked into a subordinate position relative to the European culture of the dominant master class, both cultures forming 'differentiated parts of a single socioeconomic system'. (39) Having said this it is crucial to realise that the African slaves and their descendants were by no means the inactive victims of slavery or the passive recipients of European culture. Even Rex has recently argued that '... those who are descended from the original slaves have always, and increasingly in recent years, been concerned to reassert their cultural identity'. (40)

While we welcome recognition that Afro-Caribbeans actively appropriated and subverted certain elements of British culture, moulding these together with African elements to produce a distinctive Afro-Caribbean <u>black</u> culture, we feel that it is also necessary to recognise why they did this. C.L.R. James' point that voodoo served as the black ideology in the Haitian revolution may help us here. (41) Afro-Caribbeans, though dominated by British (and other) capitalism, resisted and rebelled against that domination. Their cultures played an important part as a source of oppositional ideas and practices, and indeed still do. We do not feel that it is useful to reduce their of struggles to a simplistic notion of the 'assertion of cultural identity'. Those cultures must be seen in relation to the historical struggles of Afro-Caribbean people.

The Pathological Black Family

The effects of slavery did not stop short at the deprivation of culture in some simple sense of ideas and attitudes, but are seen as having profound consequences for the household organisation of the slaves and their Afro-Caribbean descendants. Pryce argues that the family in Jamaica with its 'proliferation of common law unions and high rates of illegitimacy' among the 'lower class folk', is an inherently unstable institution. He locates the 'peculiarities of family life in the West Indies' as stemming 'directly from the institution of slavery, which was responsible for the total destruction of <u>conventional</u> family life among slaves' (42) (our emphasis). According to him, these 'peculiarities' are only part of a 'complex of causes responsible for his (sic) inability to establish a firm, rooted sense of identity'. (43)

Cohabitation is seen to lead inevitably to family breakdown. Without the formal ties of marriage the man is able to shirk his responsibilities and run off leaving the woman to rear the children. This is not of course unknown in Britain, but for Pryce it has led to the development of a 'matriarchy' and the absence of a father figure. The resultant 'weak' family structure means that Afro-Caribbean children cannot properly be socialised and, of course, when they grow up 'without a rooted sense of identity' they merely reproduce a pathological family form and a 'weakened' culture. Pryce adds the further twist of migration, where the kinship system has to remain fluid in order to '... permit individuals to <u>abandon</u> family obligations and migrate at short notice to take advantage of economic opportunities overseas'. (44) Cashmore gets away with a cruder version. He argues that the involvement of Afro-Caribbean youth with the British police and the

> emergence (among them) of subterranean values as dominant vectors of social action, (has to do with) the lack of social control exerted by the West Indian family, due historically to the fragmentation of the family structure in slavery. (45)

We can criticise these formulations on two counts. Firstly the view of the <u>conventional</u> family that is being used is the common-sense image of the middle-class English nuclear family, with its father, mother and 2.2 children, where father is the breadwinner and mother nurtures the children. As Michèle Barrett points out, (46) this particular arrangement is the specific <u>historical</u> achievement of the bourgeoisie and even today only bears limited relation to the organisation of working class households. That this view of family life is popularly accepted as the 'natural form of household organisation' attests to the bourgeoisie's success at securing 'their definition of family life', at an ideological level.

In summary we agree with the race-relations sociologists

that Afro-Caribbean societies' sex/gender systems are different but we cannot agree that this difference is pathological. We need to remember here that their view of the family is not simply the ideological view of the white bourgeoisie, it is also a view forged historically within a white patriarchal society. It is only from this position that race-relations sociologists have been able to launch their attacks upon what they see as either a 'black matriarchy' or the black 'matrifocal' family. (47)

Youth and Identity Crisis

The idea that Afro-Caribbean people have inherited a negative self-image and weak family structure from slavery forms the backdrop against which discussion of Afro-Caribbean youth in Britain takes place. The argument is organised around the 'generation gap' which is thought to take a particularly exaggerated form within the Afro-Caribbean community. The reasons put forward for this vary from author to author, though they amount more or less to the view that the different experiences of parents and youth lead to differing responses to racism. These, in turn, provide the occasion for conflict between parents and children. Thus Cashmore contrasts the parents' withdrawal into Pentecostalism with the youths' 'truculence' and assertion. (48)

Another twist is added by the researchers' view of the Afro-Caribbean child's experience of school. The mis-education of these children within a mono-cultural/racist education system has made it difficult for them to succeed in academic terms. (49) Pryce, however, argues that this 'failure' is due to the 'mutilating colonial heritage' and 'inferior educational upbringing' of the Afro-Caribbean child. The child is therefore unable to cope with the 'demands made on him (sic) by the British school system'. (50) The experience of school is seen as merely compounding what Pryce calls the Afro-Caribbean child's 'psychic and cultural confusion' and propels them finally down the slippery slope into an 'identity crisis'. It is here that Cashmore, Pryce and Rex and Tomlinson locate the appeal of Rastafarianism for Afro-Caribbean youth. Rastafarianism is, as Rex and Tomlinson would put it, one possible step in their 'quest for a black identity'. (51)

Weinreich (52) seeks to replace the 'loose and ambiguous term "identity crisis"' with the concept of 'conflict in identification with another'. He argues that such conflicts are more often a resource than a liability and that 'ethnic identity conflicts do not generally imply self-hatred'. But while he undercuts the simplistic notions of other research his work still presents its own problems. He accepts uncritically, for example, the conclusions of Parker and Kleiner that ambivalence in identification patterns is 'realistic and adaptive for the Negro' and that 'it is the polarisation of racial identification or reference group behaviour that is psychopathogenic'. (53)

By implication those Afro-Caribbean youth with a 'consciously defined ethnic conception' who identify with Africa or the Caribbean, must be considered psychopathogenic.

Rather than enter into a detailed discussion of accounts of Afro-Caribbean life in Britain we simply point out how such accounts absolve the racist structures and practices of British society and locate the 'problem' in the black family and black consciousness. We take up instead the idea that the identity crisis of the Afro-Caribbean youth leads them into Rastafarianism. We cannot go into detail about Rastafarianism in Jamaica though we note that the movement there is uncompromisingly opposed to neo-colonialism, imperialism and racism. In this connection we also take note of Horace Campbell's point that:

> Rastafari culture remains an indelible link between the resistance of the maroons, the pan-africanist appeal of Marcus Garvey, the materialist and historical analysis of Walter Rodney and the defiance of Reggae. (54)

Young Afro-Caribbeans in Britain have been shaped by circumstances that differ considerably from those in the Caribbean. They have been subject to conditions similar to those that have given rise to the post-war working class youth subcultures, but they have experienced those conditions through the mechanism of racism. As Hall observes

> The class relations which inscribe the black fractions of the working class function as race relations. The two are inseparable. Race is the modality in which class is lived. It is also the medium in which class relations are experienced. (55)

The emergence of a British variant of Rastafari must be seen then as a part of the process of class struggle that black people have been engaged in since the fifties. Afro-Caribbean youth did not take up Rastafarian themes in order to solve their supposed identity crisis. Rastafarianism organised resistances and oppositional values that were already in existence, in a new way. The mass of Afro-Caribbean youth in Britain have taken its themes and re-organised them in the light of their particular concerns and circumstances.

Given its mass appeal in the Afro-Caribbean community, we do not find useful the tendency to define the movement in terms of a number of dogmatic tenets to which 'cultists' supposedly subscribe. (56) Instead we argue that the symbols of 'dread', by which researchers have so far identified 'cult affiliates' are found at one end of a broad continuum of belief which traverses both age and gender difference. We should add here that no researchers, except Cashmore, seem to perceive that there are female Rastafari, let alone discuss their relationship to the movement. Cashmore views rasta patriarchy as a revolt against Afro-Caribbean matriarchy, (57) a view which effectively blocks any discussion of the ideology of 'The Queen' in rasta discourse

27

and thus denies the existence of the space from which rasta women engage in their distinct form of feminist struggle. These brief remarks should indicate that the ideological designation of Rastafari as a 'millenarian cult' with psychopathogenic adherents is not the best vantage point from which to understand the movement.

ASIAN CULTURES

Opposed to the idea of weak Afro-Caribbean cultures is the equally misleading notion of strong Asian cultures. Asian languages, religious institutions and family-kinship systems survived colonialism intact. Indeed there is even a sense in which their cultures and traditions are thought to have ameliorated the worst effects of colonial subordination and neo-colonial dependence. Khan argues, for example, that

> Village life in the Indian sub-continent is neither isolated nor static. The gradual adaptation in past decades indicates the strength of traditional institutions rather than the absence of outside influence. (58)

Her treatment of relationships of power as 'cultural relations' enables her to suggest that the 'cultural pre-ferences and patterns of behaviour' of the various ethnic minorities, may actually interact with 'external determin-ants'. (59) Brooks and Singh (60) use her ideas to argue that while racism placed Asians in specific occupations to begin with, 'their own distinctive traditions and their ethnic identities ... in turn influenced their occupational and industrial distribution'. Wallman goes one step further:

> The effect of their ethnicity is ... dependent upon the state of the economic system and on their bargaining strength within it. Conversely they will not see, will not accept, will not succeed in the opportunity offered if it is not appropriate to their choice of work and their cultural ecperience. (61)

Jenny Bourne comments wryly, 'now we know why black teachers become bus drivers and skilled black workers prefer to do unskilled jobs'. (62) It is no doubt ideas such as these, and a belief that all Asians are shop-keepers, that fuels Rex's prediction that Asians have a Jewish future in Britain.

The most striking feature of these ideas about Asian culture is their failure to comment upon the impact of British colonialism. This implies that, culturally at least, the Asian sub-continent enjoyed uninterrupted development. Such an ommission is to say the least misleading and can only serve to fuel the commonly held belief that the poverty of these 'underdeveloped' nations, is the result of their 'backward' and 'rigid' cultural forms and institutions. In reality colonialism had as profound an effect on this part of the world as it had elsewhere. Iftikhar Ahmed notes that the 1857 rebellion in India provoked a change in British colonial policies:

> The intensive penetration of traditional society was replaced by <u>cautious preservation</u> of the pre-existing social order. It seemed more sensible to take Indian society as it was, to concentrate on administration and control, and to shore up the landed aristocrats, who came to be viewed as the 'natural leaders' best suited to the 'oriental mind'. (63)

Khan notes that the political instability of Azad Kashmir has also affected its economic development and future prospects (64) but says nothing about the causes of that political instability. Like others of her ilk, she fails to deal with the relations of power that lock Azad Kashmir and other parts of the Asian sub-continent into a position of dependence in the world economic system. Similarly, the systematic workings of racism in Britain and the way it locates Asian and Afro-Caribbean people in a subordinate position is more or less ignored. These failures in analysis have led the ethnicity school up a cultural cul-de-sac.

The Asian Family

The Asian household provides a contrast to the view of the Afro-Caribbean family. Circumscribed by religion and custom it provides the structured and cohesive atmosphere wherein all members of the household are made aware of their roles, rights and obligations to other members of the household and members of the wider kinship group. This arrangement promotes a 'certain stability and psychological health' in all individuals. (65) The very strength of the Asian kinship system is seen to be a source of both actual and potential weaknesses. Khan argues that the hierarchical structure of Asian households promotes 'stress-ridden relationships' particularly between sisters-in-law. Furthermore, while the family/kinship system promotes a healthy psyche, it does not 'prepare the members for change beyond that of the natural development cycle of the family'. The strength of 'traditional relationships' is thought to determine 'the skills and <u>handicaps</u> the migrant brings to his (sic) new situation in Britain'. Khan also characterises Asian women as wives who are cut off from the rest of society by custom and language, and suggests that male fiances who are new to Britain will come into conflict with their wives who are more familiar with life in England.

We have already argued the dangers of viewing one sex/ gender system through the prism of another. All we would say here is that Khan's account misrepresents life in the Asian community. Her portrayal of Asian women as oppressed wives and mothers who have little or nothing to say in relation to their families and completely dominated by their menfolk is far from reality. The militancy of Asian women on the picket lines at Grunwicks and Chix should have been enough to undermine her assertion that they do not identify 'freedom with self-assertion'. Such accounts suggest that Asian women are given quantities, incapable of manipulating their environment. We do not believe this to be the case.

Asian Youth and Cultural Conflict

Thompson's <u>The Second Generation ... Punjabi or English?</u> and
Taylor's <u>The Half Way Generation</u> argued that Asian youths'
attenuated connections with their parents' culture were a
source of family conflict. This theme was popularised by
the CRE in their publication <u>Between Two Cultures</u>. (66)
Children's exposure to British values, norms and attitudes
was thought to undermine their parents' traditional
authority and cause them to question the parents' culture.
For girls in particular the issue of arranged marriage was
thought to be a particular bone of contention. Catherine
Ballard, in her contribution, argues that the talk about
'culture conflict' merely serves to reinforce the common-
sense perceptions of practitioners and sets young Asians
apart as a 'problem category'.

> More seriously, it assumes that cultural values are
> fixed and static and that there is no possibility of
> adaptation, flexibility or accommodation between one set
> of values and another. (67)

Having thus argued, however, she then persists in trying to
explain 'the strange half-British, half-Asian behaviour of
the children', illustrating 'the kinds of inter-generational
conflicts which may occur', and assessing the 'usefulness
of the popular concept of <u>culture conflict</u>' which she has
just argued is a damaging and erroneous concept! (our
emphasis) She explores the same dreary terrain of the
<u>inevitable</u> 'gulf' between generations which 'sharpens' as
children get older and she suggests that they have never
experienced their culture 'in the totality of its original
context' in order to support what is basically a 'between
two cultures' argument. This can perhaps be explained by
her 'professional' interest, but what is unforgivable is the
fact that in pursuit of that interest, she first of all
falls back upon the parents' 'linguistic handicaps' and
then does what she has already criticised the sensational-
ist media for doing, namely arguing on the basis of extreme
cases.

Ballard's account is interesting because she is unable to
find any hard evidence that Asian youngsters are alienated
from their parents' culture or that they are opposed to
arranged marriages. Yet one gets the impression that she
still harbours doubts. Asian families, she says, provide
security and warmth, yet pressure to conform can seem
suffocating. It is also interesting that while she does not
differentiate between young women and young men in her
discussion about arranged marriages, she still feels bound
to cite the obligatory incidents of Asian girls running
away from home. It is important to remember here that white
girls run away from home as well and that the pressure to
conform is not something peculiar to the Asian community.

Conclusion

We conclude this section with a brief note on the way in which each community tends to be used as the negative reference point for the other. While the weakness of the Afro-Caribbean culture and family structure results in problems of disciplining children, the very strength of the Asian family is thought to present its own problems to white society, particularly in terms of internal violence, and difficulties of communications. Rex and Tomlinson argue, for example, that because the Afro-Caribbeans were

> ... forced into accepting British culture along with their servitude. They do therefore speak English and are better equipped to obtain employment as individuals than the Asians. (68)

And for the other side of the coin:

> ... if the West Indian is plagued by self-doubt induced by white education, and seeks a culture which will give him (sic) a sense of identity, the Asians have religions and cultures and languages of which they are proud, and which may prove surprisingly adaptive and suited to the demands of a modern industrial society. (69)

These formulations are reminiscent of children's nursery rhymes. As Goldilocks might have said:

> This culture is too weak; this culture is too strong; but this culture (the missing dimension of English culture) is just right.

RESEARCH AND STATE POLICY

We have looked at the dynamics of policy-oriented race research and situated them within the shifting framework of the social democratic race relations problematic which stretches from Dark Strangers up to Colonial Immigrants in a British City. We have also examined the conceptual limits and methodology of some influential contemporary theorists and demonstrated the relation of their work to popular common-sense racist ideologies and assumptions about the black people who comprise their object of study. It remains to explore the connections between their work - which comprises a coherent unity - and key areas of state policy and practice. In particular its relevance to a state which is at present in the midst of distinct and novel conditions of organic crisis. The study of racial politics offers a unique perspective on the transformation of the apparatuses of the British state and we argue that race research has a new-found relevance for the institutions of social control in these new historical conditions. The rest of this account develops this theme by concentrating on one aspect of the present crisis, conflict between black people and the police.

It is not simply that the 'theories' of pathological black

family life, identity crises, acculturation, generational conflict and crimogenic multiple deprivation fail to break free of the shackles of common-sense racist thinking. Rather, it is important to understand that these same ideas and images albeit in their 'untheorised' form, are at the root of a new popular politics tailored by crisis conditions. Here, Blacks are represented as illegal immigrants, muggers, Rastafarians and, most recently, inarticulate aliens whose incapacity for the English language has brought the legitimate resentment of the freeborn Englishman down upon them with disastrous results. (70) This is an important background to our discussion but cannot be developed here.

We have chosen to look at the sites where the apparently 'theoretical' instance of these common-sense racist ideas achieves its most pernicious effect. This directs us abruptly to the issue of policing under crisis conditions, in particular to the professional ideology of the community relations police officer. (71) The development of this body of theory has been intimately and extensively bound up with the problem of controlling the black communities whose grievances it recognises as both the expression of deprivation and a catalyst for insurgent behaviour. (72)

The ideological potency of the discourses of youth and race in the signification of social instability and change is scarcely in doubt. The recent convergence between the views of senior conservative politicians (73) senior policemen, (74) sociologists, state intellectuals in the race field (75) and popular purveyors of common-sense racism in the media (76) in which black youth are seen to comprise a simultaneously criminal and political threat to the social order of this country, invokes a powerful image of black youth as 'folk devil'. This appears all the more remarkable when a Home Office circular to chief constables in 1967 is recalled. This stated: 'There is little doubt that the most likely cause of friction between police and the immigrant community is the lack of knowledge and the misunderstanding of each other'. (77)

This was the era in which officialdom spoke in serious, if paternalistic, tones about the plight of the coloured school leaver, and discussed race and crime outside the syntax of 'mugging' and without reference to the USA. Such statements stand in stark contrast to more recent ones which illustrate the race/crime/politics theme. Thus Sir David MacNee told _Guardian_ readers: 'Policing a multi-racial society is putting the fabric of our policing policy philosophy under greater stress than at any time since the years immediately after the Metropolitan Police was established in 1899'. (78) In a similar vein Mrs Thatcher sagely explained: 'in their muddled but different ways the vandals on the picket lines and the muggers on our streets have got the same confused message "we want our demands met or else" and "get out of our way, give us your handbag or else"'. (79)

Accepting that the 'mugging' label has a racial reference, both statements echo the definition of the race relations problem outlined earlier. It is both sociological and systematic within its own parameters. It is also relatively secure, but has not always been so. Its relevance and its adequacy as an explanation has been won in a pitched battle in which the sociology of race relations has proved an important factor in the defeat of black interests. We must stress that we have narrowed our argument to focus on the example of black youth of Afro-Caribbean descent. However the point can be equally well exemplifed by presenting ideological theorisations of Asian communities which also operate around the themes of youth and crime. The 1971 Immigration Act and the consequent images of the illegal immigrant are only the most obvious parallel. Drawing the black communities together where other sociologists divide them, an early piece by John Brown explains:

> Characteristically, the West Indian may tend to drift into crime, as like as not by accident as design. He shacks up with a white girl for instance; likes to live at ease, playing dominos with the boys, taking a drink or two; finds it easier to let the girl work, what way better is the life, eh? (sic) By contrast the Asian attitude to poncing tends to the premeditated, organised impersonal, directly commercial. (80)

As with the West Indian community, Brown relates patterns of crime to the cultural practices of the Asian community.

> As the Asian tends to look inward so his crime tends to be internal within his community ... it tends to be more cerebral, sophisticated and organised than West Indian crime, characteristically concerned in areas such as fraud, tax evasion, conspiracy, bribery and other aspects of financial malpractice and corruption ... it is largely underground only glimpses showing even to police eyes, as in the area of illegal immigration. (81)

Suffice to say that these resonant conceptions of criminality at the heart of police practice have effects on the communities as a whole rather than simply those who fall directly foul of the law.

Cain, Holdaway and Banton (82) have all outlined the professionalisation of policing which followed the 1962 Royal Commission on the Police and the importance of both race and sociology for the managerial professional approach to police work is clear from the 1969 report of the Working Party on Police Training:

> all members of the police service must be able to show by their actions and their attitudes that they are aware of the major sociological forces which influence our way of life; that they are alert to the changing patterns of community living, the merging of social classes, and the broad effects of immigration, particularly by coloured peoples.

The consolidation of this approach under the regime of Sir Robert Mark should not be allowed to disguise the fact that its roots stretch back into the fifties and are marked by the formation of the Community Relations Branch at Scotland Yard in 1968, the introduction of unit beat policing in 1967 and the appointment of a Community Relations Officer to the Metropolitan Police in 1958. (83) Numerous pronouncements (84) present the unique double position of race in the professional approach to the urban policeman, whose attempt to kill the two birds of 'the blacks' and 'the youth' with the single stone of community relations has apparently resulted in the frequent attempt to kill the same bird twice under the different headings of 'the blacks' and 'the young blacks'.

The 1973 volume The Police We Deserve, significantly co-edited by John Alderson, presented the first hint of a partial alternative to Brown's crudities which we sampled earlier. A number of contributions to it (85) and to the Police Journal (86) demonstrate the pertinence of race. While recognising a distinction between 'managerial' and 'academic' approaches to the issue, they recognise their complementarity: 'Often (this) dividing line is obscured ... Even more often the two approaches are made together, as in the study of race relations'. (87) On one level this book was an attempt to claim academic viability for police training and research, on another it was an attempt to heal the wounds which one contributor recognised as jeopardising the relationship of the policeman and the social analyst.

> On more than one occasion, for example, senior ranking police officers have made no bones about the fact that they attribute many problems of contemporary police work to the pernicious influence of the mass media and sociology. (88)

The book appeared in the wake of work by Derek Humphry (89) and Gus John, (90) which, like Pullé's study of Ealing (91) demanded serious and detailed refutation. Brown's Theory of Police-Immigrant Relations (92) which appears to have been a text book for in-service training, can be regarded as indicating the trajectory of the official rejoinder. With John Biggs-Davidson's warning 'If we lose in Belfast we may have to fight in Brixton or Birmingham' (93) still ringing in the ears of senior policemen, and given added credibility by the Brockwell Park incident in June 1973, Brown's pamphlet was a plausible plea for what he termed 'a more rational system of social organisation in areas of community stress'. His demand that the police be given a greater voice in matters of social policy and practice echoed many of Sir Robert Mark's opinions, and was tacit confirmation of the place of race relations in the official perception and management of crisis conditions.

The move towards what may be termed a system of direct control of key urban areas had been heralded by the announcement (94) of the formation of the Urban Deprivation

Unit. This was the first step towards centralisation of urban policy and social control functions which had previously been the prerogative of autonomous local authorities. For the police, whose structure was simultaneously transformed and centralised by the 1972 Local Government Act, the growing apprehension of long term social crisis appeared in the guise of the increasingly frequent admissions, notably from the Community Relations Department, (95) that the problems they were being called upon to resolve were not of their making, and were outside their compass to resolve. These changes, as well as the growth of social studies components in police training courses recorded by Banton, (96) confirm the new-found relevance of social analysis to an increasingly coercive and repressive state apparatus. The 1972-6 period saw the police under mounting, if sporadic, pressure from black youths in the streets and forced by their new role in 'the moulding of public opinion and legislation' (97) to distinguish between efficient and merely effective modes of policing. The noted police historian T.A. Critchley sums it up: 'The paramount need is that the police should retain public support during a period of what may be intensifying social crisis'. (98)

An exhaustive catalogue of confrontations leading up to the long hot summer of 1975 can be gleaned from the pages of West Indian World, Race Today and the Runnymede Trust Bulletin. It is essential to convey the scale of this problem. As their campaign to recruit black officers floundered in the winter of 1975-6, the Metropolitan Police conceded the scale of potential disorder. In the previous twelve months, in the London area alone, there had been forty incidents of conflict which carried the potential for 'large scale disorder'. (99) They acknowledged the specifically racial politics involved in this threat to law and order:

> (the) continuing attempt by the few to 'politicise' the criminal actions of a minority of young blacks, has its effects on more moderate and constructive community spokesmen. Wherever they speak for public consumption they cannot be unaware of these negative extremists waiting in the wings to deride any constructive black approach as 'Uncle Tomism'. (100)

A series of confrontations between police and black youth established the Handsworth area as a thermometer by which the political temperature of the black community in general could be measured and led to a unique experiment in the social control of urban areas. At first glance the Lozells community policing project appears to have harmonised the activities of social services and police, fulfilling Sir Robert Mark's vision of the latter as 'participants in the role of social welfare'. Yet a senior policeman closer to the grass roots and well known post-graduate student of race relations at a local university has explained to his colleagues:

> We are not always the nice guys ... these are good,

sound operational PCs in uniform doing an operational PC's job, but they are doing it a little more effectively ... we are not trying to create a force of social workers or make claims we are getting involved in welfare. It's very much policing. (101)

Without addressing the issue of community policing in general, it is important to note that the final spur to the creation of the Lozells scheme was provided by John Brown's report Shades of Grey. (102) This cemented the signification of black criminality by the now renowned 'rastafarian in a tea cosy hat' as well as indicating its preferred resolution: the re-creation of the village in the city, complete with home beat bobby. (103)

We cannot over-stress Brown's success in setting the agenda of subsequent discussion. His report and the award winning BBC documentary of the same name managed to acknowledge the material basis of conflict and resituate it under the more resonant ideological theme of 'hot-headed youth on both sides':

> The truth I believe is to be seen in human rather than political terms. The blues - plain clothed or uniformed - with whom these blacks have the most contact resemble them in that they too are young people under intense, often frightening pressures. On the one side young dreads, brimful of unused energies, fear and resentment, aggression and ideological ardour, some with the violence aching to be out of them ... a short fuse for any police sparks. On the other the young coppers, understaffed, overworked. (104)

Brown's link between black political organisation and crime has borne strange fruit not only in 'Wolcott' but in the reporting of events in Bristol: 'It was then all the aggravation started. The crowd was jeering and shouting and two or three youths dressed in the rastafarian style began throwing stones and planks of wood'. (105) More recently at a demonstration in London: 'a television crew with commentator David McCormick was surrounded by blacks with rastafarian haircuts and threatened'. (106) Both examples operate on territory Brown created in his separation of the 'real' rasta from the 'hard-core' criminal 'dread' who 'constantly threatens the peace of individual citizens, black, brown and white'. (107)

These days it is de riguer for race researchers of all political complexions to indulge in gestural condemnation of Brown's work. Too often, as in the work of Rex and Cashmore, they kick him down the front steps only to sneak him in through the conceptual back door a few pages later. The uneasy analytic junction at which they encounter Brown has excluded discussion of his work on its academic merits. These authors and their sociological peers remain unable to face the realisation that their own understanding of the black communities in terms of identity crises, pathological family forms, generational conflict, and

36

subsequent criminality, dovetails not only with common sense racism but also, through Brown, with the operational ideologies of the policemen on the front line. One of whom, the Commander of the Handsworth sub-division explains his tasks thus:

> The need to persuade West Indian parents to relax strict discipline code (sic) which leads to strife within the family group and the consequent break up of homes is an important factor in creating future stability. Stabilising the home surroundings and drying up the flow of youngsters moving towards the squats and Rastafarianism is of paramount social importance. (108)

Although the vision of 'racial hell holes' terrorised by 'dreadlocks, rootless, squatting, pseudo-rastafarian young thugs' (109) has enabled 'the dread' to supercede the more familiar mugger as principal signifier of social disorder and black criminality, it is premature to assume that the mugger has been deracialised to the point that he cannot stage a comeback. Dr Michael Pratt, a long serving employee of the CID at Scotland Yard has recently argued for a view of mugging as a 'machismo cultural option' for disenchanted West Indian youth. Here we learn that the

> down to earth reason why mugging has emerged as the perfect cultural option for disillusioned young West Indians (is because) deep rooted in West Indian culture is the motivation to 'go it alone'. This comes initially from the not very far off days of slavery when it was very much to the owner's advantage if he could keep the slaves from communicating with each other'. (110)

It is no longer sufficient to say that the arrogance, insensitivity, distortion, bad history and sloppy scholarship typified by Pratt are par for the course in 'race-relations' today. The terrain of black culture is, no less today than it was during slavery, the site of conflict and struggle.

CONCLUSION

We have presented a picture of sociology as newly relevant to the social control of crisis conditions and sketched the distinct way in which race research has developed in this context. This leaves us with the realisation that contrary to the evidence of some publications in this field, sociologists are not yet simple state functionaries. This raises the consideration of what type of race research ought to be undertaken in the present situation, whose ends it should serve and who should carry it out. We are aware that, regardless of an author's intentions, academic analysis may serve a variety of ends. But we insist that recognition of the contours of racial politics, the historical tendency of state development, and the articulation of the plight of the black communities, demands that an avowedly critical intellectual practice ceases to regurgitate the commonsense logic of racism and repatriation. The reinforcement given to repressive state strategy by ill-considered, slapdash and inaccurate research which disregards the authority of its black subjects over their own experience, cannot go unchallenged.

We must further insist that this is not a simple matter of 'left' and 'right'. Recent work from a 'radical' perspective (111) should be viewed as evidence that the work of the so-called left can be as injurious to black interests as the work examined above. These authors with their rigid counterposition of race and class consciousness, and eurocentric conceptualisation of 'the political' distort our struggles to fit models which do not take our political traditions into account.

In this paper we have attempted to convey that black politics and cultural struggles cannot be defined beyond the boundaries of your work. We are not another 'topic' to be appropriated according to whim. In studying us you face political choices which should be acknowledged openly. Our position is simple and stands or falls on the status of black authority over the processes of researching the black communities. To sociologists we convey a simple message: forget black people and research the machinations of the racism which oppresses them.

FOOTNOTES AND REFERENCES

(1)   For a more developed argument see the forthcoming book, White Sociology, Black Struggle - Britain in the 1970s, Race and Politics Group, CCCS, University of Birmingham.

(2)   K. Little, Negroes in Britain, London, 1948, and A. Richmond, Colour Prejudice in Britain, London, 1954.

(3)   See the early work of Michael Banton, notably M. Banton, Race Relations, Tavistock, 1967; J. Rex, Race, Colonialism and the City, RKP, London, 1973; and publications from the SSRC Unit on Ethnic Relations, University of Bristol.

(4)   A. Green, 'The Political Economy of Black Labour', CCCS Paper.

(5)   Rex, 1973, op.cit, p.177.

(6)   S. Patterson, Dark Strangers, Penguin, 1965.

(7)   J. Rex and S. Tomlinson, Colonial Immigrants in a British City, London, 1979.

(8)   J. Lea, 'The Contradictions of the Sixties Race Relations Legislation' in Permissiveness and Control, Papers from the National Deviancy Conference, London, 1980.

(9)   For a development of this argument see Race and Politics Group, CCCS, op.cit, ch.1.

(10)   S. Hall et al, Policing the Crisis: Mugging, the State and Law and Order, Macmillan, London, 1978.

(11)   J. Watson (ed.), Between Two Cultures, CRE, London,

1977.
(12) C. Ballard, in Watson, _ibid_.
(13) R. Ballard, in Watson, _ibid_.
(14) See the material cited under note (4).
(15) Rex and Tomlinson, _op.cit_.
(16) For a critique see P. Gilroy, 'Managing the Uncer-
class', _Race and Class_, 21, 4, 1980.
(17) L. Bridges, 'Ministry of Internal Security', _Race
and Class_, 16, 4, 1975.
(18) J. Bourne, 'Cheerleaders and Ombudsmen: The Sociology
of Race Relations in Britain', _Race and Class_, 21, 4,
1980.
(19) R. Jenkins, 'The Production of Knowledge in the IRR',
BSA Conference paper, 1966, quoted in Bourne, _ibid_,
p.338.
(20) Bourne, _ibid_, p.339.
(21) V. Khan (ed.), _Minority Families in Britain: Support
and Stress_, Macmillan, 1979.
(22) See, for example, A. Jansari, 'Social Work with Ethnic
Minorities: A Review of the Literature', _Multi-Racial
Social Work_, 1, Derby, 1980.
(23) Cashmore spoke recently, for example, at a conference
organised by the Commonwealth Institute (12.3.81).
Among the audience were a number of Police Inspectors.
(24) K. Pryce, _Endless Pressure_, Penguin, 1979.
(25) C. Prescod, 'Black Thoughts', _New Society_, 3, 5, 1979.
(26) E. Cashmore, _Rastaman: The Rastafarian Movement in
England_, Allen and Unwin, 1979, pp.11-14.
(27) _Ibid_, p.57.
(28) _Ibid_, p.5.
(29) _Ibid_, p.11.
(30) C. Ballard, 'Conflict, Continuity and Change: Second
Generation Asians', in Khan (ed.), _op.cit_, pp.109-10.
(31) N. Foner, _Jamaica Farewell: Jamaican Migrants in
London_, RKP, 1979, pp.17-18.
(32) B. Troyna, 'Differential Use of Media Culture by
Black Youths in Britain', paper delivered to the 1978
BSA Media Conference.
(33) D. Smith, 'Women's Perspective as Radical Critique
of Sociology', _Sociological Enquiry_, 1974, 44.
(34) Prescod, _op.cit_.
(35) Pryce, _op.cit_, p.3.
(36) Rex and Tomlinson, _op.cit_, p.291.
(37) _Ibid_, p.237.
(38) Hall, _op.cit_, p.291.
(39) _Ibid_, p.161.
(40) J. Rex, 'A Working Paradigm for Race Relations
Research', _Ethnic and Racial Studies_, vol.4, no.1,
Jan. 1981, p.7.
(41) C.L.R. James, _The Black Jacobins_, Allen and Unwin,
1980.
(42) Pryce, _op.cit_, p.16.
(43) _Ibid_, p.108.
(44) _Ibid_, p.109.
(45) Cashmore, _op.cit_, p.139.
(46) M. Barrett, _Women's Oppression Today: Problems in
Marxist Feminist Analysis_, NLB, 1980, pp.199-204.

(47) Pryce views the Afro-Caribbean societies as matriarchal; Cashmore views the Afro-Caribbean family as matrifocal.
(48) Cashmore, op.cit, see ch.3, 'From Evasion to Truculence'.
(49) See, for example, B. Coard, How the West Indian Child is made Educationally Sub-Normal in the British School System, New Beacon Books, London, 1971.
(50) Pryce, op.cit, p.120.
(51) Rex and Tomlinson, op.cit, p.291.
(52) P. Weinreich, 'Ethnicity and Adolescent Identity Conflicts: A Comparative Study', in Khan, op.cit, p.89.
(53) Ibid, pp.98-9.
(54) H. Campbell, 'Rastafari: Culture of Resistance', Race and Class, vol.XXII, no.1, 1980.
(55) Hall et al, op.cit, ch.10.
(56) P. Gilroy, quoted from chapter of forthcoming Race and Politics Group, CCCS, op.cit.
(57) Cashmore, op.cit, p.78.
(58) V. Khan, 'Migration and Social Stress: Mirpuris in Bradford', in Khan (ed.), op.cit.
(59) V. Khan, 'The Pakistanis: Mirpuri Villagers at Home and in Bradford', in Watson (ed.), op.cit.
(60) D. Brooks and K. Singh, 'Pivots and Presents' in S. Wallman (ed.), Ethnicity at Work, London, 1979. Quoted in J. Bourne, op.cit.
(61) S. Wallman, quoted in Bourne, ibid, p.344.
(62) Ibid, p.344.
(63) I. Ahmed, 'Pakistan: Class and State Formation', Race and Class, vol.XII, no.3, 1981.
(64) Khan, op.cit, p.44.
(65) Ibid, p.42.
(66) Watson, op.cit.
(67) Ibid, p.109.
(68) Rex and Tomlinson, op.cit, p.291.
(69) Ibid, p.237.
(70) A view presented in 'File on Four', BBC Radio 4, 26.2.81.
(71) Supt. L. Roach, 'The Metropolitan Police Community Relations Branch', Police Studies, 3, 1978.
(72) F. Kitson, Low Intensity Operations, London, 1971; R. Evelegh, Peace Keeping in a Democratic Society, London, 1978 and 'Racialism a Threat to our Security', (editorial) Army Quarterly, April, 1977.
(73) A. Sherman, Daily Telegraph, 8.9.1976 and 9.9.1976.
(74) Sir David MacNee, Guardian, 25.9.1979.
(75) See P. Gilroy, 'Managing the Underclass', Race and Class, 21, 4, 1980.
(76) The Sun, 11.11.1980.
(77) Quoted by Assistant Commissioner C.J. Dear, The Police Journal, April/June 1972.
(78) MacNee, op.cit.
(79) Margaret Thatcher, speech in Birmingham, 19.4.1979.
(80) J. Brown, A Theory of Police-Immigrant Relations, Cranfield, 1974.
(81) Ibid.

(82) M. Cain, Society and the Policeman's Role, RKP, 1972; S. Holdaway, 'Changes in Urban Policing', British Journal of Sociology, June, 1977; S. Holdaway, 'The Reality of Police Race Relations', New Community, Summer, 1978 and M. Banton, 'Crime Prevention in the Context of Criminal Policy', Police Studies, Summer, 1978.

(83) Roach, op.cit.

(84) E. Schaffer, Community Policing, Croom Helm, 1980; Home Office, 'The Police Service and its Relations with Ethnic Minorities', Conference Paper, December, 1980. See also the Home Office evidence to the Scarman enquiry.

(85) J. Alderson, The Police We Deserve, London, 1973, see the contributions by Alderson, Stead and Chatterton.

(86) Dear, op.cit.

(87) Stead, in Alderson, op.cit, p.130.

(88) Chatterton, 'Sociology and the Police', in Alderson, op.cit.

(89) D. Humphry, Police Power and Black People, Panther, 1972.

(90) G. John, Race and the Inner City, Runnymede, 1970.

(91) S. Pullé, Police-Community Relations in Ealing, Runnymede, 1973.

(92) Brown, op.cit.

(93) J. Biggs-Davidson, 'The Role of the Armed Forces in Peace-Keeping', RUSI Seminar, 4.4.1973.

(94) Speech by Sir Robert Carr, 1.11.1973.

(95) Commander Peter Marshall, quoted in T.A. Critchley, A History of the Police in England and Wales, 2nd edition, 1978, pp.328.

(96) Banton, 1978, op.cit, p.8.

(97) Sir Robert Mark, 'Introduction', in Critchley, op.cit.

(98) Critchley, op.cit, p.329.

(99) Metropolitan Police, 'Police-West Indian Confront-ations', evidence to Commons Select Committee, 25.3.1976.

(100) Ibid, 'The Dilemma of Public Debate'.

(101) A. Leivesley, in Police Review, 7.3.1980.

(102) J. Brown, Shades of Gray, Cranfield, 1977.

(103) West Midlands Police, 'The Lozells Project - Back-ground and Objectives', undated.

(104) Brown, 1977, op.cit, p.8.

(105) Daily Telegraph, 3.4.1980.

(106) Daily Mirror, 3.3.1981.

(107) Brown, op.cit, p.8.

(108) Supt. D. Webb, 'Policing a Multi-Racial Community', West Midlands Police, op.cit, p.11.

(109) Blake Baker, 'The Softly-Softly Approach to Race Relations', Daily Telegraph, 9.5.1980.

(110) M. Pratt, Mugging as a Social Problem, RKP, 1980.

(111) R. Miles and P. Phizaclea, Labour and Racism, RKP. 1980. The work of J. Gabriel and G.S. Ben Tovim suffers from similar limitations.

3 Female Manual Workers, Fatalism and the Reinforcement of Inequalities
KATE PURCELL

THE PASSIVE WOMEN WORKER THESIS

Women and men in employment are distributed throughout the labour market in a systematically different way. The majority of women are employed in jobs and occupational areas which employ few men and which have come to be regarded as 'women's work': they predominate in the lower status occupational levels of the service sector and in manufacturing, are largely confined to semi-skilled and unskilled jobs in the clothing and textile industries, in the production of food, drink and tobacco and in the assembly of small components in the electrical engineering industry. This occupational segregation largely explains why the impact of the Equal Pay Act has been limited and women continue to have considerably lower average hourly earnings than men, as is clearly revealed by the New Earnings Surveys (DE Gazette January 1981). Throughout the workforce, women are the low status, low skilled, low paid complements to men who (all other things being equal) have more status, more recognised skills and higher remuneration. An explanation is required for the stability of this asymetrical sexual division of labour and particularly, for women's apparent acquiescence in a status quo which clearly discriminates against them as workers.

Between January and May 1980, I was employed as a semi-skilled manual worker in an electrical engineering factory in the North West of England. I had previously carried out a survey of manual workers in a similar area, investigating their attitudes to and experience of work and domestic responsibilities and their resultant political attitudes and wider orientations, particularly concerning work and gender roles.* The central objective of the research was to find out whether and how far there were differences in the work experiences and attitudes of women and men. The

*SSRC-sponsored project entitled 'Manual Workers and the Sexual Division of Labour', directed by Kate Purcell and David Bennett at Manchester Polytechnic between March 1976 and May 1979.

experience of carrying out that project convinced me that the only way to obtain an accurate impression of how people behave at work and how their beliefs about gender affect their interaction, behaviour and definition of situations, would be to work alongside them and observe their day-to-day management of their working environment and reaction to specific stimuli. I also felt that it was important for me to have subjective experience of being a manual worker in order to clarify my understanding of the pressures and practicalities of doing such work, to reassure me that my theorising as a feminist and as an industrial sociologist was based on shared practical experience rather than some sort of 'secondhand experience' (Porter, 1978) or abstract ideological perception deriving almost solely from theory.

I was particularly concerned to explore what I have called elsewhere 'the passive woman worker thesis' - the idea that women are generally more stable, passive and fundamentally exploitable workers than men (Purcell, 1979). In the survey interviews, both men and women had frequently said of women's work: 'Men wouldn't stand for it', the implication being that women are prepared to put up with a high degree of repetition, boredom and unfavourable conditions of employment that most men would find intolerable. Despite clear evidence that women in industry are less often members of unions than their male counterparts and are less often active trade unionists when they are union members (Coote and Kellner, 1981), the differences in patterns of behaviour in different industries and sizes of companies indicate that at least a significant element of this apparent gender difference is explicable in terms of the way in which women are distributed within the workforce. It is because women are employed in industries which are difficult to organise that their trade union membership is lower, rather than because women are difficult to organise that the industries are characterised by low union density (Purcell, 1979). There is also considerable evidence to suggest that women are discriminated against within trade unions, both because the social organisation of repro- duction, childrearing and marital divisions of labour conflicts with the demands of active union membership (Newland, 1980, p.24) and because of the male-dominated, homosocial nature of trade union structures and practices (Stageman, 1980, Boston, 1980) and men's attitudes to women as workers (Armstrong, 1976, pp.85-98). I wanted to see how far women's and men's actual behaviour in the work- place varied, particularly with reference to industrial relations and control of the work environment. Thus, my fieldwork began with the assumption that I was engaged upon a piece of ethnographic research in industrial sociology, but it rapidly became obvious that the scope of my analyses would have to be extended. What I initially took to be an interesting but irrelevant factor - frequent references in the course of most working days to superstition, luck, chance and the supernatural by the women I worked with - I now wish to relate to the central concern of my research: women's apparent passivity and political apathy at work. I

44

intend to explore the hypotheses:

i) that women's behaviour at work, like their behaviour elsewhere, is informed by and emerges from a fatalistic approach to life,
ii) that this fatalism is fostered by gender socialisation, women's biology and the social experience of being a woman and
iii) that it is particularly reinforced by manual working women's work and class circumstances.

THE WORKPLACE

The labour market in the area where I sought employment was far from buoyant, particularly as far as factory work for women was concerned, and it proved extremely difficult to get a job. Eventually I obtained employment as a plastic finisher (or trimmer) in a small factory on a large engineering site. The workshop where I was employed currently contained seven women workers: four other trimmers, two viewers (which is what women on inspection are called to distinguish them from males doing the same job, who are called inspectors and paid more, ostensibly on the grounds that they have a job history of skilled work) and a production clerk. There were twelve moulders (semiskilled men, who worked shifts), a production engineer, a moulding engineer, the foreman, the labourer and an inspector. In addition, considerable numbers of other employees passed through the workshop daily, either on specific business or merely in passing, and most of these were men: rate fixers, maintenance workers, technical staff, management, representatives of the firms we supplied, and assorted white-coated personnel who had no clear job specification of relevance to our workshop. In this, it mirrored the distribution of women and men in industry as a whole: men were classified as more highly skilled, were more highly paid and apart from the moulders, had more intrinsically interesting work, more discretion about how and when they did it, more authority and appeared to have more freedom generally. Although males and females were formally segregated insofar as their actual work areas did not generally overlap there was constant communication and some need for practical co-operation. For example when the women have filled heavy boxes with completed 'jobs', there is nearly always a convenient male to lift them down from the bench and take them away from the trimming area. This may be the foreman, labourer or one of the moulders, and by and large they 'labour' for the women cheerfully and ungrudgingly: the only hint of animosity is minor irritation on the part of the women when some men offer to lift easily manageable loads in exaggerated reinforcement of gender differences. There was little evidence of sexual harassment (McKinnon, 1979), of violent, repressive reinforcement of sex and gender differences and inequalities (Whitehead, 1976) or of 'mock-courtship' to the extent described elsewhere (Morgan,1969, Wilson,1963). Perhaps this was partly a function of the ages of most of the people concerned, because there was a considerable amount of sexual badinage and mock chivalry, particularly in the relationship of the foreman and the 'girls' (all but one over thirty-five). On the whole, however, such joking behaviour and sexual allusion which does take place is less related to exploitation or explicit denigration of the women than referring to the women's greater 'earthiness', perpetrated by the women themselves. Men said to me jokingly when I started work: 'you don't want to sink to their (the women's level) ... the language is enough to make your hair curl'... which is in fact quite inaccurate. Apart from a few minor expletives, the women's mode of expression was positively genteel compared to that of the average sociology department. An element of collective bawdiness contrasted with individual shyness and prudery and might be seen as an attempt to exert protective solidarity in a predominantly male environment, capitalising on primitive male uneasiness about women's natural 'unclean' powers relating to sexuality and reproduction (Mernissi, 1975). The women revelled in 'embarrassing' shy men. Fred the foreman (a father of daughters) could be sent scurrying to the other end of the workshop redfaced by the mention of Tampax. This had become ritualised to the extent that, if the women were talking about something amongst themselves that they didn't wish Fred to overhear and he came into sight, one of them would raise her voice and say: 'So I said ... 'ang on a minute and I'll get the Tampax ...' which invariably sent him scuttling away, jocular but blushing. Similarly, one of the white-coated regular passers-through who always stopped by the bench for a chat and to collect the pools money was known to the women as 'Never 'ad it' because apparently, on some occasion in the past, the details of which were long forgotten, he had shown naivety on some sex-related topic. The older women jestingly flirted with him: 'When are you going to take me out? - Your wife wouldn't mind ... you don't miss what you've never 'ad!'. He always came back for more.

This sort of joking relationship illustrates the general atmosphere in the workshop. The management style is very much to leave workers to get on with the work at their own pace subject to acceptable productivity and although the women work hard, the effort is accompanied by and interspersed with frequent social interaction and relaxed relationships. As in Donald Roy's 'Banana Time' study, 'Our work group was not only abandoned to its own resources for creating job satisfaction, but left without that basic reservoir of ill will toward management which can sometimes be counted on to stimulate the development of interesting activities to occupy hand and brain' (Roy, 1958, p.159). Supervision was very low-key and not at all authoritarian. The supervisor himself extolled the view that: 'We operate like a big happy family here. We all work together and if we 'ave a problem we sort it out quickly. I pride myself on knowing my girls well, and I trust them and they trust me'. The 'girls' didn't quite see it like that, treating Fred's

frequent demonstrations of paternalism and chivalry with
disdain and belittling and mocking him behind his back,
but there was an element of ritual even in this, almost as
if they were reacting to the supervisory role rather than
to the incumbent: in practical terms, relationships did
operate amicably and approached Fred's model quite closely.
Diatribes about Fred's alleged inefficiency, mendacity,
megalomania, dishonesty, unreliability and two-facedness
always ended: '... but I s'pose he's not such a bad old
stick really ... 'e means well, most of the time. 'E's 'is
own worst enemy'. However, it is important to note that
the apparent freedom of the workers was very clearly
circumscribed and was contingent freedom within well-
defined constraints. Indulgency patterns (Goulder, 1954)
were understood to extend only so far and the arrival of
management in the workshop prompted a conspicuous expenditure of effort. Similarly, traditions like the stopping
of work at 4pm for 4.30pm and clock-watching for the last
half-hour (a dubious privilege) was enjoyed with an eye on
the door for the possible approach of management. All of
the informal freedoms were thus constrained. There was a
clear working awareness of 'them and us' and the power
differentials therein, which has been described elsewhere
as 'factory consciousness' (Beynon, 1976).

The work which we women were doing was boring, repetitive
and had little intrinsic satisfaction. Mainly, it consisted
of manually filing the rough edges (known as 'flashing')
off moulded bakelite-like commodities, ranging from tiny
screw-heads to fairly large parts of industrial components.
We also spent considerable time shot-blasting such items,
and trimming and boring holes in them with a variety of
electrical power-operated machines. The job of trimming is
tedious, pernickety, quite hard physically, causing
calloused hands, aching wrists, aching back and eyestrain,
as well as being generally debilitating because of the
atmosphere in the workshop and particularly, the dust from
one particular moulding material used, which causes throat
dryness and if bits get on your skin, an itchy, red rash.
In summer we all had tiny red pinhead rashes all over our
legs and feet.

The workshop generally provides a paradigm example of
British industry as it is portrayed by its most vehement
critics of the left: industrial relations are in fact
pretty good, measured in terms of union-management co-
operation and lack of overt conflict, but there appears to
be negligible investment in plant, very little communication between management and workers or stewards and
workers (although management see communication as good) and
technologically it is really archaic, with positively
antediluvian equipment. One day, after I'd been asking about
the technical aspects of production, Bill the moulding
engineer brought in a few brochures of moulding presses -
glossy pictures of shiny modern equipment which bore a
passing resemblance to the well-worn, grubby presses in the
workshop, which, he assures me, do the same job. Later I

said to Rosie, one of my workmates who has worked with the firm for over forty years: 'Funny thing is, I never see anybody referring to manuals here', to which she responded:

> Oh no!... Well, the manual wouldn't be any good any more on most of them, because they alter them and tinker about to make them suit our particular specifications. That, and the fact that they're all at least second-hand - the manual doesn't come with them, I don't s'pose. Bill goes round scrapyards - yes 'e does! - looking for bits, and he sees something and says 'We'll have that' and brings it in. That's the trouble here - half the machinery is falling to bits and the other half they don't know how to operate it.

This sounds ludicrous, but it _is_ the general perception of the women workers and it was substantiated by my experience. An allegedly new deflashing machine was installed soon after I began work there and as far as I know, after several extensive but erratic attempts to get it to work, it is still not in use. Much of the machinery looked ancient and Rosie claimed that it had been there longer than her, and productivity is limited by 'bad jobs', scrapping and waste caused by mechanical failure, 'bad moulds' and alleged inefficiency on the part of the moulders. The women work for piece rates and their ability to 'make good money' is very much dependent on the moulding process being carried out properly with high quality materials. Too much powder in the mould makes moulded items heavy or crumbly with thicker flash than usual, which slows down the pace of trimming and increases the reject rate. Working conditions are noisy, dirty, with erratic, unexpected noises super-imposed on a constant buzz and whine of machinery, sudden explosions of steam and air, and sudden bangs of heavy weights descending. People exposed to these conditions eventually become relatively immune to them, and develop lipreading and telepathic techniques to manage communica-tion so that I rapidly became accustomed to the noise level whilst working there: now, when I play tapes of interviews supposedly recorded in quiet corners and empty adjacent workshops I find it extremely difficult to make out what is being said. The women's work is exactly the sort of work which could be easily replaced by microelectronic equip-ment, and carried out much more quickly and efficiently, as is already happening elsewhere. This is unlikely to happen in this particular company, in the short term at least, because of the small batch production involved. It would not be economically viable to replace labour with machinery because the women are more flexible than currently available mechanical alternatives.

THE WOMEN'S WORK

The job of trimmer is an absolutely classic 'woman's job', insofar as it is boring, repetitive, requiring 'nimble fingers' and very little thought, although as Donald Roy has pointed out, it is possible to invest even the most mundane task with interest and to derive satisfaction from any slight suggestion of variation or skill (Roy, 1952). On one hand, it is imprisonment, exploitation, a continuous deadening of the soul, of which it might legitimately be asked why people should have to tolerate such circumscribed daily existences, relatively low incomes and attacks on their faculties. Marianne Herzog has graphically documented the working conditions of similar women workers in West Germany (Herzog, 1980) and Ruth Cavendish describes the stultifying daily grind of women on the line in the car components industry in this country (Cavendish, 1981) but in the experience of both these researchers, working conditions were unremittingly worse than where I worked. When the relationship between capital and labour is mystified by laissez-faire supervision, friendly relationships and the experience of relative freedom, people who have experienced more constraints at work elsewhere are apt to compare their lot favourably with other jobs and individuals where conditions are worse, rather than challenge the limitations of their present working conditions. The women at my factory 'liked' working there and so did I. Such work provides a pattern to life, a sense of belonging, a sense of making a contribution to society, friendly interactions, 'good laughs', all of which are precarious and dependent upon daily reinforcement but which give the individual a clear sense of legitimacy and membership, an almost Durkheimian sense of social solidarity. The women I worked with were apparently typical of the stereotype of woman worker: atypically they were all members of a trade union as required by the union shop agreement which operated in the company, but they could not be described as active trade unionists. Their involvement in the union was minimal, they had low expectations of job satisfaction, they were pretty passive at work - certainly not challenging any norms.

At one stage, the department's male shop steward resigned because he wanted to maximise his earnings by working shifts and this was incompatible with carrying out his union duties. No one was willing to take on the job, but the obvious candidate was the informal leader of the women, a spirited and politically astute person who can always be relied upon to pursue and defend her interests and those of her workmates on a day-to-day basis on the shopfloor. When her name was canvassed, she responded: 'Oh no, they wouldn't have a woman. Well they couldn't have a woman to deal with the men's claims'. So I said (low profile, value-free participant observation!): 'Why not? You've had a man for the last five years; what's the difference?' The response was: '... come on, Kate. There is a difference. Now, isn't there?' And indeed there is. Further persuasion caused her to move her defence to: ,Well, I'd be no good, I'm no good in an argument. I'd get too angry. I'd lose my temper, I'd burst into tears.' Observation and friendship suggest that these excuses have little substance. Her final position of retreat was: 'Anyway, it's a hopeless job. You end up not pleasing anybody and you can't get anything done in this place anyhow ...It's a waste of time to go to meetings to hear them bleating on about how poor the company is and how lucky we are to have jobs! There's no point, it's not worth it ... apathy, that's what it is.' Me: 'But that's not apathy is it?' Jane: 'Apathy - not interested, can't be bothered, not worth the trouble, waste of time, couldn't care less ... I don't know what else I'd call it but apathy.'

It is important to note, however, that the women are very well able to control their own wage bargaining situation, have an astute grasp of the balance of power in the work-place, and manage to manipulate their own working con-ditions and family lives as efficiently as seemed possible within the externally-imposed constraints which they experienced. For example, their management of the piece-work system was highly sophisticated and definitely several jumps ahead of Bert the ratefixer and the management generally. I also noted several instances when injustices were done to individuals and the work group sprang to the defence of the people concerned and advised them how to retaliate or have the wrong redressed. One girl was sent unwillingly to another part of the factory where there was a rush on, to a job which she hated but had previous experience of and was repeatedly sent to. Managers cajoled her, flattering her that she was the only person with the experience to fill the gap in production. The male shop steward joined in trying to talk her into it, saying: 'You've got to see it from their (the management's) point of view'. To which Jane expostulated: 'Bloody hell, if he goes around seeing it from their point of view, what hope do we have?' The women had an informal meeting and advised the girl being transferred to go, but only on condition that someone else would also be put to learn the job alongside her, so that the same thing need not happen again.

The work, although repetitive, is fairly varied and if ultimately the workers have no influence over their work flow, they generally can choose from amongst a range of jobs and alternate amongst them except when there's a 'rush job' on. If you get tired of filing black boxes, you can spend an hour on the machine shot-blasting contacts, or change to red knobs for a bit. Shopfloor relationships are relaxed and amicable. The pace is not harassed. In fact, one of the ways in which the trimmers control their working conditions is to work very fast and 'buy' tea-break extensions and extra breaks. As far as relationships with management are concerned, they have a clear notion of 'them' and 'us' and the differences of interest and values between the two, but there is very little conflictual grievance indicated by their behaviour. They are positively not deferential: whilst paying lip service to rule follow-ing and respectful attitudes to managers, their behaviour occasionally verges on the insolent: 'Oh yes, we're all very hard workers here, Mister Burger', in response to a half joking reference to their extended tea-breaks by a passing middle manager. They have little respect for those whose decisions and judgement control their supply of work, and are astutely critical of the inefficiency, short-sighted planning and ill-judged attempts to improve communication between management and workers. After being shown a film advocating increased productivity, there was a cynical response on the women's part: 'They're always telling us we've got to work harder, save electric, make more effort! Huh! I don't notice them making any sacrifices. What about all them big company cars in the car park.' They feel that the identities of workers as individuals, both males and females, are undervalued in the workplace and that management sees them merely as cogs in the machine.

Whilst they only fleetingly resent these 'hidden injuries of class' (Sennett and Cobb, 1977) they do articulate awareness of them, as the following instances demonstrate, and the scars left by such injuries reinforce their feelings of powerlessness and lack of importance. 'They'll rush around and tell you how good you are when they've a rush job on, but the rest of the time they're not bothered. There's no getting away from it ... you're just a name and a number to them.' Talk then turned to redundancy. Several men and women had recently been made redundant. One man had been made redundant after forty-eight years: 'and they treated him very badly', said Rosie. 'D'you know ... even after all those years, Burger didn't even shake 'is 'and!'

They perceive inequality and inefficiency in both management and the unions at the factory, but they do not mount a challenge. However, it is not accurate to describe their basically acquiescent acceptance of conditions as pragmatic acceptance (Mann, 1969) because that implies that their continued consent in the mode of production and particularly within the sexual division of labour, is con-tingent upon lack of opportunity for alternative organisation, and is inherently unstable. As a feminist, I would like to think that this is the case but my impression after working alongside these particular manual working women at least was that their acceptance was more securely rooted, more unquestioning than that suggests: more like fatalistic tolerance - 'that's the way things are and ever will be'.

FATALISM

In fact, this ties in very clearly with another sigificant feature of daily life at the factory: the workers' interest in the supernatural, fortune-telling, horoscopes and spiritualism. Part of the ritual of every day was reading aloud the horoscopes in the popular daily papers and whilst this was generally done in a spirit of scepticism and joking, it was the quality rather than the nature of the commodity which was in question. In addition, hardly a day went past when previous visits to fortune-tellers were not

relived, analysed and evaluated in the light of recent
events in the lives in question. All but one of the women
I worked with and those I interviewed claimed to have
visited a fortune-teller or medium of some sort on at least
one occasion and most had been considerably more frequently.
None of the men admitted to having done so. Participating
in talk about visits to fortune-tellers and what happened
- the advice and prophecies given, the description of what
'she' (the medium) said and how they responded - it is
clear that such expeditions fulfil a variety of functions
by no means all of which are related to fatalism. Going to
the fortune-teller is in part a social event which reinforces the social solidarity of the work group and is, on
one level, a culturally legitimate 'night out with the
girls' and 'a bit of a giggle'. It is also an opportunity
for them to derive psychological benefit from counselling,
enabling them to analyse their work and personal lives with
the medium in a way that they would be unlikely to do with
anyone else. It is, after all, often very satisfying to
talk about oneself for an hour or more, and my experience of
interviewing manual workers and others suggests that the
majority of people derive considerable interest and enjoyment from interviews, often expressing the sentiment that
it has done them good to talk about their work and other
things, to 'get it off their chest'.

Much of the advice given by fortune-tellers that
individuals repeated to me was very much practical counselling advice rather like that purveyed by agony columnists.
The seers obviously start from the assumption that there are
at least some causes of dissatisfaction in the lives of
those who consult them, and by careful questioning and
speculative clues, discover what the problem is and help
the customer to think it through. For example, women were
told that they would be divorced, and this would be a new
beginning for them, which they must take advantage of. A
single woman in her fifties was told:

> Your main trouble is you're not prepared to take risks.
> You're very choosy who you go out with, you care too
> much what other people think. You should get out a bit
> more - have you ever been to the Palace on a Friday
> night? You ought to go, it's really nice. Perhaps you
> will, I see you meeting a man there ... he might be
> a married man, so watch it!

A great deal of the advice and prophecy concerns relationships with men and members of families. Despite the
fact that most of the women have no illusions about the
realities of love and marriage and living happily ever
after, they still want to be told that they will meet an
attractive, economically viable man who will solve all their
problems. This reflects their socialisation into the
feminine role, but it probably also accurately reflects the
fact that the experiences of warmth and sharing which
characterise romantic love do provide a sense of urgency
and an illusion of escape from a pretty routine, uneventful

existence. Married or single, they see the only real hope of major improvement in their lives in these terms. Thus, I was gleefully informed: 'Flo was told she'd be divorced and she'd meet another fella. It 'asn't happened yet, but she can't wait!'

Alongside the frivolity however, there is a serious investment in the fortune-telling. Everyone is nervous about going and unless a medium gives very unsatisfactory or inaccurate readings, in which case she is denounced as fraudulent, there is an underlying assumption that she has extra-sensory powers which enable her to see and foretell relationships and events in the future. There is consequently a fatalistic belief that the individual's life is preordained, 'what will be, will be', and the nearest you can get to controlling it is to be prepared for what is to come through the offices of one of these peculiarly talented people who 'can see more than the rest of us'. In this sense, visiting a medium is to some extent an attempt to exert control, but it is not in order to change events, merely to 'know what's in store', to be prepared. It is also an attempt to illuminate the present and to come to terms with unsatisfactory aspects of it by focussing on the future.

WOMEN'S INTERESTS

The interest of the women in social and political events outside their particular experience appeared to be limited. Like the housewives interviewed by Dorothy Hobson they regarded politics, most current affairs and industrial relations as presented in television news bulletins as '(a) depressing (b) boring, but (c) important' (Hobson, 1980, p.111). 'Human interest' news, as purveyed by the popular press, interests them more because it relates more closely to their concerns. The other main topic of conversation at work, apart from anecdotes of families and particularly, children's 'cuteness', was health. Stories were repeatedly told of relatives and acquaintances who were suffering, or had suffered from illness or physical misfortune, almost as if telling the story was an insurance against being similarly afflicted oneself.

The popular press is also full of stories of grotesque misfortune - children dying of cancer, families having terrible runs of accidents and bereavements, couples being slaughtered in road accidents on their way to honeymoon hotels ... every day there are several examples of this sort of tale. Whilst I was working in the factory I found that I was very vulnerable to this kind of information. I'd catch myself thinking terrible morbid thoughts, particularly when I was working alone on a machine. When I remarked about this to the others, they all agreed that they were similarly affected. Daily exposure to the Sun and the Star induces a view of the world as awfully dangerous, fate as capricious and such pleasures in relationships with significant others

53

that one has, as transient and contingent upon the whims of fortune and chance. The popular dailies frequently run week-long serials about the 'inside story' of the lifestyle of a popular celebrity - often a pop star such as Rod Stewart - invariably of working-class origins - who has risen to fame, wealth, endless access to luxury and particularly, excesses of sex and decadence - and who is 'really' lonely and unhappy. The clear moral which shines through is that money and sexual variety don't bring happiness, indeed, they probably promote wretchedness and you're better off the way you are. The tales are generally told by a former henchman, now working away from the tinsel and glamour of showbiz or big-time sport in an 'ordinary job', declaring that he wouldn't change places with the celebrity for anything.

FATALISM AND SUPERSTITION

It is obvious that there is a relationship between people's image of the world and their perception of their situation in it, and their attitude to work and social organisation. It seems to me that the key to understanding much of what passes for acquiescence at work: tolerance of poor working conditions and conditions of employment, unwillingness to become active in trade unions and take militant action amongst the majority of unskilled and semi-skilled female and male workers, is fatalism. Fatalism has been defined as: 'the degree to which an individual perceives a lack of ability to control his (sic) future. Fatalistic individuals believe that the events in their lives are pre-ordained and determined by fate or supernatural forces. Their attitudes towards self-control of future events includes passivity, pessimism, acceptance, endurance, pliancy and evasion' (Rogers, 1969, p.42). Richard Hoggart, writing about working-class attitudes, says:

> When people feel that they cannot do much about the main elements of their situation, feel it not necessarily with despair or disappointment or resentment but simply as a fact of life, they adopt attitudes toward that situation which allow them to have a liveable life under its shadow, a life without a constant and pressing sense of the larger situation. The attitudes remove the main elements in the situation to the realms of natural laws, the given and the raw, the almost implaceable material from which a living has to be carved. (Hoggart, 1960, p.322)

He quotes the sorts of sayings that crop up in illustration of this: 'what is to be, will be', 'if ye don't like it, ye maun lump it', 'grin and bear it', 'worse things happen at sea', 'take life as it comes', all of which had wide currency in the factory where I worked, along with aphorisms of a more superstitious nature, like 'touch wood', 'please God', 'God willing'.

The interest in fortune-tellers, palmists, tarot card

mediums, astrologers and the like, reinforce this even more and when I came to interview people after my period of participant observation I specifically asked them questions about religion, fate, luck and superstition to see whether in fact there does appear to be any correlation between gender or any other variable and a fatalistic attitude to life. From my sample, it seems that the women are more fatalistic than the men on every dimension: they avoid 'tempting fate' more, as in not walking under ladders, they believe in luck and fate, they believe in God although they are not on the whole practising Christians. A typical response to 'do you believe in God' was a semi-joking, semi-furtive glance heavenwards and the answer 'I'd better say yes'. Men tended to be more positive, either they did, they didn't or they didn't know and saw that as being a perfectly reasonable response. Surveys of people's attitudes concerning religion and superstition reinforce this. The classic study Exploring English Character (Gorer, 1955, pp.269-70) found a high incidence of superstition and consultation of various oracles amongst both women and men, but the incidence was higher for women on all religious and superstitious items tested. A more recent study also found that women are consistently more superstitious and that there is a strong correlation between social class and superstition, working-class people being generally more superstitious, which, it suggests, may be related to degree of ability to control circumstances.

> One would expect those people who are least able to control their situation to be most superstitious. One can argue that women are more superstitious because their situation is to a considerable extent outside their own control. Moreover, this is particularly true amongst working-class people whose life situation is anyway fairly insecure. (Abercrombie et al, 1970, p.123)

Men refer to 'luck' in similar ways, and devote considerable amounts of energy and interest to gambling, but they are generally less fatalistic. Their political responses indicate an awareness of the links between luck, material advantage and social inequalities. Contentions like 'You've got to look out for yourself' suggest a greater consciousness of instrumentality.

FATALISM AND WOMEN'S ROLE

I would like to contend that things happen to women more than they happen to men. Firstly, the lives of the majority of women are measured out in terms of major biological and physiological events like menstruation, pregnancy, childbirth, lactation, the menopause, or the avoidance and containment of one or more of these. On the whole, these are things which happen to women largely independently of their control, or have physical and social ramifications which 'take over' more of the woman's life, time and energy than her initial inexperienced 'choice' might have taken into account. Hilary Graham has described how women experience pregnancy and more particularly, motherhood, as a largely unstructured and unpredictable package of demands with which they must learn to 'cope' (Graham, 1979). Secondly, women's life chances are frequently restricted and determined with reference to other people, especially spouses, children and other dependent relatives (Oakley, 1974, Finch and Groves, 1980) and by systems of social organisation and legislation which assume that women are primarily homemakers and erect obstacles and penalties for those who do not conform to the prescribed norm. This is not to argue that working-class men's lives are not restricted and limited by their material circumstances and familial obligations, which they clearly are in many ways. But I would maintain that generally they experience less aspects of their lives over which they have no control, or which get out of control.

There is a great deal of sociological and psychological material which suggests that not only are women in general more passive than men in practice and in response to test situations, but indeed that such passivity, and the ability to defer to the needs of others, is an essential component of most feminine roles and of 'femininity' itself. The differential power of men and women in the labour market and in marriage promotes a 'deferential dialect' in many marriages (Bell and Newby, 1976). Examples such as managers and their wives (Pahl and Pahl, 1972) and clergymen's wives (Finch, 1980) are merely extreme and explicit examples of a tendency in most marriages for the man to be the main actor and the woman the supporting cast of thousands. Should there be any suspicion that such patterns are confined to middle-class career persons, an example of almost any of the women in my factory sample can be used to illustrate how women arrange their lives to fit in with husbands and others. They change jobs when husbands do, arrange their work to fit in which school hours, stop work to care for aged parents and change jobs to alleviate family stresses.

The effective exclusion of the majority of women from technology and politics may also reinforce the tendency for women to experience low control of their environment. If you do not understand the mechanics of household equipment, for example, or the way in which political processes operate to achieve policies, you are more likely to see such things as arbitrary and outside your control. Science is, for those who do not understand it, akin to magic. The advertising of household products, which is specifically beamed at women, emphasises this element, as in 'miracle' cleaners and futuristic marvels of technology which will 'transform your lifestyle at the press of a button'. There has been a considerable amount of psychological research into the attributions which people give for success or failure which indicates that social class (Wheaton, 1980) and gender (Dweck and Goetz, 1978) are closely correlated with instrumental behaviour and fatalism, and which sees fatalism as 'a socialised disposition' (Wheaton, 1980, p.105). The basic premise behind attribution theory is that people who repeatedly experience frustration, failure or lack of control over their environment or some aspect of it, will be unable to exert control when there is in fact an opportunity to do so. They will attribute both success and failure to external factors, which are outside their control. Such behaviour is referred to as 'learned helplessness' and controlled experiments amongst adults and school children indicate clearly that females more often exhibit this tendency than males. Wheaton (p.108) concludes that:

> In the case of sex differences, for instance, it is clear that fatalism is a way of explicating differences between the sexes in their dependence on the external environment. The problem with the traditional female sex role may be that it socialises more dependence behaviour, and thus more fatalistic orientations in the world.

I think that there is an element of truth in this but, more importantly, I think that the relative powerlessness of women, and particularly manual working women, is continuously reinforced by their membership of the working class and their position as workers.

WOMEN AND ACTIVISM

Women are not invariably passive and acquiescent at work. There are instances of industrial action where women patently did not maintain fatalistic passivity. Some of the most bitter and long-lasting examples of industrial action, particularly in the recent past, have been, or have grown from, strikes of female workgroups or work groups where women predominated. 'Women's strikes' said a trade union commentator at the time of the Salford Electrical Instruments Strike in 1974, 'are always blockbusters'. By this, he meant that in industrial relations, examples of women's militancy are nearly always triggered by situations of extreme inequity and frequently are either threats to the stability of what might objectively be considered to be a pretty miserable status quo, or responses to worsening of conditions of employment or working conditions. Such strikes tend to be defensive rather than offensive, and they tend to be long and bitter once they begin. It is clear that industrial action itself influences attitudes and perceptions and there are well-documented examples of growing activism and work group solidarity amongst women once they take action (Friedman and Meredeen 1980, Cavendish 1981). It is interesting that the Ford sewing machinists were initially not interested in the principle of equal pay and in fact many did not expect to get equal pay with men; they merely wished to redress a patently legitimate grading grievance. It was their male union colleagues and articulate parliamentary feminists who prevailed upon them to consider the political expediency and ideological importance of considering their claim in the light of the equal pay issue. Women activists I have interviewed described how they had

57

become progressively more critical, active and self-confident having once taken a stand on a particularly infuriating issue. Sheila Cunnison's findings on women workers' trade union participation amongst teachers and local authority manual workers produce a similar picture (Cunnison, 1980). There is no doubt, however, that the majority of women in both the research projects that I have worked on were less sympathetic to industrial action than men working with them, both ideologically and in practical terms and were more acquiescent at work. They saw very clearly that the first and often the most significant effect of industrial action is loss of pay to the workers and the emiseration of the households involved.

When women _are_ active in trade unions, as in politics generally, they tend to be particularly concerned with 'women's issues' such as provision of day-nurseries, welfare of employees and health care such as cancer screening at work, partly because they are directed into this role by male colleagues, but also because they, too, see it as their domain. The women shop stewards I interviewed in the earlier study saw themselves largely as representatives of the women as women and workmates rather than as workers or as representatives of an oppressed class, representing them and defending their interests within the workplace. They were considerably less often involved in the wider trade union organisation, attended meetings and conferences less and declared less interest in union affairs outside the factory than their male counterparts did. However, there is clearly a degree of male collusion in this, since they less often were given information about and invitations to such activities. The women don't expect to be asked, and the men don't expect them to go. Where women were activists, their political and industrial relations attitudes were more consistent and their commitment to the trade union movement more ideologically based than those of their male colleagues, who tended to have more instrumental attitudes in general.

It has been suggested that perhaps the major barrier to women's participation in trade unions and politics is their gender socialisation and the reinforcing experiences of adult womanhood, particularly the extent to which it promotes a separate women's sphere (Hobson, 1980, Elson and Pearson, 1980). It might thus be expected that women's activism and instrumentality might be greater outside the workplace, in relation to 'women's concerns' in the community. In fact, instances of women's activism in the community are not hard to find (May, 1977) and like the examples of women's action at work, tend to be wholehearted and unyielding. Cynthia Cockburn points out that because women are relatively inexperienced in political action, the very unexpectedness of action and their ignorance of pressure group norms are powerful weapons - because the nature of women's action: '... is to cut across all the fossilised expectations of industrial negotiation and electoral politics; thus it is less easily bought off'.

(Cockburn, 1977, p.70). But like women's industrial action, women's action in the community tends to have been erratic, relatively infrequent and usually in response to some major grievance, threat or event. Ann Gallagher, surveying women's action in the community, has concluded that, except in a few dramatic instances: '... in spite of the influence of the women's movement and the fact that the community is women's domain, community development has not meant very much to women' (Gallagher, 1977, pp.139-40).

CONCLUSION

It should not surprise us that women's behaviour in the community is similar to their behaviour at work, since their power position in both is at base similar. Despite there being women's domains where women appear to be relatively autonomous, as in the family and in family consumption patterns, they turn out on analysis to be, at best, areas of potential power and control, very much contingent upon the material circumstances and personal relationships of the women in question. A woman may exercise considerable private power (Stacey and Price, 1980, 1981) but the fact that such power is, by definition, mediated through or permitted by her relationships with men means that it is privatised individual power, opposed rather than predisposed to collective action.

Veronica Beechey has argued that economically active women workers are analogous to workers in developing countries, insofar as women's subsistence needs are presumed to be subsidised by their husbands' earnings in the same way as the peasant economy underpins the emerging capitalist one and negates the need for workers to be paid the full cost of the reproduction of their labour power. I think we can fruitfully take this analysis further and argue that the ideological predispositions of the peasant are very much the same as those of most low-skilled, low-paid industrial workers, particularly women workers in whom class and gender predispositions are combined. If 'women' are substituted for 'peasants' in the following quote, the fit is remarkable:

Peasants ... are class segments in a larger population (with their own partial cultures) ... that is, in contrast to primitive tribal groups, they are in no way autonomous, culturally self-sufficient units. They can be understood only in the broader setting. Throughout history peasants have been a peripheral but essential part of civilisations, producing the food that makes possible urban life, supporting the specialised classes of political and religious rulers and educated elite who carry what Redfield called 'the Great Tradition' ... the peasant is essentially powerless in large areas of life, because the basic decisions affecting villages are made by other classes ...Before injustice, the arbitrary and the incomprehensible they must be passive acceptors, for they lack the power and knowledge to be otherwise. (Foster, 1967, pp.7-8)

On the other hand, as well as reinforcing this picture of fatalistic apathy, studies of peasants which I have consulted emphasise the rationality and good management of those aspects of life which are experienced as being subject to control. (Foster, ibid, Rogers, 1969, Banfield, 1976) Like the inmates of Goffman's Total Institutions, people in relatively powerless situations learn to maximise any control that they do have (Goffman, 1961, pp.157-281). Whilst there are clearly limits to how far the analogy between peasants and women holds, quite apart from the fact that peasants are male and female in roughly equal proportion, the common factor I wish to stress is relative lack of control over circumstances. Peasants' capacity to fight exploitation and to develop autonomous structures through political action has been demonstrated often enough and to great effect (Scott, 1976, Shanin, 1966) but like women, their militancy has most often been aroused by perceptions of relative deprivation - excessive deprivation relative to their expectations - rather than the deprivation or exploitation per se.

Given the realities of the dual labour market (Barron and Norris, 1976), in which most women's work is in general less secure than most men's (Breugel, 1979) and is relatively more threatened by technological innovation (CSE Micro-electronics Group, 1980), women's perception that they are virtually powerless in the world of work is substantially accurate. Most of the women in the factory where I worked have observed the operation of the dual labour market at first hand: they have seen twilight shifts introduced and dispensed with according to productive need, they have had friends who have been made redundant and workmates who have retired or resigned and not been replaced. The nurseries which their children and grandchildren attend have been closed or are threatened with closure. They are aware of, and some even accept, the argument that in a period of high unemployment, perhaps women's jobs should be the first to go. All around them men are being made redundant and asked to retire early, and their teenage children are unemployed or, if employed, seen to be 'lucky to have a job'. They are aware of the technological threat; of the new machine that hasn't been used yet, Beryl said: 'We call it the white elephant, but maybe it's just as well they can't get it to work. They say it could do the work of three women'. At the time of writing this paper (February 1981), some of the employees of the factory, including the women I worked with, are working a three-day week as a result of the economic recession.

Under such circumstances, the realities of people's particular position in the labour market is less important than what they believe to be the case. The women in the factory where I worked believe that the company is in danger of economic collapse, that their own department is inefficient and liable to be moved to another site within the company, that their own jobs are insecure because of technological innovation and they are unsure whether they have any right to expect job security. Jane's reaction to her nomination as shop steward quoted above illustrates the profound lack of control of not only their working conditions but of themselves. Their gender and class socialisation and virtually everything that has happened to them since has predisposed them to experience their lives as contingent upon the whims of fate, mediated by husbands, families and employers. Such experiences erect undeniably daunting barriers to consciousness raising and political activism and help us to understand why there are not more instances of working women's militancy. But in the end, it is important to stress that fatalism and passivity are examples of learned behaviour and, as the psychologists quoted above are always anxious to point out in defence of their experiments, learned behaviour can be <u>unlearned</u>. The dialectical relationships between gender and class, and between ideology and practice, are highly complex and I do not wish to minimise the importance of class and material circumstances, which I believe to be the main determinants of, and restrictions on, industrial relations and political attitudes and practices. However, I am concerned to explore the mechanisms whereby such attitudes and practices develop and are reinforced or modified by experience. It seems to me that gender is both an attribute and experience, the material and ideological characteristics and ramifications of which are of crucial importance in understanding social organisation and the perpetuation of inequalities.

REFERENCES

Abercrombie, N, Baker, J, Brett, S and Foster, J, (1970), 'Superstition and Religion: the God of the Gaps' in Martin, David and Hill, Michael, A Sociological Yearbook of Religion in Britain, vol.3, SCM Press, pp.93-129.

Abramson, L.Y, Seligman, M.P and Teasdale, J.D, (1978), 'Learned Helplessness in Humans: Critique and Reformulation' in The Journal of Abnormal Psychology, vol.87, no.1, pp.49-74.

Armstrong, P, (1976), 'Workers Divided: the Case of Six Women' in Nichols, T, and Armstrong, P, (eds.) Workers Divided - A Study in Shopfloor Politics, Fontana.

Banfield, E.C, with the assistance (sic) of Banfield, L.F, (1967) The Moral Basis of a Backward Society, The Free Press, NY.

Beechey, V, (1977) 'Some Notes on Female Wage Labour' in Capital and Class, no.3.

Bell, C and Newby, H, (1976), 'Husbands and Wives: the Dynamics of the Deferential Dialect' in Barker, D.L and Allen, S (eds), Dependence and Exploitation in Work and Marriage, Longman.

Beynon, H, (1976) Working for Ford, E.P. Publishing.

Boston, S, (1980) Women Workers and the Trade Unions, Davis-Poynter,

Bruegel, I, (1979) 'Women as a reserve army of labour: a note on recent British experience', Feminist Review no.3, pp.12-24.

Cavendish, R, (1981) Women on the Line, Routledge and Kegan Paul.

Cockburn, C, (1977) 'When Women Get Involved in Community Action' in Mayo, M (ed.), Women in the Community, Routledge and Kegan Paul.

Coote, A, and Kellner, P, 'Hear this Brother' - Women Workers and Union Power, NS Report 1, 1980.

CSE Microelectronics Group (1980), Microelectronics: Capitalist Technology and the Working Class, CSE Books.

Cunnison, S, Trade Union Activity Among (Married) Women in Relation to their Family Roles, SSRC Final Report - publication of findings forthcoming.

Dweck, C and Goetz, T (1978) 'Attributions and Learned Helplessness' in Harvey, J.H, Ickes, W and Kidd, R.F (eds.), New Directions in Attribution Research, Lawrence Erlbaum Associates, New Jersey.

Elson, D and Pearson, R, The Latest Phase of International Capitalism and its Implications for Women in the Third World, IDS Discussion Paper, University of Sussex, June, 1980.

Finch, J (1980), 'Devising Conventional Performances: the Case of Clergymen's Wives', Sociological Review, vol.28, no.4.

Finch, J and Groves, D (1980) 'Community Care and the Family: A Case of Equal Opportunities?' in the Journal of Social Policy, vol.9, Part 4.

Foster, G.M (1967) Tsintzuntzan Mexican Peasants in a Changing World, Little, Brown and Co. Boston.

Friedman, H and Meredeen, S, (1980) The Dynamics of Industrial Conflict - Lessons From Ford, Croom Helm.

Gallagher, A (1977), 'Women and Community Work', in Mayo, op.cit.

Goffman, E, (1961) Asylums. Essays on the Social Situation of Mental Patients and Other Inmates, Penguin, Harmondsworth.

Gorer, G (1955), Exploring English Character, The Cresset Press.

Gouldner, A (1954), Patterns of Industrial Bureaucracy, The Free Press, NY.

Graham, H (1979), Unpublished paper given at the Women's Research and Resources Centre Summer School at Bradford University in September 1979.

Herzog, M (1980), 'Housewives and the Mass Media', in Hall, S, Hobson, D, Lowe, A and Willis, P, Culture, Media, Language, Hutchinson University Library.

Hoggart, R, (1960) The Uses of Literacy, Penguin, Harmondsworth.

Mann, M (1970),'The Social Cohesion of Liberal Democracy', American Sociological Review, vol.35, no.3.

Mayo, M (1977), Women in the Community, Routledge and Kegan Paul.

MacKinnon, C.A (1979), Sexual Harassment of Working Women, Yale University Press, New Haven.

Mernissi, F (1975), Beyond the Veil: Male-Female Dynamics in a Modern Muslim Society, Wiley, Schenkman, Cambridge, Massachusetts.

Morgan, D.H.J (1969), Theoretical and Conceptual Problems in The Study of Social Relations at Work: An Analysis of Differing Definitions of Women's Roles in a Northern Factory, Unpublished Phd. Thesis, University of Manchester.

Newland, K (1980), Women, Men and the Division of Labour, Worldwatch Paper 37, Worldwatch Institute, Washington DC.

Oakley, A (1974), The Sociology of Housework, Martin Robertson.

Pahl, J.M and Pahl, R.E (1972), Managers and Their Wives, Penguin, Harmondsworth.

Porter, M (1978), 'Consciousness and Secondhand Experience: Wives and Husbands in Industrial Action', Sociological Review, vol.26, no.2.

Purcell, K (1979), 'Militancy and Acquiescence Amongst Women Workers', in Burman, S (ed.), Fit Work For Women, Croom Helm.

Rogers, E.M (1969), Modernisation Among Peasants - The Impact of Communication, Holt, NY.

Roy, D.F (1958) 'Banana Time' - Job Satisfaction and Informal Interaction, Human Organisation, 18.

Roy, D.F (1952) 'Quota Restriction and Goldbricking in a Machine Shop', American Journal of Sociology, no.57, pp.427-42.

Scott, J.C (1976) The Moral Economy of the Peasant, Yale University Press, New Haven and London.

Sennett, R and Cobb, J (1977), The Hidden Injuries of Class, Cambridge University Press.

Shanin, I (1966), 'The Peasantry as a Political Factor' in Sociological Review, vol.14, no.1, pp.5-27.

Stacey, M and Price, M (1980) 'Women and Power', Feminist Review, no.3.

Stacey, M and Price, M (1981), Women, Power and Politics,

Tavistock.

Stageman, J (1980), <u>Women in Trade Unions</u>, Industrial Studies Unit Paper, University of Hull.

Wheaton, B (1980), 'The Sociogenesis of Psychological Disorder: An Attributional Theory', <u>Journal of Health and Social Behaviour</u>, vol.21, pp.100-24.

Whitehead, A (1976) 'Sexual Antagonism in Herefordshire', in Barker, D and Allen, S, <u>Dependence and Exploitation in Work and Marriage</u>, Longman.

Wilson, S (1963), <u>Social Factors Influencing Industrial Output. A Sociological Study of a Factory in North West Lancashire</u>, Unpublished Phd. Thesis, University of Manchester.

4 The Generation Game: Playing by the Rules
JOHN FITZ AND JOHN HOOD-WILLIAMS

INTRODUCTION

This paper is an historical study of the legal rules of inheritance. Inheritance, in the enlarged sense with which we use the term, refers to the familial transmission of values throughout the life of family subordinates and at crucial moments in the life cycle - the death of the patriarch, marriage, and the age of majority. Inheritance is therefore the process of the circulation of familial capital: a process of circulation or transmission unlike the transmissions within capitalism itself. The logic of these transmissions tell us about the patriarchal form of the family and about the character of intergenerational relations.

If we wish to understand 'youth' and childhood we have to proceed not by studies of discrete phenomena but by studies of relationships, since youth is not a function of age but a social category constituted in relation to, indeed in opposition to, the category adult (as is feminine to masculine). The key institutional setting for this relationship is the family and familial relations between adults and children are referred to variously as kinship, lineal or intergenerational relations. Of course adults and children or youths meet on grounds not staked out by the family but it is significant to note the extent to which the shadow of family life, captured for example in the doctrines of <u>parens patriae</u> and <u>in loco parentis</u>, falls upon these meetings.

The family itself, however, is rather different from popular characterisations which speak of it, quite erroneously, in relation to notions of 'reproduction' and ideology. It is in fact a complex of relations between the sexes and ages that are, significantly, economic. The dependants within familial relations are typically wives and those children and youths who are 'of the family'. Family heads are typically male - the patriarchs. The dependencies, exclusions and protections of wives and children are not of course the same, neither are they confined to the economic realm.

In this paper we explore one aspect of the relation of dependency of children or youths which involves the transmissions of values. Because we stress the significance of a relationship to understanding the 'youth question' we prefer to speak of the adult-minor relation. We intend to stress in this formulation the sense in which 'minor' is constituted in opposition to adulthood; the subjection, exclusion and dependence of the latter relative to the former and the significance of patriarchal family forms to this relation. In addition we want to emphasise the extent to which minor is a category riven by sex differences: the exclusions and the dependencies of girls are different from boys and there exists a complex cross-cutting between age and sex. We refer to these below. Lastly, although we focus upon common features of the social status 'minor', that status is of course riven by differences in the social class background of the patriarch to whom they belong, and by different racial traditions.

The dependency of minors is secured in a variety of ways - their inability to act as legal subjects, to hold capital, their exclusion from waged labour, the contemporary obligation to attend school and the process of socialisation. Their dependency however, significantly derives from the status of minors within the family, particularly with respect to divisions of family labour, the familial structuring of the waged labour market, and, especially historically, the ownership of familial property. We examine the rules governing the circulation of this property because they give us the template of historically approved family forms and the status of family members, even with regard to that majority of families who had no property to transmit. For the purpose of analysis we divide this process of transmission - inheritance - into two types: diachronic and synchronic. Diachronic inheritance refers to transmissions over time and down the family line at specific and crucial moments in the life cycle. Synchronic inheritance refers to gifts inter vivos and to those familial transmissions referred to by writers such as Bourdieu (1976) as 'social reproduction'.

Because of a failure to recognise the importance of the family as an economic system, it is seldom observed that in the midst of capitalism we have an entrenched system of distribution which is not capitalist but upon which capitalism relies. There is in fact no necessity for capitalist accumulation to be transmitted through the patriarchal systems we discuss. This vital part of the processes of circulation of values in capitalist societies, especially in regard to its consequences for women and minors is, conventionally, completely unregarded. To speak of transmissions only in class terms is to reduce family members to mere appendages of the heads of households. The historical changes in the mode of patriarchal transmission that we trace, are in part the product of the development of capitalist production. None the less what is remarkable is the persistence of these patriarchal forms.

Our concern in this paper is principally with diachronic inheritance which, historically, provided a relatively fixed structure, in which the rules of transmission spoke the patriarch. Our discussion of the changes in the rules, which signify changes in the principles of social control, focus upon the transformations that occur around 1660 and then transformations occuring in the nineteenth century. The historical development has been one in which the significance of diachronic inheritance has been reduced. The fixed powers and obligations of the patriarch, despite in practice always allowing a certain freedom of movement, have given way to a highly individualised and personal form of authority. For the children of the property-owning class, for example, this meant the ending of some of the guarantees of inheritance but an increasing freedom to marry when and whom they pleased.

This stress on the importance of studying youth as a relationship, the primacy that we accord to the family and the significance of the economic character of inter-generational relations may seem somewhat obvious and simple to many readers but it is a simplicity and obviousness not reflected in the literature. Many of the most fashionable forms of youth studies seem preoccupied with the male and the bizarre, and ignore the importance of the family. To take just two examples. The 'cultural studies' approach is still widely influential. For example, the new Open University Course E353 contains one unit telling the familiar culturalist and masculinist story (Davies, 1981). However, writers associated with this tradition are now perhaps aware of the 'structural neglect' of the family, as McRobbie puts it (McRobbie, 1980).

Secondly, the Sociology of Education effectively concerns itself, within the 'reproduction' paradigm, with two questions. Firstly with schooling as an institution 'reproducing' the technical divisions of labour (Bowles and Gintis) and secondly with schooling as an institution transmitting and distributing culture/knowledge ('cultural capital') both processes functioning to reproduce social class divisions. Recent feminist writings have added in, on a somewhat ad hoc basis, the significance of sexual divisions - an addition without need of political justification and theoretically justified by the extreme vagueness of the parameters of the concept 'cultural capital'. (1) However, although this recent writing is extremely valuable, systematic explanation for the undoubted sexism of schooling cannot come from invoking Bourdieu or Althusser but requires an elaboration of the character and determinations of the family itself.

It should already be clear that our own approach derives from the work of feminists who have, undoubtedly, produced the most insightful accounts in this area. Early writers at the centre of the launch of the second wave of feminism, such as Millett and Firestone, understood from the very beginning that patriarchy referred not just to relations

67

between sexes but also to those between ages, however these sets of relations may be understood (Millett, 1971, Firestone, 1970). Firestone, for example, wrote of the 'special tie' between women and children: a tie that was essentially a 'shared oppression' which is, for her, but not for us, biologically based. However, despite these early hints the question has not been taken up subsequently, (2) there being no systematic analysis of adult-minor relations. Indeed, in the interim, the whole question of what Millett referred to as old (male) dominates young (male) seems to have slipped out of the meaning of patriarchy itself. (3)

Later feminist writers have developed extremely sophisticated accounts of the family (Delphy, 1977, Delphy and Leonard, 1980). The central propositions of this approach, which we have adopted, turn around a concern to speak of familial relations as economic, or labour, relations. We do not believe (nor can we find any evidence that Delphy and Leonard ever implied) that the economic features of familial relations are exhaustive and certainly not that all that there is to say about familial/patriarchal relations can be contained within the designation 'economic'. However, we do believe that there is a crucially important area of study to be pursued in considering the economic characteristics of familial relations. In fact we argue that important features of adult-minor relations cannot be understood without attention to economic features of this relation.

In order to proceed logically the paper begins with an account of the conception of the family that we are working with, paying particular attention to the subordinate status of minors. Then, through a description of the historical development of the legal rules of inheritance we uncover important principles governing the dependency of minors.

THE HOLY FAMILY

This discussion of the family draws upon the work of Delphy and Leonard and in particular, 'The Family as an Economic System' (Delphy and Leonard, 1980). Their basic premises that concern us are, that:

(i) The family both historically and currently, constitutes a form or system of producing and consuming goods and services and transmitting property, in the broadest sense, according to a logic quite different from that of capital.

(ii) That there are two modes of recruitment to the family system. Firstly, the marital relation which recruits women-wives and is of 'primary importance' in explaining the 'multiplex nature of women's oppression'. Secondly, the kinship and/or lineal relations which recruit minors and are significant in explaining their dependency.

(iii) The family is not unitary but a system of

differentially distributed power and status relations.

Premise (i): forms of producing

If 'economic' means anything at all it means a concern with
the processes, practices, relations and forces of production, distribution, consumption and transmission or
circulation of goods and services (capitals or values). It
means a concern with the work (labour) done, the divisions
of that work, both technical and social, the relations
within which that work is undertaken and the rewards
received for it (the distributions, circulations, transmissions of the social product). (4) Delphy and Leonard
set out to demonstrate the considerable extent to which the
family is involved in all these activities despite prevailing accounts of the family that if 'Marxist', relegate
to the superstructure, (5) if bourgeois, consign it to an
'affective' tie wrapped in and based upon 'personal
relations' of romantic, heterosexual and nurturant loving.
(6)

Delphy and Leonard argue that family production today is
one form but that variation between families exists according to the extent to which a particular family produces
goods and services for the market (i.e. goods that are in
fact exchanged: one end of the family continuum) and those
in which little or no goods and/or services, other than
labour power, reach the market (the other end of the family
continuum). There is nothing illogical, of course in
supposing that the familial form is the same even though
the destination of the goods varies, since the ultimate
destination of the goods and services is irrelevant to the
character of the relations within which they are produced.
Indeed it may often not be clear at the time of production
whether a particular value is for the market or for self
consumption. Differing, local historical conditions, for
example, can effect the destination of goods. A family that
suddenly, because of hardship, takes in lodgers, is providing goods/services for exchange without any change in
family form. (7) Familial forms are, of course, subject to
historical change. Examples of families which continue to
produce extensively for the market today are in agriculture
(the English smallholding and small farm, the French
peasants); craft; small businesses (including professions
which are businesses - doctors, lawyers, dentists, solici-
tors); small hotels, boarding houses, restaurants; retail
traders, small shop keepers. It is likely, given the
growth of the 'black economy' and the deepening recession,
that such families, already substantial in number, will
increase.

What characterises familial production today and how does
it differ from capitalist production? Familial production
has the following features. It is a system within which
family members provide unpaid labour for the (usually male)
head. The head is legally and <u>de facto</u> obliged to maintain
family members, who receive upkeep and a share of the family

property at his death. The relationship is governed by reciprocal duties: the obligation to maintain on the part of the head; the obligatory provision of work and/or obedience by the subordinates. The crucial differences between capitalist work relations and familial ones are that the former take the commodity form: they are waged, based upon exchange and equivalence (8) and upon class dependence (wage labourers are formally free in Marx's sense). On the other hand familial relations do not take the commodity form: they are unwaged, are precisely <u>not</u> based upon exchange and equivalence, and are relations not of class dependence but personal dependence. Wives and children are not free, in Marx's sense, but are imbricated within an inclusive dependence comparable to forms of indenture, and signalled by the compulsory character of familial work, the infrequency with which wives change their husbands, and children their parents (i.e. the absence of a market in wives and children) and by the central role of physical force in patriarchal relations. (9)

It ought not to be too difficult to grasp the fact that the contemporary family is a producer of the sorts of goods and services which, when produced by capitalist enterprises are exchanged on the market for money. Despite this ease, it is still taking considerable time for it to be recognised that it is illogical to grant the term 'economic' production to a meat pie factory that buys in meat, fat and flour and turns out pies and to refuse to grant it to a wife or daughter who, within different social relations, does the same thing. The English contributors to the domestic labour debate have argued that the difference between the two processes is that the factory produces exchange values whereas the wife or daughter produces use values. (10) As we have already pointed out the destination of a value (and therefore in Marxism, its form) and the mode of its circulation (whether it be exchanged, a gift, burnt or buried with the dead) need have no necessary connection whatever to the relations within which it is produced.

Premise (ii): the marital and kinship relations

Delphy and Leonard argue for the importance of the marital relation as a key to the oppression of women. They designate this relation as one in which the unpaid labour of women-wives is appropriated by male husbands.

It is so obvious that it goes unremarked that this relation consists of a man who is always the husband and a woman who is always the wife. Thereby, the features of patriarchy, coupledom, heterosexuality and some assumption of monogamy, are united. The marital relation is the procedure of recruitment to family work today which simultaneously assigns women to a particular status within the family. The subordinate position of wives is legally guaranteed, reinforced by the tax and welfare systems, physical violence, and a sexist labour market. (11) Since the opprobrium offered to women who decide to opt out of

70

marriage is considerable, the recruitment net is widely cast.

The kinship system, and particularly the notion of the family line, operates comparably for minors. Minors are recruited to the family, not simply through a biological commonplace, but through social practices (see, for example, our discussion of adulterine bastardy). Historically, it is quite clear that minors engaged in productive family work. However, our suggestion is that, to an extent not yet properly appreciated, they continue to do so today.

Premise (iii): family members

We have anticipated this discussion by speaking of family heads and family subordinates and rightly so since such distributions of power and status significantly derive from positions within a system of producing. Delphy and Leonard argue that families are not to be regarded as 'units' but as complexes of relations between sexes and ages. These relations represent differing status positions within the family and differing distributions of power. Families have a single head, the (usually male) patriarch, and subordinate members who provide unpaid labour and/or obedience to that head. In contemporary western society these subordinates are, primarily, wives (always women in our society) and children. These constitute what we describe as immediate or household family members.

The division of labour and the rewards received in families depends upon the status of the family member and not on the nature of the work done or on any measure of ability or need. The general principle behind familial divisions of labour is that tasks performed by women and minors are low status and attract least rewards. This is exemplified by the character of the tasks, the work conditions, control and supervision of the labour, time taken, and by the quality and size of meals etc. consumed. Delphy and Leonard illustrate this principle by a specific study of agriculture in France in which it is clear that across sub-cultures, and over time, tasks may be assigned to different people and the tasks themselves may change and be divided differently, but, the general principle holds: that familial subordinates do low status work and work that familial subordinates do is of low status. Of course, at the level of cultural description, subordinates' work is designated as, for example, 'light', non-productive or non-essential.

MINORS, OWNERSHIP AND WORK

Immediate familial relations are a complex of relations between women-wives and men-husbands and between adults and minors, complicated by the sexual divisions, boy, girl. These sets of immediate familial relations are distinctive. In law, for example, they are distinguished by the concepts of espousal rights, and of guardianship and wardship. We are now concerned with the second set of relations, and the ways in which they articulate with the first and are cross cut by sexual divisions. This second set of relations is constitutive of what in law is referred to as the family 'line' i.e. relations over time and across ages between adults and their (usually biological) children - children who are 'of the family'. Families are therefore three-dimensional institutions in a particular sense. Of course many institutions exist over time, as do many social relations, but families are partly composed of relations across time. They are also of a distinctive longevity: they unite, contemporarily, particular non-exchangeable subjects for periods of time unequalled in other institutions.

Adult-child/youth relations, as familial relations, operate within the broader parameters of a patriarchy already described, taking on many of its features while retaining a distinctiveness. Transmissions between adults and minors take the form of inheritance in our enlarged sense and this relationship represents the family line, or at least a short piece of it in time. At present it represents, for all but a minority of aristocratic families, the most significant piece of the family line as the importance of a lineage stretching beyond three generations is almost extinct. This is no doubt partly due to the change in the prime form of productive property, from land to financial and industrial capital.

Clearly, family life has a massive presence for minors. It is the institutional setting for their lives which structures the rhythms of their day through meal times, bed times and family chores; it is where they spend the majority of their time; it significantly determines their destinations in the labour market; it is where they are subject to the closest affective relations and to the most pervasive authority. Naturally, the social class and race of their patriarch governs the character of these interactions.

Patriarchal relations, then, are characterised by a number of features: legal obligation/compulsion, personal dependence, the appropriation of unwaged work and control through emotional and physical force. These characteristics apply to children/youths as to all family subordinates, the differences are those of sex and age. Familial power is to be associated with maleness and adulthood. There are therefore contradictory statuses within the family. Women are adults but not males, boys are males but not adults, girls are doubly dependent. Since childhood is a temporary dependence in our society, at least for boys, there are further complications in determining when a boy is an adult man (when his father dies, if he is the eldest son?, when he leaves home?, when he enters waged labour?, when he marries?; as numerous writers have pointed out, there is no clear demarcation) and when a girl is an adult woman (when she marries?). The adult-minor relation is always riven by sex differences and mediated by the class position of the

familial head. This means that time itself has a sexed
quality, with different meanings for boys and girls.
Indeed it is a serious question as to whether girls can
ever be said to become 'adult' - the step from daughter to
wife is short.

So far we have suggested that the position of women-wives
and minors is similar and different. The similarities of
their position as familial subordinates turns on a shared
non-ownership of the familial means of producing. The
difference in their position turns on a legal obligation
on the part of minors to attend school and the consequent
restrictions on their ability to participate in waged and
familial work.

Similarities: For wives and children, the family of which
they are members is different than it is for the family
head. The family belongs to the family head in a way that
it does not belong to the other family subordinates. Therefore the work done by family members means different things
to the head and to the subordinates. For homely examples
of this ownership of the family we can begin with the family
car, in which wives and children typically ride (and in the
case of the latter, perhaps, typically clean) but which is
owned and driven by the family head; the family home is
lived in by all the family members but again, typically, it
is owned by, or tenured to, the family head; the family
head can squander, spend or devise testate the patrimony:
it belongs to him. In families that produce significantly
for the market the concept of ownership by the family head
is even more clearly pronounced. The farmer's small holding,
the brewery tenancy, the retail shop, the doctor's surgery
belong to family heads and are frequently not transferable.
(12)

Differences: It might seem that, having focussed upon the
work done in families, we should include the unpaid work of
minors as a feature uniting their condition to women-wives.
In the following discussion we suggest that children/youths
do do considerable amounts of family work. However, in the
last analysis, we cannot conclude that their unwaged work
is appropriated in ways entirely comparable to that of
wives. It is clear that historically, children were productive members of familial systems for producing goods and
services. With the increasing extension and importance of
waged labour and the decline of petty commodity production
(a prolonged process ocurring from the sixteenth to eighteenth centuries) the dependence of minors, and wives, is
increasingly regulated through their relationship to the
waged labour market. Later we discuss, historically, the
status of minors and wives in relation to the ownership of
property. However, we remain aware of the crucial importance
of the labour market. In the eighteenth and early nineteenth
centuries the extension of the waged labour market meant an
increase in the number of minors in waged work. It became
more profitable to place them directly on the labour market
than to have them as producers within the family - a common

occurrence for present-day wives, who are frequently earning directly on the market and engaged in family work. Like wives today, the wages of children who, historically, entered wage labour were subject to appropriation by the family head (Corrigan, 1977). This is so whether the children worked in mills, mines or in domestic service, and it was partly due to the fact that minors could not contract (or at least that contracts entered into by children were and are voidable). The importance of the increasing extensivity of wage labour for wives, historically, was however mediated by legislation, notably Hardwicke's Marriage Act 1753 (13) and the Married Women's Property Acts of the nineteenth century.

To what extent do children continue to work for the family today? Children's exclusion from the wage labour market is now legally guaranteed: the result of a nineteenth century struggle regarded with suspicion by working-class children themselves, their parents and factions of the bourgeoisie. Despite this legal regulation, to what extent do children continue to work in waged labour? There is considerable evidence of children in waged work in Second and Third World countries but less for Western Europe and North America. We would hypothesise only that the numbers for these latter two areas are considerable and far greater than generally realised. The most likely concentrations are in the retail trade (part time and Saturday work), newspaper delivery, small businesses e.g. small shop keepers, market stalls and home workers. Much of this work is unseen. We do not know its extent, or what happens to the money paid to children: is it appropriated by family heads, set against 'pocket' money or kept by the children?

What of the unpaid familial work undertaken by children? Again very little is known about such work since very little is known about what goes on inside families today. It would seem likely that considerable amounts of domestic work are undertaken by minors and especially by daughters, the 'natural' inheritors of a wife's work. (14) Daughters, typically, may be involved in the child care of younger siblings, in cleaning, in cooking and in shopping. Both boys and girls shop, run errands, clean cars and garden. We would suggest a relation between the amount of work undertaken by children and the family form into which they are born. Thus, if the family produces significantly for the market, child work is proportionately greater than if the family produces exclusively for self-consumption. This does not map neatly with the class position of the familial head, except for the number of petty bourgeois heads in this group. Another significant variable would be race, which is related to different traditions of family work.

Despite the neglect by social scientists of the degree to which children are engaged in waged and unwaged work and despite the significant similarities in the family work of daughters and wives, (15) there remain crucial differences between wives and minors. Whereas it is possible to demonstrate, despite a contrary ideology, that the labour of wives is appropriated by husbands, it is no longer possible to argue similarly for minors. There is little doubt that minors represent a net financial loss for adults if the value of their labour is calculated against their cost. Even if adults make the assumption that care in old age will be provided by familial minors, it is an assumption that they cannot rely on or enforce (though daughters are significantly more reliable in this respect). Daughters or sons' wives <u>may</u> provide care in old age and this may, over a lifetime, represent a reasonable return on investment, but despite this it remains difficult to argue for a description of minors (particularly sons) as providers of unpaid labour for familial heads.

This difference between minors and wives is marked by the legal compulsion upon minors to attend school. This obligation clearly constitutes the dependent status of minors, disallowing them the possibility of the relative autonomy of waged labour and subjecting them to conditions of subordination not dissimilar, in some respects, to those of wives. The compulsion to attend school and the length and constancy of the school day, effectively occupies children/youths in ways that restrict the possibility of waged labour and, indeed, familial work. Of course it is technically possible for minors to work extensively for the family: 'working' wives frequently spend the equivalent of school hours in waged work in addition to family work. Nevertheless, minors are not typically expected to do so, though expectations differ significantly for girls. Although to a degree freed from the subjection of familial labour and, to a considerable degree, freed from the exploitation of waged labour, they are released only to endure the monotonies of school work. Indeed their status is that of dependent subjects, like the aged.

We have suggested some way of getting a better understanding of the positions of boys (as sons) and girls (as daughters) in relation to wives and to the familial head. What of the position of wives themselves, as adults on the one hand, and women on the other? If power goes with maleness and adulthood, wives stand in a contradictory relation to minors. They stand as adults and as women/mothers. As adults they occupy a position within the patriarchy, with power over children/youths. This relation is further complicated by the gender of the children/youths: the mother-son relation being rather different from the mother-daughter one (increasing age makes these differences more acute). The latter relation <u>may</u> be one in which sex (male) overrides adulthood. (16)

In the light of our earlier discussion we regard child care as part of familial work and in an important sense, therefore, it is work done <u>for</u> the familial head. Although children benefit from child care (though they cannot control such benefits) we have to regard such care, like that which wives provide for sick and elderly family members and for the able-bodied familial head, within the broader economy of the family. When this is done it becomes clear that the care and control over minors that wives have is mediated by their position within the family as a whole. The axis of power between wives and children depends upon the sex and age of the children and the family head.

THE LEGAL RULES OF INHERITANCE

In our discussion of familial inheritance below, we shall be taking up some of these points, particularly the position and status of family subordinates. However, we begin with some introductory remarks about the nature of familial, as opposed to capitalist, forms of transmission.

Firstly, it is worth pointing out that inheritance is most importantly concerned with familial transmission. There is no such thing as capitalist inheritance. Capitalist transmissions are synchronic, occurring as 'free' exchanges between subjects or entities united through the exchange relation as and when chosen by the subjects or the representatives of entities (trusts, stock companies etc.). Familial transmission takes, as we remarked above, two forms: synchronic - gifts inter vivos, the whole bundle of practices that make up 'social reproduction' (cf. Bourdieu, 1976), and diachronic - transmissions over time and down the family line. The diachronic transmissions and their historical transformations concern us here. They occur not between free subjects but between familial members. Indeed forms of inheritance contribute towards the construction of who is 'of the family' (see our discussion of adulterine bastardy below). They also involve discussions and assumptions about the status and validity of the marital relation, and thirdly, since they are transmissions over time, they constitute the notion of family line itself. To take a short section of this line is to consider familial inter-generational relations: relations between adults and minors. State regulation, through legal forms and judicial processes, of diachronic inheritance concerns itself with questions of the valid family form which varies historically but is composed, as our earlier discussion makes clear, of conjugal, kinship and lineal relations. The legal rules give us, historically, the approved forms of the family: they are, in a sense, the rules of order.

We have pointed out that whereas capitalist transmissions are 'free', family transmissions are between fixed, nonexchangeable subjects: family members. However, despite the presence of a family form given through the rules of intestate, succession (see below) and the obligation to maintain, there developes historically an increasing freedom for family heads to devise patrimony.

Two further differences between capitalist and familial transmissions remain. The first is, that while the timing of capitalist exchanges is determinable, diachronic inheritance occurs at significant moments in the life cycle, the most important, typically, are the age of majority, marriage and the death of the patriarch. The determinants here are rather different from the 'freedoms' of capitalist exchange. The death of the patriarch is determined only rarely by family members! The age of majority is culturally fixed. The age of marriage is fixed by cultural norms, the will of the patriarch and the efforts of the minors. Secondly, just as familial relations were argued to be non-equivalent exchanges, so is inheritance. For example, when inheritance takes the form of primogeniture, it means effectively that the familial labour of the wife and other subordinates is appropriated _de facto_ and _de jure_ by the eldest son.

This chapter focusses on the legal forms and judicial processes regulating the familial transmission of _real property_ in England and Wales. Particular attention is paid to the legal rules of _intestate succession_. These rules are invoked, in the absence of a will or testament, by and through the judicial process. They are an open example of how the church, the crown and then the state were concerned, firstly, with the orderly transmission of property from one generation to the next, and secondly, with the family, a particular form of which is promoted and maintained by the rules of inheritance and by common law rules of property and marriage. The legal rules of intestate succession were written by and for a property owning class, concerned with the preservation of the material basis of its political power and social status. However, the propertyless classes were subject to the same or similar rules. The common law, even though it evolves through disputes between the crown and the great fiefs, and disputes between and within property holding families, is just that - 'the common law' - and therefore applicable to 'common' people as well.

This last point is of particular concern because what we look at here is not simply the construction of a familial form, but part of the process by which the unequal distribution of a prime form of productive property, land, is maintained and reproduced by familial means. The importance in England and Wales of the rules of intestate succession, the system of marriage alliances, bastardy and legitimacy, the system of primogeniture and the notion of impartibility, as a system of inheritance rules and practices derives from the fact that these are the very means by which economic advantage, political power and familial property are transmitted 'down the line'.

Here we shall look at the family processes of transmission at the death of the familial head, by exploring the important changes occurring around 1660 with the capitalising of property relations external (but not internal) to the family, and those nineteenth century changes which, for the first time _de jure_, saw women/wives as property owning subjects.

The remarkable long _durée_ of the legal forms of intestate

succession, compared with marked changes in capitalist transmissions, suggests the validity of regarding familial forms as feudal sedimentations. Internal familial relations were once structured in a manner similar to the external relations given through tenurial obligations and services, and have survived as distinctively uncapitalised parts of the social and economic world.

We are also able to get some sense of a long-standing state concern to maintain, define and support a patriarchal family form privileging maleness and seniority. The concern on the part of a property owning class, to consolidate and expand its non-partible property is suggested in legal rules preoccupied with legitimate transmissions. While legitimacy, primogeniture and the position of other family subordinates are legal issues they clearly have social consequences. To take a number of examples. The consequence of the histori- cally increasing power of familial heads to wilfully devise patrimony meant for the wives and children of property- owning men an increasing subjection to a patriarchal power which had decreasingly fewer obligations to provide for heritable subjects. This meant increased control over the lives of wives and minors. In the case of the latter, this was particularly at the crucial moments of majority and marriage, and for both categories at the death of the patriarch. It was now possible for him, from the early modern period, to make no provision whatsoever for his familial descendants. On the other hand, later nineteenth century developments such as the creation, de jure of property-owning women had subsequent significance for their political rights and marks a small gain for the wives of the bourgeoisie. Hence, women moved increasingly towards a contemporary notion of 'citizenship'. Minors however, re- mained outside the polity.

With regard to wives and children within working-class families, developments such as the nineteenth century Factory Acts and the male union demands for a 'family wage' drove women and children from crucial areas of the waged labour market. The consequence of this for wives was an increased dependence upon their husbands and an increasing confinement within the domestic sphere. For children of the working class a concomitant dependence was coupled to an increasing obligation to attend school. This schooling meant, by the end of the nineteenth century, increased gender differentiation, increased age grading and increased infantilisation. In short, a cultural process resulting in subjects that we today consider to be 'children'. In very broad terms, we can characterise the qualitative shift in the modalities of patriarchal control, derivable from the principles of transmission, as a move from clearly specified rules, to the personalised, 'free', regimen that we recog- nise today.

To take another example concerning daughters of the property-owning classes. Up to and during the nineteenth century, the sexual regulation of daughters and a continuing concern for virginity and appropriate marriage, is taken up at the level of legal forms by the intricate and convoluted considerations in case law of adulterine bastardy.

Despite these suggestions, we do not claim to have written a social history of diachronic and synchronic familial inheritance. Such a study would require a book-length presentation and considerable study. This is not a study of customary practices but of legal regulations and despite suggestive theories of the relations between the two (Bourdieu, 1976) no ultimate claim to their validity can be settled without considerable advances in our knowledge. Even if such a study is restricted to the nineteenth century, during which less than ten per cent of the population left wills, the problem of evidence is considerable. Recent changes, such as the introduction of various forms of taxation, justify (at least in relation to increasing numbers of the middle class) the emphasis placed by social scientists upon synchronic inheritance and the reproduction of class positions through the transmission of cultural capital. Nevertheless, the study here identifies the distinctively _familial_ quality of a mode of transmission of value (both economic and cultural) which persists and through which a considerable amount of the total social value is passed.

INTESTATE SUCCESSION

We begin with the rules of intestate succession because these rules, invoked independently of familial or individual choice, represent a class view, expressed through legal forms, of what the appropriate familial order was and should be. The legal rules on the intestate succession of real property are succinctly stated:

> The first class of persons called to the inheritance comprises the dead person's descendants; in other words if he leaves an 'heir of his body' no other person will inherit. Among his descendants precedence is settled by six rules.
> (i) A living descendant excludes his or her own descendants.
> (ii) A dead descendant is represented by his or her own descendants.
> (iii) Males exclude females of equal degree.
> (iv) Among males of equal degree only the eldest inherits.
> (v) Females of equal degree inherit together as co-heiresses.
> (vi) The rule that a dead descendant is represented by his or her own descendants overrides the preference for the male sex, so that a grand-daughter by a dead eldest son will exclude a younger son. (Pollock and Maitland, 1968, p.260)

Some preliminary comments. Firstly, these rules were settled by the early thirteenth century (_ibid._). They remained operative until 1926, when statute law (the Administration of Estates Act) effectively merged real and personal property. In the same year, by statute law, marriage could retroactively legitimate children born to a couple prior to wedlock. Secondly, the rules were invoked at the death of a landowner who did not leave a will; at the death of those absolutely disqualified as testators (the infant, the married woman and the mad); and, significantly, where the form of tenure precluded a land holder transmitting by will, a category including numbers of major land holders pre-1660. Our interest lies in the family form constituted by the rules because they concretise some of the arguments we advance concerning the differences between capitalist and familial property relations. Fundamentally, the rules not only assign a destiny to property, but they are expressly concerned with who is 'of the family' and the hierarchy of status of those in the family.

ELEMENTS OF THE LINE

Lineal Consanguinity

Through the notion of lineal consanguinity (Blackstone, 1776, p.203) land was destined to proceed along one of two paths: either it descended to blood relations of the original grantee, or passed by reversion back to the superior lord. The legal rules thus provided definite limits to the dispersion of productive property. Familial practices required the production of an heir (17) in order to retain the family-land nexus and in order to defeat the second destiny. The pivotal position of the heir in continuation of the land-line nexus was perfectly clear and much hung on it for the interests of the family and the superior lord. The family was required not only to produce children, but to produce legitimate issue, that is, an heir of the body of the married couple, for the bastard, the nullius filius (the child of nobody), which is no more than a legal construct, could not legally take the inheritance. The bastard per se represented no real threat to the family but did present a threat to the superior tenant. The changeling, or the suppositious child was in fact a strategy used when necessary by families, to secure the land-line nexus. When we look at common law cases concerning inheritance (Nicholas, 1836), they are obsessively concerned with problems of legitimacy.

Adulterine Bastardy

The common law definition of the heir conceived the status in terms of an heir of the body of known parents, with known parentage conceived as a married couple, thus distinguishing the heir from the nullius filius. However, problems about known parentage stem from the wide interpretation given through ecclesiastical courts. For the Church, nuptials were prima facie evidence of legitimacy, for it regarded all children born to a married couple, prior to or during wedlock as legitimate. The Church's attitude in effect denied the King's Courts of Common Law any say in the destiny of land. Furthermore, it was the ecclesiastical courts which determined the validity of marriage, a criterion at the heart of common notions of legitimacy, so the common law was doubly distanced from the regulation of inheritance.

In effect, the common law accepted the strong presumption (and it remains with us today) that all children of the marriage are legitimate, but it did not ever accept the retroactive power of marriage to legitimise children born of a couple prior to wedlock. However, arising out of this strong presumption that all children of a wife in <u>couverture</u> of her husband were legitimate, there is one species of bastard which presented a threat to the husband, his representatives and cadet branches of the family: the <u>adulterine bastard</u>, the child whose paternity is other than its mother's husband's. The sexually promiscuous wife was, in law, a danger to all parties in the inheritance system. The philandering husband could acknowledge the paternity of children fathered outside the marriage, for the absence of nuptials <u>prima facie</u> protected the inheritance against claims by bastard children of single or married women other than his wife. Adulterine bastards presented a threat in so far as they would be the means by which land would be removed from 'the family' and diverted elsewhere. The adulterine bastard has further significance in our analysis. Its very existence as a category (formulated in case law from the thirteenth century) establishes that 'the family' is coterminous with the paternity of a particular male. The maternity of a child establishes no <u>positive</u> claim to be 'of the family', nor to the inheritance. By the fifteenth century common law cases had settled the grounds on which paternity could be challenged and rebutted. These were (a) that the husband was under fourteen years old, therefore incapable of procreation (b) non-access (c) impotence (d) divorce. These principles still operate in modern law. The assumption embedded in adulterine bastardy, is, we argue, <u>that property shall devolve only on the legitimate offspring of the husband,</u> not simply the legitimate children of a marriage. In this sense the law asserts the primacy of the husband as transmitter of real property, down the line, which is constituted by the laws of inheritance as <u>his</u> 'line'.

Paternity is of some importance at the moment; we await the Law Commission's Final Report and Draft Bill on illegitimacy, for example. Looked at historically, categories such as the heir, the bastard, legitimacy and illegitimacy and paternity can only be considered as categories which emerged in and through the law's concern to regulate the transmission of real property. These categories, however, have a much wider application. Thus, Finer and McGregor (1974) indicate that the Poor Laws, and local customary practices, presumed that even in the absence of nuptials, the putative father had obligations to maintain his offspring. The unacceptable face of paternity still resides in the procedures of the paternity

81

suit where claim for maintenance still means the inspection (judicial in court, administrative in the case of benefits) of the sexual life of unmarried mothers, and in the concern over custody of children.

The outlines of the family form constituted by the legal rules of intestate succession of real property should now be clear. Real property moves down the line, not sideways to the wife or upwards to parents. (18) It is propelled along the axis of blood relations. The claim is advanced by the possession of genes and chromosomes, not stocks, shares or capital interests, and thus the protracted struggles to exclude the bastard serve to define the family and secure the destiny of real property. However, the functioning of lineal consanguinity is never simply a mechanism for tying real property to the family; it is also a crucial reproducer of the blood related family itself. For what is inherited by descendants is not only the family property, but also the system by which it devolved on them, which, in turn, includes positions and statuses (the heir and the bastard) and which stands one descendant in relationship to another. That relationship is clearly elaborated in rules (iii) and (iv), where primacy is accorded the eldest male and the younger and the female descendants are allotted a destiny of subordination.

Primogeniture

Primogeniture and the allied notion of impartibility (i.e. that property should devolve as an unbroken bundle) is sometimes regarded as the English system of inheritance, in contrast to the Continental system of morcellation (enshrined in the Code Napoleon) where all sons (or in the absence of sons, daughters) have an equal claim on familial property. Foreign observers have in past times commented on the pervasiveness of primogeniture and its malign effect of impoverishing younger sons (Thirsk, 1976). Despite its privileged position in the legal rules, however, the significance of primogeniture needs to be reappraised.

Firstly, primogeniture is not the overarching principle of the legal system of inheritance. It is always subject to the principle of testamentary power (i.e. that land holders and owners won the right to dispose of real property by will or testament). Testamentary power signals an important difference between the English and Continental systems in that heirs in English law have no birth right (property could be alienated without their consent) and that there is no legal notion of the family as a property-owning entity, even though the gentry conceived land as belonging to the line and took great care to preserve the nexus. The contradiction between the legal existence of testamentary power and practice of preserving the land-line nexus was settled by the device of strict settlement. Without pursuing all the technicalities, the strict settlement was a bargain struck between males of two generations and implicating a putative (and perhaps yet unborn) grandchild. The deal left the land in the hands of the father, with annuities to the son for the life of his father; on the death of the father the son assumed control of the estate. But it exacted from the son a promise to resettle the land on the heirs of his body in the same manner (Robertshaw and Curtin, 1977, Laurence, 1978). Taltrum's Case of 1472 and the difficulties encountered by this system of strict settlement in meeting extraordinary needs demanding cash (marriage portions, investment opportunities) led to a more flexible system of strict settlement (a portion of the estate, e.g. rent charges, was set aside to meet contingent liabilities).

It will be apparent that strict settlement granted only a limited economic existence to potential heirs until the death of the father. In the case of younger descendants their dependence is first on the father, and then the heir, for marriage portions and the other forms of economic provision. Strict settlement underscores the age of majority, marriage and the death of the patriarch as the crucial moments when familial property is propelled down the line, but these moments do not signal the end of parental control.

Secondly, Thirsk (op.cit.) argues that although primogeniture was to be found commonly in the seventeenth century as an inheritance practice among the yeomanry and lesser landholders, it was by no means the only one. Elsewhere we can find examples of primogeniture as an imposed practice, especially on the villein tenants of kights fees (Pollock and Maitland, op.cit, p.278) where the superior tenant was probably more interested in the impartible nature of the tenancy: property was to be held by one person who was in turn liable for the dues and services. There were also considerable regional and local variations to primogeniture: Kent Gavelkind, Borough French and English systems provide for the youngest descendant to be entered as heir. Ultimogeniture benefits the parents to the extent that the youngest member was the one still left in the home; on taking the inheritance they were expected to provide free bench for any surviving parent.

Thirdly, studies indicate that although the legal rules suggest that the eldest was advanced as the heir, the inheritance was hedged so that provision was made for the younger descendants. Only the wealthiest could provide separate parcels of land for younger descendants, but in the case of lesser landholders, some provision was made in cash, goods or beasts (Cooper, 1976, Spufford, 1976, Thompson, 1976).

With these caveats in mind, why the persistent interest in primogeniture? Firstly, primogeniture plainly exists in the common law rules of intestate succession of real property. However we may conceive common law, it applied to great and small at times when land was the prime form of productive property. Great landowners defeated the rules through the equity courts, lesser landowners got round it by local customary practices, but in both cases the strategies merely confirm (Bordieu, 1976) that certain hard and fast rules did exist, and clearly embedded in them is the principle of primogeniture. Secondly, if we consider the manoeuvres of the landowning gentry, strict settlements were bargains between fathers and, where they existed, eldest sons, or eldest daughters. Land in the 'agrarian grid' (19) was not equally distributed but was held in the hands of a few families, and their practices (strict settlement, marriage alliances etc.) privileged primogeniture. Thus, in 1848, two-thirds of all land in England was tied up by strict settlement (Robertshaw and Curtin, op.cit, p.298). The correspondence between the concentration of productive property and a particular form of inheritance is difficult to dismiss. That the process of accumulation of land and its maintenance in the hands of a few families involved a particular familial form (given in the legal rules and the system of strict settlement, the customary practice of the great landowners) suggests that the familial system of transmitting property should be central to our understanding and analysis of the reproduction of class, political power and state action.

While the system of primogeniture is not inimical to capitalist accumulation and concentration of the means of production, there is no requirement that property should devolve only on eldest sons. That it did so is a function of particular notions of the family embedded in marriage laws, the common law rules of property ownership and the rules of intestate succession of real property, some of which we have tried to tease out here. Capitalist property relations, developing through the commodification of land, the classification of 'things' into real and personal property (subject to different inheritance systems), the apportioning of things to owners (the concept of private property), of themselves signal no necessity for individual, gender or age specific ownership. They are, of course, destructive of communal property and collective ownership. However, the significant fact that 'things' are allotted to, and owned by, male adults is a product of familial relations, structured by legal rules, customary practices and state action. This might be compared to the similar process of the exclusions of women and minors from the labour market in the nineteenth century. There was nothing in the changes in the labour process that necessarily precluded the employment of women and minors, as fractions of the bourgeoisie pointed out, rather, the expulsions were accomplished by legislation arising from agitation by male combinations for a family wage (cf. Hussain, 1976, Hartman, 1979).

In one sense, the legal rules of intestate succession announce the 'plan', or 'template', for the transmission of real property down the line. In the absence of a will, in the case of an invalid will, or where land is held by those absolutely excluded from testamentary power, then the rules take effect. The elements of the plan describe the valid inheritance of property, and also define the familial

relations necessarily associated with its secure transmission. We have said that they are rules of social order,
elaborated for and by a land-owning class, which, by their
presence in the common law, have a wider application. The
principal concerns of the rules, as we have discussed them
are:

(i) The centrality of the marital relationship in
defining who is considered to be the heir of the body
and promoted as claimant to the inheritance. By the
same process the marital relation is central in
defining who is counted 'of the blood', for in the
absence of nuptials the common law provided for the
absolute exclusion of some biological children: the
bastards.

(ii) The destiny of land is 'down' the line, to descendants, not sideways or upwards. Although this is
taken to be obvious and unremarkable, descent is a
historically and culturally specific inheritance
practice. As we point out later, changes in the form
of productive property entailed a system different
from descent.

(iii) By common law, the eldest was advanced as heir,
though there were local and regional variations
(ultimogeniture). The practice of primogeniture was
partly in the interests of transmitting the inheritance
as one unbroken parcel. But it was a system which not
only entailed the unequal distribution of property to
descendants, but also, the unequal distribution of
political and social advantage.

(iv) Women were, by the rules, merely 'postponed males'.
They took the inheritance until such times as a male
heir was produced (cf. Bourdieu, op.cit.).

(v) The familial form announced by the rules (the male
- adult head of house, the privileged eldest son, the
subordinate position of the younger and female descendants and the equally distanced and subordinate
position of the married woman) is actually transmitted
and reproduced at the same moment as property is passed
on down the line.

The relationship between the family and the land is a
complex and subtle one. There is a constant intertwining
of the economic and the familial event. Simpson catches it
nicely:

To the wealthy landed classes, real property was the
essential endowment not of individuals but of the
family, a continuing but constantly changing entity
forming and reforming around the basic family events
- birth, the attainment of majority, marriage and
death - and rendered continuous by the concepts of
blood and inheritance (Simpson, 1979, p.x, our
emphasis).

But it is precisely at these 'basic family events' that land

is <u>not</u> 'of the family', for the family does not democratic-
ally decide the destiny of the land, this is determined by
the patriarch. In its devising the place of minors was often
no more than as pawns in the matrix of alliances and
settlements. Even in the case of strict settlements, where
the patriarch's control over the inheritance was somewhat
restricted, the settlement was a bargain struck between
him and his father, between him and his eldest son. Moreover, the basic family events were occasions in familial
life most strictly controlled by adults, often by the
application of violence, (20) or by threats of disinherit-
ance. The crucial family events are, in fact, the points
at which the minors' dependence and subordination are most
naked.

Patriarchal Property

We understand the significance of the Abolition of Tenures
Act, 1660, in the light of the commodification of land as
'property' and, with it, the transformation of landholders
into potential owners. This is an important moment in the
capitalising of the property relations, and yet, the
statute hardly disturbs familial property relations. The
systematic exclusion of married women and minors from the
ownership of property was continued in two different ways.
In the case of the minor, the Act of 1660 marks their
extended separation from the ownership of real property.
Prior to 1660 it was possible for minors to assume control
of socage tenures at the age of fourteen, after 1660 the
'military' age of the majority of twenty-one was extended to
all minors (Fitz, 1981).

The dependence of minors on adults (parents and guardians)
was legally given by their absolute exclusion from owning
property until the age of twenty-one. Through the seventeenth and eighteenth centuries, political and juridical
theorists, such as Locke and Filmer, based their arguments
against extending citizen and political rights to minors
on this legal exclusion from property ownership (Richards,
Milligan and Graham, 1981).

The exclusion of the married woman from property ownership was somewhat different. Women, <u>feme sole</u>, divorced or
widowed, were never excluded from property ownership.
However, in common law the principle was that on marriage,
a husband assumed proprietary interests (use, enjoyment
and disposal) of any real property brought into the
marriage. This has to be seen alongside marital rights to
the body of the wife herself, and rights over minors, given
through guardianship laws. In the case of land after 1660
the appropriation of real property by the husband presented
a threat to the married woman's father, in so far as it
meant the alienation of land from 'the line'. To prevent
husbands assuming control and disposing of ancestral
property, the landed classes through their lawyers, developed the elaborate and complex legal instrument of the
strict marriage settlement (Graveson and Crane, 1958,

pp.14-15). Family lawyers used the Court of Chancery, i.e. the system of equity, to defeat the common law rights of the husband. During the seventeenth and eighteenth centuries equity developed the doctrine of a wife's separate estate, whereby property could be endowed on trustees for the wife's exclusive enjoyment. While this ensured a married woman's limited economic independence, her status was similar to that of a minor: she had no rights to the capital, only claims on the income. Furthermore, she could not devise any gift or will any of the property held in trust. In fact the married woman could not devise real property at all, for such property was owned either by the trust or by her husband. It was not until the Married Women and Tortfeasers Act, 1935, that she acquired 'full power to dispose of property as if she were _feme sole_ (Bromley, 1976, p.603).

It is significant that the landed classes, drawing on private resources, protected their interests through the equity courts in the face of the state, which by merely allowing the common law rules to lie unaltered until the nineteenth century, severely disadvantaged the lot of <u>all</u> married women. As Dicey suggests, the equity courts were not as concerned with the legal status of married women, as with the power of their fathers to prevent ancestral land being alienated from 'the line' by common law rules (Dicey, 1914, pp.371-98). And yet as we demonstrate in some detail below, the common law concerning the familial transmission of real estate was by no means immaterial to the needs and interests of landed classes, for the rules of intestate succession served to tie land to the family and the family to the land. The common law and statute law, post 1660, celebrates a patriarchal family form (adult male owner, the excluded and dependent wife and minor) which stands in some contradiction to the 'free' capitalist relations of property and labour of the period.

The historical specificity of this family form stands in relief when we consider the important changes it underwent during the nineteenth century. An earlier paper (Fitz, <u>op. cit.</u>) indicated the manner in which the equity courts, through the doctrine of <u>parens patriae</u>, provided the state with the legal basis to intervene in the familial sphere in the interests of the 'welfare of child'. It suggested that the doctrine of <u>parens patriae</u> rewrote the relations between parents and children in so far as the state assumed the mantle of the supreme parentage of all children. We are concerned here with some other dimensions of the state regulation of family form.

What is striking about familial property relations in the mid- and late-nineteenth century is the resurrection of the married woman as a property-owning subject. Interestingly, it is the equity courts which provide a point of departure. Recognising a significant shift in the form of productive property from land to investment in stocks, shares and bonds, (21) they entertained a new form of marriage

87

settlement, the personal settlement, which grew in importance from the middle of the century (Crane, 1957, p.235). Strict settlements did not disappear, but the personal settlement took a place alongside them. The difference between the forms of settlement resides in the different forms of property held in trust (crudely, land in the first case, industrial and finance capital in the other). Crane generally argues that the wife's property was either held for her separate use (in trust, from which she had the income) or she took a joint interest in the trust alongside the husband. In terms of transmission, he argues: 'Hereby the parents could determine distribution of capital among the children or remoter issue as they saw fit, even to the total exclusion of some.' (Crane, op.cit, our emphasis.)

What he fails to say is: (a) while the husband could not alienate or use the wife's capital, neither could the wife, for it is 'owned' and controlled by trustees appointed by the father; (b) whereas he could devise or alienate his own property, the wife could not; (c) the destiny of 'her' property was not of her devising but of her father's representatives. Therefore the point that 'parents' determined the distribution is misleading. As in the case of strict marriage settlements the intention is to ensure that, in the absence of children, the wife's property goes back to her family (i.e. to her father), or if there is a son, the contract is between the grandfather and the grandson, to the exclusion of the feckless husband. At the same time, the settlement represents a contract, over time, reaffirming the continued existence of the patrilineal form.

Strict and personal settlements were, at best, class-specifically advantageous for a minority of married women. Those unable to use the equity courts, were by common law, still required to surrender any property or income to the male head of household. The Married Women's Property Acts (22) put into statutory form an already existing legal practice in which wives were able to control and dispose of property which fell to them by inheritance. The feminist struggles of the period centred on something quite different. This was property, in the form of cash income, earned by married women through labour and talent (celebrated examples involved women authors and actresses whose income was spent or squandered by feckless husbands). The Acts gave married women something denied by common law and early property statutes, the right to dispose of property without the consent of the husband or her father (or his representatives). The Acts do not construct a formal legal parity between husband and wife in relationship to property until 1935. This point marks the end of the historic similarity between the married woman and the minor in property law.

With respect to property, married women and minors part company in 1935, but with respect to their abilities/inabilities to contract, their paths ran different courses.

88

Minors have, historically, had only limited ability to contract (23) and this remains the case today. At the age of majority the significance of the sexual division comes into play. While _adult_ sons could contract, wives could not. _De facto_, therefore, many women were _never_ able to contract. As we have suggested, the step from daughter to wife is short.

We have pointed out that formal legal equality is not granted to wives until the Married Women and Tortfeasors Act, 1935. However, given our argument for the persistence of patriarchy and the importance of forms of transmission of real property to its maintenance, how was it possible for _de jure_ equality to be enacted in 1935? The answer is that by then the importance of diachronic transmission of property had diminished significantly. This was due to the imposition of death duties from the early years of the twentieth century. The result was, and is, an increase in the significance of gifts _inter vivos_, i.e. synchronic transmissions. Therefore, it has been possible in recent years to write a _de jure_ equality of sexes into laws regulating inheritance, without in the least disturbing patriarchy. The process of patriarchal continuance now reside in synchronic transmission.

CONCLUSION

This discussion of familial transmission has concerned itself with one of the economic processes with which families are involved. The legal rules governing these transmissions give us the outlines of what, for ruling fractions, constituted proper familial relations. These relations are starkly patriarchal in the inclusive sense of privileging maleness _and_ seniority. The dependence of wives and minors is historically related to their inability to contract and their exclusion from wage labour. We have focussed in this paper upon the first of these exclusions which have been maintained and reproduced in and through systems of inheritance. The transmissions of real property down the line, the common law rules of intestate succession, testamentary power, the customary practices of strict and personal settlements, the transfer of gifts _inter vivos_ and the reforms of The Married Women's Property Acts, have operated to maintain the power of the familial head. The twentieth century revisions to these rules, granting formal equality between wives and husbands, came after the first taxations of real property and consequently at a time of the decreased importance of diachronic inheritance.

The legal rules give us a sense of 'proper' familial forms, which after Hardwicke's Marriage Act, began to have increasing significance outside the classes for whom they were written. They also give us the _lineal_ dimension to familial relations and indicate its patrilineal character. The lineal transmission of property is constitutive of the family line itself, and therefore, in part, of adult-minor relations. Our discussion of lineal consanguinity and adulterine bastardy (a limit case as to who is/is not of the family line i.e. 'of the family') reveals the social practices by which minors are recruited to the family. The commonplace mapping of biological children of the wife and husband as being 'of the family' hides the social rules that order family membership. We have compared such lineal rules to the marital relation. Historically both lineal and marital relations were recruitments to, and appropriations of, familial productive labour.

The dependence of today's minors is still given through the exclusions and inabilities we have listed. Although the appropriation of minors' labour (including waged labour) by the family head has a long history, this does not constitute the basis of their dependence. Their subordinate status results from a legal obligation to attend school and a concomitant exclusion from waged labour (Millward, 1968, Leonard, 1980). Currently, as a result of taxation and the partibility of inheritance, the diachronic transmission of real property is of decreased significance. This is particularly true for a middle class that ensures class comparability for fathers and sons through the transmission of cultural capital. For daughters, marriage is still the process through which a mediated social class position, and familial dependence, is obtained. However, the dependent, excluded status of minors today and its articulation to that of women-wives will not be understood without study of the family and of the economic significance of that institution.

NOTES

(1) The sexism of schooling is demonstrated by Byrne (1978), Deem (1978) and Spender and Sarah (1980). The beginnings of a more systematic exploration of the familial character of the English school system is to be found in David (1980). Nava (1981) has also written sensitively in the area.
(2) The exception would be Mathieu (1977).
(3) For example, Beechey's oft quoted discussion of the concept of patriarchy (Beechey, 1979) makes no reference to age relations.
(4) To speak more accurately we could offer this distinction: the social product transmitted through familial inheritance consists of (i) capital and cultural capital, accrued through capitalist relations, and (ii) patrimony, accrued through familial relations. In practice, of course, these products are indistinguishable.
(5) For example, Althusser (1971).
(6) For example, Blood (1969).
(7) This is clearly not what Marx thought when he was considering wage labour. However, he discusses the productive and unproductive labour of cooks and musicians from the point of view of the market. In these terms the remarks are valid. In terms of familial relations,

in which Marx was uninterested, they are not.

(8) Even the unequal exchange within the capitalist relation assumes an equivalence: an equivalence that is never met. There is no comparable notion of equivalence underlying familial relations. The argument here is lengthy and cannot be properly developed in this article.

(9) Increasing evidence for the centrality of physical violence to patriarchal relations has come from Dobash and Dobash (1979) and Pahl (1980).

(10) To us, the English variant of this debate always suffered from the insistence on asking questions about familial relations from the standpoint of the market,

(11) See, respectively, Leonard (1980), Land (1975, 1978), Dobash and Dobash (op.cit.) and Hartman (1979). For a general survey see Hood-Williams (1981).

(12) This, as often as not, is because of the non-transferability of social skills and/or credentials between family members.

(13) Social historians such as Gillis (1981) and O'Donovan (1979) point out (i) that this Act worked to extend the remit of the legal forms of marriage of the property-owning classes (which we discuss in this paper) to other social classes, and (ii) the ways in which this development disadvantaged women who had previously been relatively independent.

(14) For a critical review of the literature that is available on the patterns of distribution and consumption of resources within the family see Pahl (op.cit.) and Grey (1979). For children and wage work see Challis and Elliman (1979). For accounts of minors' contributions to family budgets see Millward (1968) and Leonard (1980).

(15) In addition, daughters, unlike wives, are not typically expected to sexually service familial heads. However our increasing knowledge of incest, by far the most common form of which appears to be father-daughter (Armstrong, 1978, Jeffreys, 1981) suggests that even in this regard the difference between the obligations of daughters and wives is nothing like absolute.

(16) Dobash and Dobash note that the second most common form of domestic violence, after husbands to wives, is sons to mothers. Also, recent news reports alleging increasing numbers of attacks by school pupils on teachers fail to specify the extent to which these are boys attacking female teachers.

(17) Women were 'postponed' to men as heirs (i.e. a younger brother takes the inheritance) but also, they were postponed males in the sense that while they were not expected to bear arms (part of the feudal obligations) they were expected to provide a substitute.

(18) 'Upward' transmission or ascent is not now excluded, nor are the bastards.

(19) The concept of 'the grid of inheritance' comes from E.P. Thompson (1976). The grid comprises the form of property to be devised and the practices and means (law, custom, expectation) of its devising. See p.358

for the different 'grids'.

(20) See Stone L. (1977) especially 'The Reinforcement of Patriarchy', pp.179ff.

(21) The point at which land ceases to be the prime form of productive property and is superseded by commercial and industrial capitals, is quite difficult to determine. The Habbakuk (1940) thesis and contributions to the ensuing debate, Clay (1968), Beckett (1977), discuss at length the 'new' function of land in the eighteenth century as security for venture capital. For discussion of the rise of finance capitalists and industrialists, see Rubenstein (1977) and Rogers (1979).

(22) For a full discussion of the Married Women's Property Acts see Dicey (op.cit.). The Act of 1870 gave married women the limited right to pursue actions in court in her own name. However:

'until 1883 (after the 1882 Act) the wedding ceremony conveyed to the husband all the wife's personal property, the right to manage, control and draw the income from any source, and, after the abolition of her legitimae portio the absolute right to dispose of all 'his' property at his death as he chose, leaving his wife and children destitute'. (Stone, 1977, p.24.)

(23) The issue at law turns on whether a contract by a minor is voidable. They are bound by 'a beneficial contract' of employment, education or training, and they are bound to pay a reasonable price for the provision of 'necessaries'. Contract for the acquisition of a permanent interest in property is voidable (Hood Phillips and Hudson, 1977, pp.346-7).

REFERENCES

Althusser, L, (1971) <u>Lenin and Philosophy</u>, NLB, London.
Armstrong, L, (1978) <u>Kiss Daddy Goodnight</u>, Pocket Books, New York.
Beckett, J.V, (1977) 'English landownership in the later seventeenth and eighteenth centuries; the debate and the problems', <u>Economic History Review</u>, 2nd series, vol.30.
Beechey, V, (1979) 'On Patriarchy', <u>Feminist Review</u>, 3.
Bernstein, B, (1977) <u>Class, Codes and Control</u>, vol.3, RKP, London.
Blackstone, W, (1976) <u>Commentaries on the Laws of England: vol.II: The Rights of Things</u>, University of Chicago Press, facsimile edition, 1979.
Blood, R.O, (1969) <u>Marriage</u>, The Free Press, New York.
Bonfield, L, (1979) 'Marriage settlements and the "rise of great estates", the demographic aspect', <u>Economic History Review</u>, 2nd series, vol.32.
Bourdieu, P, (1976), 'Marriage strategies as strategies of social reproduction', in Forster, R. and Ransum, O, <u>Family and Society</u>, John Hopkins University Press.
Bromley, P, (1976) <u>Family Law</u>, (5th edition), Butterworth, London.
Byrne, E.M, (1978) <u>Women and Education</u>, Tavistock, London.
Challis, J. and Elliman, D, (1979) <u>Child Workers Today</u>, Quartermaine House, London.
Corrigan, P, (1977) 'Feudal Relics or Capitalist Monuments?' <u>Sociology</u>, 2, 3, September.
Clay, C, (1968) 'Marriage, inheritance and the rise of large estates in England, 1660-1815', <u>Economic History Review</u>, 2nd series, vol.21.
Cooper, J.P, (1976) 'Patterns of inheritance and settlement by great landowners from the fifteenth to the eighteenth century', in Goody, Thirsk and Thompson (<u>op.cit.</u>).
Crane, F.R, (1975) 'Family settlements and succession', in Graveson and Crane (<u>op.cit.</u>).
David, Miriam E, (1980) <u>The State, the Family and Education</u>, RKP, London.
Davies, D, (1981) <u>E353; Education, Society and the State</u>, Open University Press.
Deem, R, (1978) <u>Women and Schooling</u>, RKP, London.
Delphy, C, (1977) <u>The Main Enemy</u>, WRRC, London.
Delphy, C, (1979) 'Sharing the Same Table: Consumption and the Family', in Harris (<u>op.cit.</u>).
Delphy, C. and Leonard, D, (1980) 'The Family as an economic system', Kent Conference Paper, 1980.
Dicey, A.V, (1914) <u>Law and Public Opinion in England</u>, Macmillan, London.
Dobash, R.E. and Dobash, R, (1979) <u>Violence Against Wives</u>.
O'Donovan, K, (1979) 'The Male Appendage - Legal Definitions of Women', in S. Burman (ed.), <u>Fit Work for Women</u>, Croom Helm, London.
Finer, M. and McGregor, O.R, (1974) <u>Report of the Committee on One-Parent Families</u>, vol.2, HMSO, Cmnd.5629.
Firestone, S, (1970) <u>The Dialectic of Sex</u>, Granada Books.
Fitz, J, (1981) 'The child as a legal subject', in Dale, I.R, Fergusson, R. and Macdonald, M, (eds.) <u>Education and</u>

the State: Politics, Patriarchy and Practice, OU Course
Reader, vol.2, Falmer Press.
Gillis, J.R, (1964) Youth and History, Tavistock, London.
Gillis, J.R, (1981) 'Resort to Common Law Marriage in
England and Wales, 1700-1850', Past and Present.
Goody, J, Thirsk, J. and Thompson, E.P, (1976) Family and
Inheritance, Rural Society in Western Europe 1200-1800,
Cambridge University Press.
Graveson, R.H. and Crane, F.R, (1957) A Century of Family
Law, Sweet and Maxwell, London.
Grey, A, (1979) 'The Working Class Family as an Economic
Unit', in Harris (op.cit.).
Habakkuk, H.J, (1940) 'English landownership 1680-1740',
Economic History Review, 1st series, vol.10.
Harris, C, (1979) The Sociology of the Family, Sociological
Review Monograph, University of Keele, no.28.
Hartman, H, (1979) 'Capitalism, patriarchy and job segreg-
ation by sex', in Eisenstein, Z.R, (ed.) Capitalist
Patriarchy and Socialist Feminism, Monthly Review Press,
London.
Hood Phillips, O. and Hudson, A.H, (1977) A First Book of
English Law, Sweet and Maxwell, London.
Hood-Williams, J, (1981) 'Social Science on the Family',
Social Science Teacher, 11, 1.
Hussain, A, (1976) 'The economy and the education system in
capitalistic societies', Economy and Society, 5, 4.
Jeffreys, S, (1981), in Friedman, S, (ed.) Heterosexuality,
Couples and Parenthood, WRRC, London.
Land, H, (1975) 'The myth of the male breadwinner', New
Society, October 9.
Land, H, (1978) 'Who cares for the Family?' Journal of
Social Policy, 7, 3.
Leonard-Barker, D, (1978) 'The regulation of marriage: re-
pressive benevolence', in Smart, B. et al, (eds.) Power
and The State, Croom Helm, London.
Leonard, D, (1980) Sex and Generation, A Study of Courtship
and Weddings, Tavistock, London.
Laurence, P.M, (1978) The Law and Custom of Primogeniture,
Yorke Essay Prize, J. Hall and Son, Cambridge.
Matthieu, N, (1977) Ignored by Some, Denied by Others,
WRRC, London.
McRobbie, A, (1980) 'Settling Accounts with Sub-Cultures',
Screen Education, 34.
Millett, K, (1971) Sexual Politics, Hart Davies.
Millward, N, (1968) 'Family, Status and Behaviour at Work',
Sociological Review, 16, 2.
Nava, M, (1981) 'Girls aren't really a problem', Schooling
and Culture, 9.
Nicholas, H, (1836) On the Law of Adulterine Bastardy,
William Pickering, London.
Pahl, J, (1980) 'Patterns of money management within
marriage', Journal of Social Policy, 9, 3.
Pollock, F. and Maitland, F.W, (1968) The History of English
Law Before the Time of Edward I, 2nd edition, Cambridge
University Press, Cambridge (2 vols.).
Robertshaw, P. and Curtin, C, (1977) 'Legal definition of
the family, an historical and sociological exploration',

Sociological Review, 25, 2.

Rogers, N, (1979) 'Money, land and lineage: the big bourgeoisie of Hanoverian London', _Social History_, 4, 3.

Richards, J, Mulligan, L. and Graham J.K, (1981) '"Property" and "People"; political usages of Locke and some contemporaries', _Journal of the History of Ideas_, XLII, 1.

Rubenstein, W.D, (1977) 'Wealth, elites and the class structure of modern Britain', _Past and Present_, 76.

Simpson, A.W.B, (1979) _Introduction to Blackstone, Book II, Commentaries on the Laws of England,_ University of Chicago Press.

Spender, D. and Sarah, E, (1980) _Learning to Lose: Sexism and Education_, The Women's Press.

Spufford, M, (1976) 'Peasant inheritance customs and land distribution in Cambridgeshire from the sixteenth to the eighteenth century', in Goody, Thirsk and Thompson (_op. cit._).

Stone, L, (1977) _The Family, Sex and Marriage in England, 1500-1800_, Weidenfeld and Nicholson, London.

Stone, O, (1977) _Family Law_, Macmillan, London.

Thirsk, J, (1976) 'The European debate on customs of inheritance', in Goody, Thirsk and Thompson (_op.cit._).

Tilly, L. and Scott, J, (1973) _Women's Work and European Fertility Patterns_, mimeo.

Young, M. and Willmott, P, (1957) _Family and Kinship in East London_, RKP, London.

5 Aging and Inequality: Consumer Culture and the New Middle Age
MIKE FEATHERSTONE AND MIKE HEPWORTH

Gerontologists and biologists suggest that built into the genetic structure of man is a pre-set clock of aging which determines that our bodies will age and die and that this process will occur at a specific rate. (1) To the aging individual the signs of this process become more noticeable in its advanced stages: wrinkled and sagging flesh, greying hair, hair loss, the inability to sustain physical performance, and declining sexual powers. Despite the promise of science and technology to hold back and eventually master the aging process, individuals have to face the fact that it is ultimately irreversible: their bodies will run down and decline. Yet the cultural responses to aging, and the social meaning it has for the individual, can vary a great deal. In some societies adulthood is conferred much later than in the contemporary west, and is perceived as being independent of physiological maturation. Among the Western Apache, for example, single persons are regarded as 'youths' or 'maidens', adult status only being granted with marriage. Arensberg reported that amongst the Irish peasantry as recently as the 1930s, a male was considered a 'boy' until he inherited from his father and would not be permitted to marry or to function in other ways as an adult even if he was thirty or forty years old. Conversely in other cultures an individual could have the status of old prematurely conferred upon him: the Maricopa Indians of Arizona regard an individual as 'old' if he has a grandchild, thus the terms 'old man' and 'old woman' can be ascribed to individuals in their early forties. (2)

In contrast the definition of old age in contemporary western societies is increasingly becoming a temporal one: (3) the old are those who are known to have lived a certain number of years. It is impossible to exist without having had the exact date of one's birth recorded and individuals are constantly required to give information about their age in educational, occupational and administrative contexts, as well as being frequently reminded by the media that age is a major guide to the categorisation of individuals. This progressive tendency towards temporal reification fixes the emergence, presence and absence of individual capacities to chronology. The age of consent, for example, is considered to be a matter of chronology rather than physiological or psychological maturity and retirement follows a similar pattern. It has also been suggested that the current fascination with the lifecycle developmentalist view of life as an obstacle course, embodies the awareness that success in life depends upon reaching certain goals on schedule. (4) One of the prime means for the individual to record and verify his progress through life is through photography. Photographic images encourage the individual to engage in self-surveillance and compare the effects of the aging process on his appearance against cultural norms which have been created within a society which depends upon a proliferation of visual images. (5) As a consequence individuals are constantly exhorted to monitor their physical appearance and performance for signs of decline and to take steps to remedy these reverses. In this social climate the age at which people are expected to be sensitive to the ravages of time has noticeably decreased. If the attributes of youth are to be preserved preventative action must be taken long before the first physical signs of bodily betrayals of chronological age appear.

In this new climate of sensitivity towards some of the less physically disabling changes which are a part of aging, experts and other commentators have observed that the middle years have a special status in the life history of the individual because it is during these decades that the physical signs of aging are often detected for the first time. Irene Friese writes:

> Theorists agree that there is a point in the lifecycle when people experience a major transition into middle age (age 44-47). As people age they become aware that they no longer look young, may no longer feel attractive, and can no longer rely on their body to function unflaggingly. Their grown children and aging parents also make vivid their own halfway status in the adult lifespan. No longer able to think of themselves as young, they confront the disquieting prospect of becoming old. The feeling that time is running out creates a psychological pressure to make the most of one's remaining good years; to seek out desired experiences before it is too late. There seems to be a 'now-or-never' feeling that underlies decisions made during the midlife transitions. (6)

There is abundant evidence, therefore, that middle-aged people are being increasingly encouraged to become sensitive about physical aging and its social implications. An analysis of representations, discussions and descriptions of middle age in the media (7) reveals mounting pressure on individuals in all walks of life to feel self-conscious about their appearance and to compare themselves with certain cultural ideals. In other words, we are witnessing a systematisation of discourse and a restructuring of images of middle age which are not in themselves totally new but which have been disciplined and elaborated to meet the demands of both state bureaucracies and consumer culture.

In the traditional stereotype of middle age, physical appearance was expected to deteriorate and little concern was shown about diet, weight, body image, fashion or keeping fit. Growing old was seen as a natural and inevitable process: as 'fate', something which according to the norm, could not be combatted by energetic self-maintenance and attempts to 'stay', 'dress', 'look' or 'be' young. Resignation characterises phrases such as 'growing old gracefully','becoming set in your ways', and 'it's old age creeping on'. George Orwell, in his pre-war essay on the art of the famous postcard illustrator Donald McGill, points out that in these popular cards there are no pictures of good-looking people beyond their first youth, and in effect we are presented with two opposing types: the 'spooning' couple and the 'cat and dog' couple.

> Sex appeal vanishes at about the age of twenty-five. Well-preserved and good-looking people beyond their first youth are never represented. The amorous honey-mooning couple reappear as the grim-visaged wife and shapeless, moustachioed, red-nosed husband, no inter-mediate stage being allowed for. (8)

In this traditional imagery, middle age was generally presented as a period of inevitable physical and sexual decline: a time of the 'sexual hush' as one writer around the turn of the century put it. Impotence and frigidity were apparently a common fate. The vulgar and farcical aspects of middle-aged sex were subjected to an endless series of jokes, where frigidity and impotence are approached with what Nutall and Carmichael refer to as 'survival humour'. (9) In the old tradition sex was there-fore seen as the province of the young and it was corres-pondingly difficult to imagine older people engaging in sex. (10)

But the signs are that this traditional image is gradually being refurbished and the media are playing an important role in this process. The typical, middle-aged, working-class 'slob' is currently under assault from a number of quarters. The widely publicised British Health Education Council, 'Look After Yourself' campaign, for example, put out a television advertisement showing an overweight, middle-aged husband being taken in a collar and lead by his wife for a walk in the park. To the accompaniment of a whimsical commentary extolling the advantages of regular exercise, he was shown capering around, fetching sticks and barking at other females. This was followed by two full-page advertisements in The Sun, Mirror and News of the World in January and February 1978 which were reprinted in June 1978. Their headlines ran: 'You'd Enjoy Sex More If You Had a Pair of Plimsolls' and 'Is Your Body Coming Between You and the Opposite Sex'. The first advert began: 'If you sit at home all evening you're a sitting target for heart disease, obesity and depression. Your body is just running down'. It asked the reader to fight back, walk to work, repaint the house, buy a dog, take up a game or exercise. A whole range of benefits was offered:

> You'll sleep better, shake off depression, you'll enjoy
> going out, work more effectively and think more
> clearly, you'll mend the kid's bike. And yes, frankly
> you'll be more inclined to enjoy sex. And as you're
> in more attractive shape so will your partner. There
> are more exciting things than the late night movie -
> and they're better exercise.

The government-backed campaign had middle-aged people
very much in mind, and in particular (given that the
advertisements appeared on commercial television and in the
popular press) the working-class 'slob' image. It was
clearly attempting to break through the old idea that body
shape and fitness are something inherited and the body
naturally deteriorates and 'spreads out' with age.

A new image is therefore emerging which views middle age
as an adjunct to youth and emphasises that individuals who
look after their bodies and adopt a positive, sensible
attitude towards the aging process will enjoy the benefits
of youthfulness deep into the middle years. Individuals are
led to believe they can hold the negative aspects of the
aging process at bay: the tendency to be unfit, overweight,
wrinkled, to go grey, to lose one's hair, to suffer from
declining sexual powers, to look 'out of date', to look
defeated. Moreover, with the adoption of a rational
conservationalist attitude towards one's own body one can
prolong the positive attributes of youth: flexibility,
adaptability and an energetic outlook. Hardly a week goes
by without extensive feature articles in the popular media
on one or another of the elements of the new imagery: aging,
slimming, vitamins, health foods, appearance, sex or
physical fitness.

When asked on the BBC television series 'Feeling Great'
why he bothered to keep fit, actor William Franklin began
to make conventional references to feeling good, having a
demanding job, etc, and then checked himself: 'No, I'm
going to be honest. The real reason is that when I take my
clothes off at night, I like hearing my wife say "You look
bloody good"'. (11) The undoubted implication is that 'if
you look good you feel good', and more importantly, looking
good is not a fixed quality which we do or do not possess,
but something which everyone can achieve with effort. This
reflects a society in which bodily appearance and demeanour
are beginning to assume a major importance for the
individual's sense of self identity. Where social interactions take on a more fluid, precarious nature, and
individuals move through a world where careful presentation
of self and impression management (the awareness of the
body as a means of expression) become mandatory. (12) At
the same time it may be objected that all cultures have
placed a high value on beauty and appearance and the present
day preoccupation is nothing new. This contention can be
placed in historical perspective through a consideration of

Richard Sennett's <u>The Fall of Public Man</u> (13) where he discusses the relatively recent origins of the belief that appearance and bodily presentation are 'achievables' which express one's self.

Sennett argues that in 18th century public life, appearance and bodily expression were more playfully distanced from the self and not regarded as revelations of personality. An individual's character was given by birth, and was not something which could be developed or modified. Decisive changes took place in the nineteenth century which resulted in the intrusion of personality into public life. This was, in part, a consequence of the substitution of a traditional holistic world view, in which every entity had a fixed place in the order of things, with a more fluid, existentialist view of the world in which each individual was responsible for the development of his potential. It was also the result of the manufacture and availability of cheap, mass-produced clothing, subsequently to be advertised and displayed in the new department stores, which had the effect of investing clothes with an aura of mystery. A person's dress and demeanour were gradually seen as a sign of his personality, an expression of his individuality. Clothes became, in the words of Thomas Carlyle, 'emblems of the soul'. (14) Modern man, according to Sennett, is still concerned with the intrusion of personality into public life and spends much time decoding the minutia of others' appearance which are taken as signs of their inner selves. In public the individual feels increasingly estranged, vulnerable and is scrupulous over the management of impressions when moving through a world of strangers. At the same time he is fascinated by the 'gastronomy of the eye', the plenitude of possibilities in a world of appearances, each of which offers some clue to the bearer's own personality. Yet Sennett's analysis is centred on the 19th century and although he projects it forwards to the present day (where he notes the cultivation of self takes a more extreme and narcissistic form) he does not consider the intervening social changes which have contributed to this process.

The rationalisation and expansion of techniques of mass production in the early decades of the twentieth century laid the foundation for consumerism and these processes have been subjected to theoretical analysis by Georg Lukacs and members of the Frankfurt School. An analysis grounded in Marx's theory of the fetishism of commodities which, they argued, could be extended beyond the merely economic to offer a critical method of understanding changes in the socio-cultural realm. In <u>Capital</u> Marx outlined how under capitalism all useful objects became commodities and relations based upon the exchange of commodities (market relations) begin to dominate and control the distribution both of products and of producers. (15) Eventually, the laws of commodity exchange dictate what will be produced, who will work, where men will work and the value of their labour. Social relations between individuals become governed material relations and take on the strange and unnatural form of relations between things. At the same time material things (commodities) seem to take on a social life of their own, they become personified, move around, engage in social intercourse.

In History and Class Consciousness (16) Lukacs develops his theory of reification (Verdinglichung) which was based upon a broadening out of Marx's theory of commodity fetishism using insights taken from Weber's theory of rationalisation. For Lukacs, Marx's analysis had demonstrated the dehumanising effects of commodity exchange where the tendency was to regard all qualities, use-values, including the person as quantifiable, calculable, measurable. Formal similarities exist between this type of exchange calculation and the calculation of the worker as a factor of production through the use of an increasingly sophisticated division of labour where tasks become progressively specialised and fragmented (Taylorism is an important part of this process) and the worker becomes 'a mechanical part incorporated into a mechanical system'. Where Lukacs goes beyond Marx is to bring out the parallels between this process and Weber's theory of the increasing rationalisation of society. Weber had drawn attention to the progressive disenchantment and bureaucratisation of the world through the outward penetration of formal rationality - the subjection of human action to abstract, quantifiable and calculable rules - to all areas of life. By following Weber's use of rationalisation Lukacs was able to show that commodity fetishism now extended beyond the purely economic. The instrumental rational calculation of men and social relationships in everyday life was similar to those of the factory. Indeed, the factory became the model for all social relationships and the 'fate of the worker became the fate of society as a whole'. (17)

Lukacs' theory of reification proves useful in understanding the societal changes behind the growth of consumerism and a new attitude to middle age because it pinpoints the progressive development of the capacity to calculate all social relationships, and even one's self, in terms of formal and instrumentally rational criteria. There is a tendency to demystify all aspects of personal existence. The body, health, the life course, presentation of self, and even death, become divested of their traditional transpersonal cultural meanings and are seen as capable of rational control. This process can be grounded in the 'helping professions': experts who seek to codify and administer the new information as well as educating the population to their changing needs in purely instrumental terms. Also directly relevant to the new image of middle age are the development of a pseudo-science of the body (which includes the calculation of 'normal' weight and optimum calorific levels for age, sex, height and build); the development of home economics which provides systematic information on hygiene, nutrition, diet; the calculation of the effects of varying levels of fitness and dietary control on longevity, health and energy levels. The machine imagery of the body tells us it should be serviced like the motor car and can be repaired and parts replaced on a modular basis: spare part surgery, transplants, plastic surgery, hormone therapy, and vitamins can renovate and keep it in peak condition. The view is that the span of life can be controlled and extended into a future where ultimately death itself can be mastered. Body shape, height, beauty, ugliness can be dissected and remodelled and embodied existence can be purchased and achieved.

The rationalisation of everyday life and culture was furthered during the inter-war period by the development of the popular media coupled with the rapid extension of advertising. Radio, motion pictures, tabloid press and mass-circulation magazines helped to discredit traditional mores and create new standards of behaviour, and stereotypes which encouraged individuals to become more critically self-conscious of their appearance and presentation of self. The erosion of the traditional mores and the receptivity of individuals to the dissemination of new norms, stereotypes and lifestyle images can be illuminated by examining Adorno's elaboration of certain aspects of Marx's theory of commodity fetishism. Adorno's analysis centres on the effects of the extension of the commodity form to culture, whereby capitalism not only subordinated the original use-value of objects by making them commodities, but allowed exchange-value to take on the function of use, facilitating the substitution of a new artificial use. Marx had indicated the two-fold nature of the commodity whereby its exchange-value (monetary value) tended to dominate its use-value, the intrinsic or unique quality of the object. Adorno takes this analysis a stage further by suggesting that in late capitalism the dominance of exchange-value is such that it has completely obliterated the memory of the last traces of use-values, and in addition entails the substitution of a secondary, ersatz use-value which masquerades as 'pure' or 'true' as value:

> ... if commodities consist of exchange-value and use-value then in advanced capitalist society an illusion of pure use-value as displayed by cultural goods has been substituted for pure exchange-value. This exchange-value has deceptively taken over the function of use-value. (18)

In his cultural criticism Adorno constantly refers to this tendency of increasing reification where everything becomes subjected to the sign of the commodity. At the same time, his maxim 'save the particular' can be understood as a plea to seek out and highlight resistance to exchange-value, in order to show the contradictions that occur within all levels of culture. While the dominance of exchange-value places everything on the same illusionary scale, allowing cultural goods to take on the mantle of a fetishised use-value, this 'false' use-value appeals because it represents an attempt at regression, an attempt to escape the abstract equivalence of mass production. In an essay on Veblen, Adorno says 'Men prefer to deceive themselves with illusions of the concrete rather than abandon the hope which clings to it.' (19)

In the early decades of the 20th century the rationalisation of industrial production through the development of scientific management greatly increased the productive potential which laid the foundation for a consumer way of life based upon the mass production and consumption of commodities. Outside the workplace, traditional mores and values were weakened both through the general reification of everyday life and the way in which the predominance of exchange-value (the extension of consumer purchasing into more and more areas of life) had the effect of weakening the traditionally conceived qualitative use of things, freeing them to take on whatever designated use commercial interests could dream up. As Horkheimer and Adorno remark: 'Everything is looked at from one aspect: that it can be used for something else, however vague the notion of this use may be.' (20) Of crucial importance in this process was the growth of advertising which drew upon a pool of imagery highlighting the good life, especially a sense of well-being based on a new equation of beauty with youth, freedom, and flexibility. The endowment of commodities with an aura of romance and mystery produced a proliferation of imagery which merges and becomes interchangeable with the imagery presented in the mass media: a society of appearances, where images become hard to distinguish from, and at times preferable to, reality. Images invite comparisons, constant reminders of what we are not, and what we might be.

In their paper 'Advertising Needs and Commodity Fetishism' (21) Kline and Leiss help to further our understanding of this process. They open with a criticism of Marx for overemphasising the intrinsic use-value of goods in assuming that every commodity has an objective value in relation to human needs which is threatened by the growing dominance of exchange-value under capitalism. Instead they prefer to follow Marshall Sahlins in adopting a culturalist critique of the notion that use-values satisfy objective human wants. 'Use' and 'need' are not universals, they function within specific cultural orders. (22) Rather than talk about true needs Kline and Leiss refer to the 'symbolic constitution of utility'.

They want to examine the production (the manufacture, sale and advertising) and the reception (the symbolic associations used by consumers in constructing lifestyle models) of the symbolism of commodities. Their orientation therefore switches from the analysis of the larger scale reification effects of the exchange economy to a consideration of the construction and reception of the symbolic meaning of commodities within consumer culture. Attempting to understand the symbolic properties of goods by examining the imagery used in marketing, especially media-based advertising, Kline and Leiss note that goods are much more than the sum of their physical properties and are increasingly presented as offering more diffuse feelings of happiness and well-being to their users. Advertising imagery constantly utilises a range of lifestyle models in which psychological associations such as family happiness, career success, youth and freedom, become loosely symbolically associated with goods. Since the early stages of consumerism in the 1920s there has been a gradual shift in advertising from the use of textual material and explicit statements of value: '... the commodity seems to become a projective field in which the human states of feeling achievable in consumption are fluidly super-imposed upon non-human, physical-sensory aspects of the commodity.' (23)

These processes cannot be understood simply as leading to mass deception. The re-symbolisation of commodities which took place within the expansion of consumer culture did not confront individuals as a total ideology. The discrediting of traditional use-values and mores entails a critical element which individuals may perceive as 'reasonable'. The values challenged were not only based upon brotherhood and community, the romanticised side of Gemeinschaft, but also involved the subjection of individuals to dogmatic authority: for tradition also means patriarchal domination. As Habermas has pointed out, while scientism becomes a technological ideology, it also involves a critique of arbitary structures of prejudice. (24) Consumerism under the guise of enlightenment offers a critique of traditional, restrictive attitudes towards family activities, child rearing practices, sexuality and leisure time pursuits. It appears to offer freedom of choice and control over dogmatic and fixed natural and social categories: youth and beauty, for example, are presented as 'achievables'. The penetration and expansion of the market into everyday, non-work activities provides some of the freedoms and equalities of the market, however illusory they might turn out to be.

In the inter-war era, consumer culture often stimulated popular desires (long suppressed in the working class) for the romance and exotica of far away places, a sense of action and movement captured by the motor car, the promise of excitement, things happening, of social relationships which triumphed over fate. (25) In a similar way these industries were able to latch onto the movement for sexual freedom and present the freer sexual atmosphere which emerged in the 1920s as a necessary correlate of the consumer life-style. S. Kern grounds the changes which occurred in the 1920s in the emergence of a more aggressive female sexuality in the First World War. (26) Within this context the old ideas of chastity and self-control were eroded and an increase in pre-marital and extra-marital affairs took place. Changes took place in women's fashions: hemlines rose, necklines plunged, women began to wear provocative coloured underwear and started to use cosmetics. Likewise the emphasis placed upon health, fitness, body maintenance and sport in the 1920s was not simply the result of the strategies of the advertising and cultural industries. Rather, as Haley's discussion of the Victorian obsession with bodily health implies, they latched upon genuine needs and a cultural attitude towards the body which can be traced back to the mid-nineteenth century. (27)

Consumerism thus sought to socialise individuals to the needs of expanding mass production. It did so by transforming genuine needs into reified appearances, and through its critique of traditional values offered a greater freedom of choice which was not completely illusory. Recent debates on whether or not 'one-dimensionality' did manage to administer everything out of existence are misplaced (28) for reality both then and now is essentially Janus-faced. A contradictory reality exhibits the tendency for culture to be subsumed under the general concept (reification), yet culture also resists the tendency for integration and represents the perennial protest of the particular against the general. Towards the end of his life Theodor Adorno spoke of symptoms of double consciousness whereby individuals were able to resist total manipulation:

> It seems that the integration of consciousness and leisure time is not yet complete after all. The real interests of individuals are still strong enough to resist total manipulation up to a point. This analysis would be in tune with the prognosis that consciousness cannot be totally integrated in a society in which the basic contradictions remain undiminished. (29)

Also instructive in this context is McCarthy's comment on the case for a motivational crisis presented in Legitimation Crisis, where he argues that Habermas' formulation poses too broad a dichotomy between the acceptance of decisions without reasons and the acceptance of decisions as the expression of a rational consensus and misses out the middle ground, that individuals may accept decisions because nothing better seems practically possible in the given circumstances. (30) Individuals can be motivated to accept a given way of life (consumerism) not simply because they have been absorbed, but (and perhaps cynically) because it provides an acceptable flow of rewards and is the only realistic alternative available.

In Captains of Consciousness (31) Ewen argues that the rise of consumerism in the 1920s should not be seen as part of a gradual evolution of capitalism. Instead it represents a survivalist strategy on the part of business leaders whose response to the increasing capacity for mass production was to create new habits and form a larger buying public. Traditional values had to be broken down: puritan notions of thrift and moderation, traditional 'folk' cures and remedies for the problems of everyday life had to be discredited to make way for the new consumer values. Advertising played a crucial role in this process, it sought to make individuals emotionally vulnerable, conscious of their bodies and appearance. In effect it helped create a world in which fear reigned, where individuals must guard

106

against the 'betrayals' of bad breath, dandruff and a spotty face. These bodily imperfections could no longer be regarded as natural, the advertisements established new standards and norms emphasising that the individual's self-image depended more and more upon the opinions of others, thus laying the foundation for a world in which interactionist social psychology could readily function.

Youth was elevated to the position of one of the most important values in consumer culture. In part this was a response to the de-skilling of the labour force, itself a consequence of the introduction of the new techniques of mass production. Youthfulness was not only an industrial ideal, but through advertising became a wider cultural ideal with the concept of the successful youth becoming the healthy, energetic, high performance stereotype used to provide a definition of the successful adult. (32)

The 'flapper' was born. Ewen characterises her as a new type of woman, full of restless energy, living for the moment, trying out everything new and discarding the old, demanding the same social freedoms men enjoyed. She was: 'pure consumer, busy dancing through the world of modern goods. She was youth, marked by energy not judgement'. (33) With her boyish, slender figure, short skirt and flat chest, the flapper symbolised little girlhood and set a new stereotype for the young mother, a style which was particularly hard on the middle-aged woman, and which superannuated the older woman. Advertising encouraged greater self-consciousness and constant self-scrutiny. Women, in particular, were encouraged to become narcissistic and to look at themselves as objects to be compared to other women. For those who fell short of the ideal, and there were many, appearance was something which could be purchased and achieved. In the 1920s the advertisements for body care and presentation were predominantly directed at women. (34) For the first time in large numbers they put on rouge and lipstick, they wore short skirts and rayon stockings, they abandoned the corset and wore rubber 'weight reducing' girdles. (35)

Hollywood reinforced the new stereotypes acclaimed in the advertisements. After the First World War the movies helped to modernise and homogenise sex, women were presented as sex objects who had to work and strive to present and maintain their sexuality; sexuality had become a duty of leisure. C.B. de Mille's 'Why Change Your Wife' (1920) captured this new consumer sexual morality: Gloria Swanson played a drab housewife who drove her husband to another woman, but then bought a new wardrobe, got a new hairstyle and won him back. (36) The movies broke down the old taboos, they offered a modernised view of sexuality which cut through Victorian sentimentality, they set new fashions and helped to establish new norms and stereotypes of behaviour; as Daniel Bell states: 'Films glorified the cult of youth (girls wore bobbed hair and short skirts), and middle-aged men and women were advised to make hay while the sun shines.' (37)

With weekly attendances of a hundred million in the United States in 1930, (twenty million in Britain in 1937) a new pool of imagery, centred around a glamourised consumer lifestyle, was held up to large numbers of people who could draw out various elements to augment their daily lives. Films set the fashion in clothes, hairstyles and christian names, like Marlene, Gary, Shirley. The inter-war years also saw the development of radio broadcasting; the tabloid newspaper, the New York <u>Daily News</u> being the first in 1919, with the <u>Daily Mirror</u> the first British tabloid in 1937; mass circulation magazines, the <u>Saturday Evening Post</u>, <u>Life</u>, <u>Ladies Home Journal</u> and <u>Cosmopolitan</u> in the United States. In Britain, where the attempts to establish a uniform taste met with more resistance, it was not until 1937 that <u>Woman</u> was launched. (38) All these magazines celebrated the consumer lifestyle, they offered expert advice on appearance, presentation, body maintenance, and homemaking and carried advertisements which reiterated the message. The media also played an important role in the elevation of sport to the position of a national pastime.

Such images make individuals more conscious of externals, appearances, presentation and 'the look'. In this context it is interesting to note that Bela Balazs in 1923 speculated that film was transforming the emotional life of twentieth century man by directing him away from words towards movement and gesture. A culture dominated by words tends to be intangible and abstract, and reduces the human body to a basic biological organism, whereas the new emphasis upon visual images draws attention to the visible body, to clothing, demeanour and gesture. (39) In the last twenty-five years, television has also led to a shift from textural information and descriptions of the intrinsic qualities of commodities to looser, more ambiguous lifestyle images, which surround the commodity with associations of youth, active recreation, familial and sexual love, personal maintenance, the good life, and the natural-historical (nostalgic) existence. (40)

Alongside the growth of consumer culture a number of demographic changes have occurred which have radically altered the nature of midlife. Peter Laslett (41) has outlined some of the most important of these changes. He refers to the reduction of family size from around six children in late Victorian times to just over two today. Women formerly spent two-thirds to three-quarters of their reproductive cycle pregnant or near pregnancy, now it amounts to only one-eighth of the time. Furthermore, the average family would expect to lose two or three out of their six children, with only half of the children reaching the age of twenty. With the growth in life-expectancy from fifty years around the turn of the century, to between sixty-five and seventy today, more people are living into middle age and beyond. Changes in the nature of work, the reduction in the numbers of individuals employed in physically demanding occupations and the length of the working day, (42) coupled with better nutrition, has meant that health in general has improved and the possibility of a more active middle age created.

All these changes have resulted in a massive increase in the time a couple can expect to spend with each other in the middle years, time which is less likely to be punctuated by the intrusion of what were formerly routine, yet frequently traumatic, family occurrences: the birth, sickness, or death of a child. Put simply, less happens in the family today. In mid-life, husbands and wives have more time to spend with each other, which taken together with the reduction in working time, has opened up an expanding zone of free time (soon to be channelled into the category of 'leisure' time) alongside the growth of consumer culture.

The emergence of the 'empty nest' and the increase in time and purchasing power of the middle-aged couple, have also opened up a new market ripe for commercial exploitation. In the past, commercial opportunism responded to the knowledge that, at certain periods in the life cycle, people whose income was formerly tightly committed had more money to spend (the creation of the teenager and the development of youth culture in the 1950s can, of course, be seen in this light). (43) Similarly, the changes in the nature of the life course leading to the 'empty nest', as well as the wife's return to full-time employment, have created the possibility of a new middle-aged market in the 1960s and 1970s and concommitant commercial interest in creating a new image for middle age. (44) Mark Abrams has pointed out that the period between the late forties and early sixties represents perhaps the most prosperous years of the married couple. (45) These are also the years in which the problem of what to do with the additional free time begins to emerge. (46)

We have now reached a position where one of the most socially acceptable ways of filling in time in middle age is by keeping fit. Jogging Magazine recently featured an interview with a middle-aged man whose response to the question 'why jog?' was that he experienced a 'general feeling of well-being and alertness, being taut and crisp'. He went on to observe: 'Then of course, there is the slight smugness when you think, I'm better than the next man, I also feel that my chances of survival are better ... the obvious benefit is that you never get bored. You say to yourself, what shall I do next? Oh yes, go for a run.' (47)

Over the last few years, first in the United States and now in Britain and Europe, jogging has been promoted as an inexpensive way of improving the physical health of all the family. A recent British study of 18,000 middle-aged male office workers over an eight-year period discovered that those who were involved in various methods of keeping fit (jogging included) had a lower incidence of coronary heart disease, the main cause of death in middle age, than their colleagues who did not involve themselves in vigorous exercise. (48) However, another recent study of 1,000 joggers in Liverpool showed that well under one in ten obtained any benefit from jogging and concluded that exercise had to be hard, long and regular to be effective. (49) In other words, jogging can actively promote health but only if it is part of a vigorous and sustained keep fit programme. Occasional exercise is almost useless.

Physical fitness is of course notoriously difficult to measure. Medical researchers, physiologists and sports specialists have some way to go to determine precise indicators of health and well-being. The promoters of jogging, therefore, also hold out the promise of an additional set of benefits which operate on another level: the subjective. Jogging, it is urged, can provide a sensuous experience which reawakens in the individual a new awareness of his bodily needs. In the same way that the 'wilderness experience' can heighten individual sensitivity to the surrounding natural environment and the relationship of the body to it, jogging can stimulate a new pleasurable relationship between man and nature. Here the body is no longer treated primarily as an instrument of labour, but as a source of pleasure and delight in a manner closely parallel to Kant's concept of the aim of art: 'interesse-loses Wohlgefallen' - purposiveness without purpose. Whilst, therefore, the measurable physical benefits of jogging may be less than joggers imagine, jogging can be seen as a source of personal satisfaction: a subjective sense of mental and physical well-being.

It must however be remembered that jogging and its rewards are not untouched by consumer culture 'where everything has a use for something else', and where the market has moved in to redefine use and value. Notwithstanding the alleged need for only rudimentary and inexpensive equipment, joggers are continually urged to monitor and improve their performance with the aid of stopwatches, pedometers and even jogging machines. Specially tailored shorts, singlets, 'jogging suits' (some following the dictates of haute couture) and 'scientifically designed' running shoes, are marketed on the basis that they not only improve efficiency but look good too. The jogger who buys these products will not only improve his health and fitness but will also compete more effectively with his fellows and enjoy their reaction to his smooth appearance. Under the appropriate conditions exercise can be physically beneficial, but the problem is that it tends to be subordinated to the market requirements of the expanding leisure industry and its aims and consequences become redefined and reified. Almost all advertisements for do-it-yourself exercise (rowing machines, body builders, weight lifting kits, sit-up benches, cycling machines, jogging equipment, etc.) under-score the cosmetic rewards of looking slimmer and therefore more attractive.

Jogging may also point to a preoccupation with longevity and survivalism: lengthening the odds against sudden death or incapacitating illness. This aspect is epitomised in an

110

article by Bruce Tulloh entitled 'The Over-Forties: How Jogging Can Make You Age Backwards'. Tulloh, aged 43, explains that a number of reports have concluded that jogging and other forms of exercise actually increase life-expectancy. Chronological age is not the most important factor, for exercise can make the middle-aged biologically younger. This doesn't just make the body look and actually 'be' younger, but also according to Tulloh, 'The biggest bonus is the feeling of youthfulness that running gives us.' It is this feeling of youthfulness which itself contributes to making us young:

> It is the person who allows the pressures to build up, and who never gets out of his grey tunnel into the real exciting world, who is being pushed to an early grave. The runner too, will have to go, sooner or later, more likely later, but until then he really can enjoy per-petual youth. This summer I went up a mountain with a man of 90 who was younger than many of my 35-year-old colleagues. (50)

The adoption of an ascetic and disciplinary attitude towards one's body is presented as a sensible way of avoiding illness and maximising one's life chances. Since the oil crises of the 1970s, governments have become more conscious of energy conservation, and economic pressures towards ecology on a societal level are accompanied on the individual level by the injunction to adopt body mainten-ance techniques in order to achieve 'inner ecology'. This tendency to regard not only one's appearance, but bodily health and life expectancy, as no longer ascribed qualities but 'achievables', can be traced back to the early part of the nineteenth century. Samuel Smiles, a champion of self-reliance and individualism, stressed in Self Help (1859) that good health is a prerequisite for success and a necessary condition to enjoy the fruits of success, and that it was incumbent on the individual to exercise prudence in health matters. (51) In the late 1970s this form of self-help individualism (a persistent strand in our culture despite the emergence of the welfare state) is undergoing a revival, primarily it would seem as a means of reducing government expenditure. A return to a more general disciplinary ethos throughout society and a reinforcement of the work ethic have also been encouraged by the present high level of unemployment. (52) The notion of do-it-yourself health care further resonates with more deep-seated features of consumer culture, which encourages individuals to approach their personal and interpersonal relationships and free time activities in a calculating, instrumental frame of mind.

Longevity is held out as a reward of body maintenance. 'Will You Live to a Ripe Old Age?' asks the headline of a feature article in The Sun: 'Mr. Average dies at 69, Mrs. Average at 75. But what is your chance? How you live and what you eat can have an amazing effect on your lifespan say doctors and scientists ... The Sun quiz designed with expert medical advice could help save your life.' (53) This fascination with longevity is behind the steady procession of western scientists and journalists who have made the trek to the remote Andean village of Vilcabamba in Ecuador to discover the secrets of the inhabitants, some of whom live to be over 120. It is not merely their longevity which intrigues the West, but the fact that far from degenerating into geriatric old age, the inhabitants lead an active healthy life, being still able to work, enjoy sex and consume considerable quantities of home-made rum and cigarettes deep into old age. (54) Even if Vilcabamba refuses to disclose its secret, some western scientists are confident that the lifespan can be progressively extended. Techniques under investigation include the adoption of a semi-starvation diet, eating chemicals and lowering the body temperature, all of which, it is held, would increase life expectancy by over fifty per cent. (55) More dramatic still are the predictions by some futurologists that we will have solved the problem of death in the next twenty years or so. (56) Evidence that these predictions are taken seriously is provided by the emergence in California of 'Cryonic Suspension', the macabre practice of freezing one's dear-departed in the belief they can be revived once a cure for death has been discovered. As yet only thirty-two people have been frozen at a cost of £50,000 each. One prospective customer summed up the new immortals' orientation: 'Cryonic Suspension is the second worst thing that can happen to you - the worst is death.' (57)

What is interesting about this current obsession with longevity, is not merely the absurdly grandiose claims of a technical solution to the problem of death, nor the widening global contradiction between the affluent areas of the west (in the 'developed' countries life expectancy is being pushed into the upper seventies and eighties and the poorer third world nations still experience a 'Stone Age' life expectancy of just over thirty years), but why longevity is becoming an important value within our culture. Of course, it would be foolish to dispute the universal validity of the desire to live a healthy life, to fend off old age and death, yet when these projects become elevated to the stature of central life goals, it should sensitise us to the changing valuation of life and death within our culture. This is not to insist that man should revert to subordinating himself to some 'irrational' (e.g. religious) value outside himself; the elimination of needless suffering, ill health and death itself is a worthy transcultural human goal. It is their elevation to a position where it appears to be the only meaningful goal for individuals, where egoistic self-preservation is the only worthwhile end, which detracts from other equally worthy ends and tends to lead to their exclusion. (58)

In the modern era death has increasingly been detached from notions of fate and destiny (59) and has been accentuated in the twentieth century because death tends to be defined as an unacceptable and essentially meaningless intrusion in the midst of a happy life. Ariès comments on this interdict:

> One must avoid - no longer for the sake of the dying person, but for society's sake, for the sake of those close to the dying person - the disturbance and the overly strong emotion caused by the ugliness of death in the midst of a happy life, for it is henceforth given that life is always happy or should always seem to be so. (60)

Franz Borkenau's discussion of the wide range of alternative cultural responses to death can help to illuminate our current inability to accept death as a meaningful part of life. Of particular interest is his notion of death-defying (e.g. Christianity) and death-denying (e.g. dark ages) cultures and the collapse of the former into the latter. (61) Faith in a life after death which is integral to salvationist religions such as Christianity, directs attention away from self-preservation. Dark ages, on the other hand, tend to devalue religion, leading to a regeneration of magical practices purporting to offer some degree of control and protection over threatening, irrational, natural and mystical forces. Speculation that we are witnessing the end of the epoch and facing the prospect of a new dark age aside (62), the concept of death-denying conduct provides us with some interesting speculative insights on contemporary society. The notion that life is governed by fate, that current injustices will be redeemed in the after-life, has been replaced by death-denying conduct, where one's health and life expectancy are vulnerable and constantly under threat from a myriad of forces, which can and should be rationally controlled by the ever-vigilant individual. (63) Concern with health care, techniques of body maintenance, also suggests an immanent conception of the body: the body is no longer seen as a medium for the expression of the soul. (64) With the destruction of its traditional religious purpose, the body, formerly a means to other loftier ends, folds back into itself to serve what appears to the individual to be the only worthwhile goal, the preservation of the self. Yet the current survivalist concern with health and longevity is caught on a fundamental contradiction. The body inevitably deteriorates over time and even those who try to stay young at heart are constantly reminded of their decline and inevitable death by wrinkles, sagging flesh and unpleasant odours. Reparative measures will inevitably fail, and within a culture unable to offer the individual significant goals which transcend the importance of his self-preservation, the only strategy society prescribes is more of the same, a renewal of his vigilance and watchfulness, supported by the knowledge that scientists work deep into the night to achieve the final elimination of disease and death.

In a society dominated by appearances and images, one of the effects of the encouragement of presentation of self and the cultivation of bodily expression, is that images are often taken as realities. Attention is focussed on a competitive comparison of appearances, and the realities behind the images, the individual's own experience of his potential and desires and need to engage in a meaningful discourse with others about his life, is constricted and denied. However, as we have indicated, the new imagery and the values which lie behind it are not without their contradictions and the women's movement has been especially forceful in drawing attention to the injustice of the dominant female stereotype which bears down heavily on the aging woman. Since their personal and social advancement depends upon their being physically attractive girls are taught from an early age to care for their appearance. Throughout their lives women encounter the message 'that their looks are a commodity to be bartered. and exchanged for a man'. (65) To the aging woman the deterioration of facial and bodily beauty is particularly bad news. She has to face the fact that failure to maintain a youthful appearance implies loss of femininity and thus acceptability as a person. Feminist resentment against the dominant definition of the undesirability of the aging women has highlighted the need for constant effort on a woman's part to maintain approved desirability as she grows older. (66)

According to this perspective the prospect of middle age holds out few benefits. It signifies the end of the woman's conventional role, not only as a youthful sex object, but also as a maternal homemaker. There is a definite absence of a compensatory role or positive image for the aging woman, except to try to 'stay young and beautiful'. Whilst society in general is making everyone more conscious of the aging process, it is, feminists argue, the middle-aged woman who feels these pressures most deeply. Even though middle-aged men, as we have pointed out earlier, are subjected to cosmetic encouragement they will have an alternative role available to them which, because it emphasises time-honoured concepts of 'maturity' and 'character', allows them to grow old more gracefully and thus to enjoy better life chances. It is this contrast which has prompted Susan Sontag to coin the phrase 'the double standard of aging'. (67) Because masculinity is identified with other qualities than simply the maintenance of youthful appearance (these include competitive autonomy and self-control) middle-aged men have an easier time than middle-aged women. As he grows older the man may thus become even more attractive and is permitted, for example, to have affairs with younger women, whereas the middle-aged woman experiences gradual sexual disqualification as her looks deteriorate.

Yet, as we have earlier maintained, this situation is by no means static. The cosmetic and fashion industries, one part only of the youth-orientated consumer culture, ensure amongst men an increasing consciousness of appearance, bodily presentation and the ravages of time. In this sense we can see the long-term tendency within capitalist rationalisation towards a universality of the commodity form which transforms all qualitative social distinctions including gender. Within consumer culture both men and women are increasingly awarded the dubious status of equal consumers in the marketplace. (68)

The women's movement is playing a part in this process by attempting to redress some of the more blatant sexual inequalities in the labour market and in the right to exercise control over one's own body. With regard to the latter, women are now claiming the sole right to define femininity and to underplay female complaints and frailties which, they say, are the historical product of a male dominated, or patriarchal society. (69) From this perspective, the centrality of the menopause as the most crucial event for women in middle-age is challenged, on the grounds that it ties a woman's identity far too closely to her biological role. Several of the self-help manuals on middle age addressed to women, de-emphasise the significance of specific female physiology and prefer the term 'mid-life crisis' to that of menopause as a label for the problems women tend to encounter during the middle years. (70)

From a class perspective, the new imagery can be more readily assimilated by the middle class whose values already encourage self-help individualism and instrumental problem solving. The debate over the relative influence of a supposedly overarching consumer culture depends upon assumptions about the differences between middle and working class life in contemporary society. For some critics the concept of a particular working class culture still persists. Raymond Williams for example, writes:

> The primary distinction between bourgeois and working class culture is to be sought in the whole way of life, and here again we must not confine ourselves to such evidence as housing, dress and modes of leisure. Industrial production tends to create uniformity in such matters, but the vital distinction lies at a different level. The crucial distinguishing element in English life since the Industrial Revolution is not language, not dress, not leisure ...The crucial distinction is between alternative ideas of the nature of society. (71)

Those who follow this approach suggest there are crucial distinctions in the meaning of the body and aging between the middle and working class. Rosenblatt and Suchman remark:

> It is as though the white-collar class think of the body as a machine to be preserved and kept in perfect functioning condition, whether through prosthetic devices, rehabilitation, cosmetic surgery or perpetual treatment, whereas blue-collar groups think of the body as having a limited span of utility: to be enjoyed in youth and then to suffer with and endure stoically with age and decrepitude. (72)

As far as the development of the overall life course is concerned, Neugarten and Datan have drawn attention to an essential difference in rhythm between the classes. The middle class see early adulthood (between twenty and thirty) as a period of experimentation and look forward to a middle age of progressive achievement and productivity: 'the prime of life'. In contrast, the working class see early adulthood as a period of inescapable responsibilities, to be followed by a decline in middle age: becoming a 'has been'. (73) Ken Rogers has also drawn attention to the increase in accident rates, suicides and signs of premature aging amongst poor whites, blacks, American Indians and inhabitants of the American urban ghettoes. For them the equivalent of a severe mid-life crisis which cannot be resolved comes early, in their late twenties and early thirties. (74)

Much of this line of reasoning depends upon evidence of the existence of distinct working class subcultures where identity is substantially derived from a strict division of labour between the sexes and a clear demarcation of skills. Undoubtedly distinctive working class communities, based upon occupations such as fishing and mining and having their own distinctive traditions and values, still exist in western society. But the signs are that these communities are slowly and surely disappearing and that, in the words of Howard H. Davis, 'as occupationally-based social identity declines, so the external influences on social consciousness (e.g. media) are likely to become more important'. (75) Davis is commenting on changing sources of identity amongst the working class in Britain and a similar line of argument has gained acceptance amongst sociologists in the United States. In his article 'Beyond Class: the Decline of Industrial Labour and Leisure', John Alt has concluded:

> the transition to monopoly capitalist society tends to shift the source of social relations, culture and ideology from a class culture of work to a mass culture of consumerism ... a shift from a daily class ex- perience, rooted in occupational communities and functionally related to the labour fetishism of early capitalism, to a relative social privatisation of daily existence rooted in the family and mediated by a mass consumer culture provided by corporate institutions. (76)

The consumer values emerging from the media are superimposed on traditional class distinctions. Advertising, for example, encourages people to identify less with the way they earn their living, the production process, and more with the products they purchase and consume with the rewards of their labour.

Increasing acceptance of the values of consumer culture takes place on two levels. Firstly on the level of media imagery, and secondly in the material arrangements of every- day life and, in particular, the distinction between public and private spaces. With regard to the media, as we have emphasised throughout, members of all social classes are subjected to a barage of lifestyle imagery in which the values of youth, fitness and beauty play an inescapable part. Secondly, the division of the world into public and private spheres and, in particular, the material arrangements of the former are such that members of all social classes are increasingly placed 'on stage' and assessed according to their appearance, style and bodily presentation when outside the home. One effect of the long-term rationalisation of capital has been the demise of the corner shop, now largely replaced by the anonymous supermarket and contemporary shopping centre. The result has been to change shopping from a quick neighbourly trip down the street, to a major, highly organised expedition into a more anonymous public space where certain standards of dress and appearance are deemed desirable. In other words, the supermarket shopper participates in a world of public display. A similar process can be observed in the transformation of the British public house where the small, intimate 'bar or snug' in the local has been replaced by the new pub with its large, one-room lounge. John Clarke has noted how changes in the organisation of the breweries have displaced the traditional pub clientele in favour of the new consumer who:

> differs from the old in terms of age (she/he is young), class (she/he is classless) and taste (campari not beer). The effect of this attempt to address the new consumer is to fundamentally change the social and economic conditions under which drinking takes place, that is, to change the determinants of a particular historically developed form of reproduction. We may borrow from Althusser to suggest that these changes in material conditions and signifying practices (and the commercial ideologists which guide them) function to interpellate a new identity for the drinker - that of the 'consumer' rather than the 'member'. (77)

If we accept there is more and more evidence that the working class are under pressure to maintain their appearance, as a condition of participation in the consumer lifestyle, then we have no difficulty in detecting even clearer evidence of these tendencies in advanced capitalism among the more advantaged classes. 'The most advanced social groups - affluent young professionals - expose most sharply the advanced tendencies of capitalism' says Russell Jacoby. (78) It is amongst this social stratum that the narcissistic tendencies associated with consumerism can be seen in heightened form. These are the people with the time and money to absorb themselves totally in consumer culture and engage in the kind of identity exploration, body maintenance and cultivation of the persona which the theory and practice of the new middle age recommends. Consumerism seeks to promote a controlled hedonism which is expressed through a secular, calculating approach to life which throws the individual back onto his own resources. If he has only himself then he must stand in dread of losing that self and one of the greatest threats to the marketability of the self is the deterioration of appearance attendant on the aging process. In consumer culture it is not only important to survive, but to survive as an active participant who has not been disqualified by the ravages time can work.

Christopher Lasch has suggested that the fear of old age and death are closely linked to the growing prominence of the narcissistic personality; a type of individual who is: '... facile at managing the impressions he gives to others, ravenous for admiration but contemptuous of those he manipulates in providing it - unappeasably hungry for emotional experiences with which to fill an inner void; terrified of aging and death. (79)

The narcissistic type is chronically uneasy about his health, excessively self-conscious, constantly searching himself for flaws and signs of decay, and haunted by fantasies of omnipotence and eternal youth. Until relatively recently aging was seen to have its compensations: parents who were involved in relations of obligation and dependence with their children could identify with, and live vicariously through them, but nowadays, the children are frequently resented as intrusions and even possible rivals. To men and women who fear growing old and cling to youth, middle age appears to be the first signs of the disaster which lies in wait. The recent publicity given to middle age as a problem phase and the emergence of the concept of the mid-life crisis, can be understood within the context of this growing fear of old age and death.

Within a capitalist consumer society a new image of middle age is therefore emerging which stresses a youthful presentation of self and a survivalist obsession with health and longevity. On the individual level these developments are paralleled by the emergence of a new narcissistic personality type. Yet the new imagery and the culture from which it springs contain inherent contradictions and however much the imagery represents itself as the harbinger and custodian of the good life, it promotes a lifestyle which isolates individuals from each other and suppresses the need to come to terms with the inevitability of old age and death.

NOTES AND REFERENCES

(1) See A. Rosenfeld, Prolongevity, Knopf, New York, 1976, p.15.
(2) See the discussion in M. Clarke and B.G. Anderson, Culture and Aging: An Anthropological Study of Older Americans, Thomas, Springfield, III, p.6.
(3) See Clarke and Anderson, op.cit. pp.7-8. E.P. Thompson in his 'Time Work Discipline and Industrial Capitalism', Past and Present, 38, December 1967, outlines the emergence of the modern belief that time should be conserved and not wasted, that individuals should keep busy and constantly plan out their time. By emphasising that rewards will follow from the productive consumption of time in both work and leisure there is a resulting repression of a more 'natural' work rhythm

and a loss of the capacity to relax in the traditional uninhibited way. For a more theoretical discussion see H.G. Reid, 'American Social Science in the Politics of Time and the Crisis of Technocorporate Society', Politics and Society, 3, 2, 1973.

(4) See C. Lasch, The Culture of Narcissism, Norton, New York, 1979, pp.48-9.

(5) Susan Sontag, On Photography, Allen Lane. London, 1978; also the discussion in Lasch, op.cit, p.48.

(6) I. Friese, Women and Sex Roles: A Social Psychological Perspective, W.W. Norton, New York, 1978, pp.179-80.

(7) We have analysed the media presentation of middle age and associated topics since 1974. The following newspapers and magazines have been systematically examined: Sun, Daily Mirror, News of the World, Observer, Sunday Times, Jogging Magazine, Choice. Less systematically we have looked at: Woman, Woman's Own, Reveille, Cosmopolitan, Tit Bits, The Weekly News, Playboy, Slimming, Successful Slimming, Here's Health, TV Times. A preliminary analysis of this information appears in M. Featherstone and M. Hepworth, 'Changing Images of Middle Age', in M. Johnson (ed.), Transitions in Middle and Later Life, BSG Publications, London, 1980. See also M. Featherstone and M. Hepworth, Surviving Middle Age, Basil Blackwell, Oxford, 1982.

(8) G. Orwell, 'The Art of Donald McGill', in Collected Essays, Mercury Books, London, 1961, p.170.

(9) G. Nutall and R. Carmichael, Common Factors/Vulgar Factions, RKP, London, 1977.

(10) A. Leigh, 'Is There Really Sex After 40?' Sunday Times, 3 June, 1977.

(11) Quoted in Jogging Magazine, 2 April, 1979.

(12) This world, of course, is the world described so brilliantly by Erving Goffman. Peter Manning argues that Goffman has been particularly sensitive to changes in Anglo-American life over the last ten to fifteen years which have resulted in a decline in civility and the thin veneer of reciprocity becomes increasingly precarious. P.K. Manning, 'The Decline of Civility: A Comment on Erving Goffman's Sociology', Canadian Review of Sociology and Anthropology, 13 January, 1976.

(13) R. Sennett, The Fall of Public Man, Cambridge University Press, 1976.

(14) T. Carlyle, Sartor Resartus, quoted in Senett, op.cit. p.146.

(15) K. Marx, Capital, vol.1, Penguin, 1976, ch.1 - esp. Section 4, 'Fetishism of the Commodity and Its Secret'. Also T. Carver, 'Marx's Commodity Fetishism', Inquiry, 18, 1975. R. Dunayevskaya, Marxism and Freedom: From 1776 until Today, Bookman's Association, New York, 1958, chs.7, 8.

(16) G. Lukacs, History and Class Consciousness, trans. R. Livingstone, Merlin Press, 1971. See also: A. Arato, 'Lukacs' Theory of Reification', Telos, 11, 1972, and A. Arato, 'Introduction to Esthetic Theory and Cultural Criticism', in A. Arato and E. Gebhardt (eds.), The Essential Frankfurt School Reader, Basil Blackwell,

Oxford, 1978, esp. pp.194-7.

(17) Lukacs, *op.cit.* p.91.

(18) T. Adorno, 'Dissonanzen Musik in der verwalteten Welt', GS 14, pp.375-9, quoted in G. Rose, *The Melancholy Science: An Introduction to Adorno*, Macmillan, London, 1978, p.25.

(19) T. Adorno, 'Veblen's Attack on Culture', *Prisms*, trans. S. and S. Weber, Spearman, London, 1967, p.85.

(20) M. Horkheimer and T. Adorno, *Dialectic of Enlightenment*, trans. J. Cumming, Herder and Herder, New York, 1972, p.158.

(21) S. Kline and W. Leiss, 'Advertising Needs and Commodity Fetishism', *Canadian Journal of Political and Social Theory*, 2, 1, 1978. R. Sennett and D, McCannell also make brief references to Marx's theory of commodity fetishism and how the commodity comes to take on new meanings which go beyond its original use. Neither refer to the development of Marx's theory by Lukacs and Adorno. See Sennett, *op.cit*, p.145, and D. McCannell, *The Tourist: A New Theory of the Leisure Class*, Schoken Books, New York, 1976, pp.19-20.

(22) M. Sahlins, *Culture and Practical Reason*, Chicago University Press, 1976, p.150, referred to in Kline and Leiss, *op.cit*, p.12. By implication this criticism applies to Adorno, who, along with other members of the Frankfurt School, is accused, by Leiss, of holding to the fiction of a layer of true needs behind the manipulated desires of the capitalist marketplace. Yet here 'true needs' need not be taken as referring to timeless universals, but to a potential within a historical tradition which has become progressively eliminated. Adorno's 'man without a memory' and Marcuse's 'one-dimensional man' both refer to the modern individual, who, under the pressure of the commodification of culture is incapable of remembering the historical and aesthetic dimensions. Adorno in particular, constantly opposed philosophical anthropology and philosophy of first principles. *Negative Dialectics* stands testament to this. Leiss's statement is in his review of S. Ewen, 'Captains of Consciousness', *Telos*, 29, 1967, p.208.

(23) Kline and Leiss, *op.cit*, p.18.

(24) J. Habermas, *Legitimation Crisis*, trans. T. McCarthy, Heinemann, London, 1976, p.84. In his paper 'Technology and Science as Ideology', Habermas tells us that 'technological consciousness ... is less ideological than previous ideologies', *Towards a Rational Society*, Heinemann, London, p.111. For a discussion and critique of Habermas' position see A. Gouldner, *The Dialectic of Ideology and Technology*, Macmillan, London, 1976, pp.257-9.

(25) J. Alt, 'Beyond Class: The Decline of Labour and Leisure', *Telos*, 28, 1976, p.72.

(26) S. Kern, *Anatomy and Destiny: A Cultural History of The Human Body*, Bobbs-Merrill, 1975, ch.15, 'Eros in Barbed Wire'.

(27) B. Haley, *The Healthy Body and Victorian Culture*,

Harvard University Press, Boston, 1979.

(28) See John Alt's review of F. Hearn's 'Domination, Legitimation and Resistance', _Telos_, 37, 1978, p.208, and Hearn's reply in the same issue. Also, P. Piccone, 'The Crisis of One-Dimensionality', _Telos_, 35, 1978, and T. Luke, 'Culture and Politics in an Age of Artificial Negativity', _ibid_.

(29) T.W. Adorno, 'Freizeit, Stichworte', p.65, quoted in A. Huyssen, 'Introduction to Adorno's "Culture Industry Reconsidered"', _New German Critique_, 6, 1975, p.10. The notion of culture as the perennial protest of the particular against the general is mentioned in T. Adorno, 'Culture and Administration', _Telos_, 37, 1978, p.97, in which he comments on the ability of culture to resist total reification (see esp. p.111). Adorno's method of 'negative dialectics', his anti-system approach, and preference for the essay form, is a necessary response to a split and antagonistic reality which cannot be adequately represented by any system which aims primarily for clarity and simplicity; see the discussion in Rose, _op.cit_, esp. p.15.

(30) T. McCarthy, _The Critical Theory of Jurgen Habermas_, Hutchinson, London, 1978, p.377.

(31) S. Ewen, _Captains of Consciousness: Advertising and the Social Roots of Consumer Culture_, McGraw-Hill, New York, 1976.

(32) According to Ostrander this emphasis on youth in the 1920s was so marked that he has characterised the decade as a 'filiarchy': rule by the young. G. Ostrander, _American Civilisation in the First Machine Age_, Harper, New York, 1970. In Britain the emphasis on youth was less marked and consumerism took off later (see note 38 below). But the perception of a generation was evident. G. West, in _The Twentieth Century_, March 1937, quoted in T. Barker (ed.), _The Long March of Everyman_, Deutsch, London, 1975, p.231, states: 'I am a young man. At least I am just thirty, and that seems to me to be young. But more and more for some while now I have been aware of a younger generation than my own growing into manhood and into achievement, and quite lately it has been brought home to me in more than one connection that I really know very little - very little - of what those younger men and women think and feel about things. One tends to believe that others of one's age and younger, agree with one by nature and necessity. But do they?' (See also Asa Briggs, 'Semi-Detached', in Barker, _op.cit_, ch.10.) Most discussions of youth culture (e.g. 'Resistance Through Rituals', _Working Papers in Cultural Studies_, 8-9, Summer 1975), concentrate on the post-war era, and do not connect these developments to earlier cultural changes in the 1920s and '30s.

(33) Ewen, _op.cit_, p.149. Ewen also quotes Helen Woodward, the head of a large cosmetic firm, 'Remember what you are selling is not beauty - it is youth', p.147.

(34) Advertisements for bodily hygiene became more prominent in the inter-war years - body odour, and the newly

121

discovered 'halitosis' had to be guarded against by men as well as women. A Gillette Razor Blade advertisement in 1930 emphasised the dangers of not shaving. Below a picture of a distraught-looking wife it implored: 'Keep an eye on your wife. Possibly she's not as happy as she seems. Sometimes you may catch her face. Is she worrying about you? After all, most wives are loyal and proud, and rather reluctant to speak up. This may be far from the fact - but there's a chance she's distressed because you aren't as careful about shaving as you were in times past ...' Quoted in E.S. Turner, The Shocking History of Advertising, Michael Joseph, London, 1952, p.224.

(35) F.L. Allen, Only Yesterday, vol.1, Penguin, Harmondsworth, 1931, p.146, notes 'Women who in 1920 would have thought the use of paint immoral were soon applying it regularly as a matter of course and making no effort to disguise the fact: beauty shops had sprung up on every street to give facials, to apply pomade and astringent, to make war against wrinkles and sagging chins of age, to pluck and trim and colour the eyebrows and otherwise enhance and restore the bloom of youth; and a strange form of surgery, "face-lifting" took place among the applied sciences of the day.'

(36) See the discussion of de Mille's films in M. Rosen, Popcorn Venus: Women, Movies and the American Dream, Coward, McCann and Gergeshan, New York, 1972, p.62.

(37) D. Bell, The Cultural Contradictions of Capitalism, Heinemann, London, 1976, p.67.

(38) This was partly a result of entrenched traditional values and partly a consequence of the more severe economic depression Britain had experienced in the 1920s. Consumerism did not really start to get a hold in Britain until the mid-1930s, and then in the Midlands and South away from the centres of unemployment in the North, Scotland and Wales. On this see C. Cockburn, The Devil's Decade, esp. ch.5, 'The New Consumer, Sidgewick and Jackson, London, 1973.

(39) S. Kern, op.cit, p.32.

(40) See Kline and Leiss, op.cit, p.23.

(41) P. Laslett, 'The History of The Life Course', unpublished paper presented to the Mid-Life Study Group, Loughborough University, June, 1979.

(42) See J.F.C. Harrison, The Early Victorian 1832-1851, Weidenfeld and Nicholson, London, 1971. Harrison quotes from the 1831 health report of Dr C.T. Thakrah about physical decline in middle age: 'Most operatives in this country prematurely sink from labour, if they be not destroyed by acute disease. "Worn out" is as often applied to a workman as a coach horse, and frequently with equal propriety in reference to premature decay.' This of course applied predominantly to the working class. F. Engels in The Condition of the Working Class in England, (1845), Panther, London, 1969, writes 'In Manchester this premature old age amongst operatives is so universal that almost every man of forty would be taken for ten to fifteen years older, while the

prosperous classes, men as well as women, preserve their appearance exceedingly well if they do not drink too heavily' (p.188).

(43) See P. Abrams, 'Age and Generation', in P. Barker (ed.), A Sociological Portrait, Penguin, Harmondsworth, 1972, p.102.

(44) Michael Frayn in his novel Towards the End of the Morning, Fontana, London, 1967, has the financial whizz-kid Morris mulling over potentially lucrative ventures: 'Lots of markets still untapped ...Take the fifties age-group. Maximum earning power, children off their hands, ten years to go before retirement. Lots of money there, Bob. Sell them sports cars, jock-straps, buck-skin boots - young men's kit. They've got the money for it at that age.'

(45) M. Abrams, 'How And Why We Spend Our Money' in E. Butterworth and D. Weir (eds.), The Sociology of Modern Britain, Fontana, London, 1970, pp.49-50. Abrams also notes that age differences lead to differences in consumption which are often greater than those generated by class differences.

(46) In the words of Neugarten and Datan, 'it might be ventured that the central psychological task for middle age relates to the use of time, and the essential polarity in between time mastery and capitulation'. B.L. Neugarten and N. Datan, 'The Middle Years', in S. Arieti (ed.), American Handbook of Aging, vol.1, Barrie Books, New York, 1974, p.594.

(47) Jogging Magazine, April 1979, p.54.

(48) See J.N. Morris, M.G. Everitt, R. Pollard and S.W. Chave, 'Vigorous Exercise in Leisure-Time: Protection Against Coronary Heart Disease', The Lancet, 6 December, 1980.

(49) Report on the research of Dr Vaughan Thomas, Liverpool Polytechnic, in the Daily Mirror, 3 February, 1981.

(50) Jogging Magazine, March 1979, p.44. Tulloh's book was also featured in The Sun, where it was given a centre-page spread.

(51) Quoted in S.W.F. Holloway, 'Medical Education in England 1830-1958', History, 49, 1964, p.319. Holloway also mentions that this attitude was prevalent in the United States; Tocqueville in Democracy in America, states 'In America the passion for physical well-being is general'. It is of course also possible to interpret the revival of self-help in the late 1970s as an indication of the generation of a possible negative critique. T. Luke, 'Culture and Politics in An Age of Artificial Negativity', op.cit, p.60, argues 'Instead of furthering integrating individuals into a standardised system, which has overloaded the once-efficient system to its cost-effectiveness breaking point, health professionals are giving individuals back their autonomy and judgement in self-help health maintenance and sick-care training.'

(52) This view is put forward by Jurgen Habermas, 'Con-servatism and Capitalism in Crisis', New Left Review, 115, May 1979. For a discussion see p. Wilby, 'Habermas

and the Language of the Modern State', <u>New Society</u>, 22 March, 1979.

(53) <u>The Sun</u>, 28 August, 1978.

(54) Their secrets are thought to include a sparse low fat diet, and regular walking up mountains. The evidence for longevity has its critics; see R.B. Mazess and S.H. Forman, 'Longevity and Age by Exaggeration in Vilcabamba', <u>Journal of Gerontology</u>, 34, 1, 1979.

(55) See V. Packard, <u>The People Shapers</u>, Macdonald and Jaynes, London, 1978. (Also serialised in the <u>Daily Mirror</u> in 1978.)

(56) Escandarian of The New School for Social Research, New York, believes we will have conquered death in the next 20 years. Rosenfeld, <u>op.cit</u>, put this date forward to 2025.

(57) Quoted in 'The Immortalists', Everyman, BBC TV, 11 November, 1979.

(58) See H. Marcuse's discussion 'The Ideology of Death', in H. Feifel (ed.), <u>The Meaning of Death</u>, McGraw-Hill, New York, 1959.

(59) L.F. Stone, <u>Family, Sex and Marriage in England 1500-1800</u>, Weidenfeld and Nicolson, London, 1977, p.251, argues that this change took place in England in the late 17th and early 18th century, with the emergence of a theology of free-will in which God was presented as a remote watchmaker of the universe who didn't interfere in individual lives.

(60) P. Ariès, <u>Western Attitudes Towards Death</u>, Johns Hopkins University Press, 1974, p.87.

(61) Franz Borkenau, 'The Concept of Death', <u>The Twentieth Century</u>, 157, 1955.

(62) See, for example, T. Luckmann, 'On the Rationality of Institutions in Modern Life', <u>European Journal of Sociology</u>, 16, 1975; R. Nisbet, <u>The Twilight of Authority</u>, Heinemann, London, 1976; G. Steiner, <u>In Bluebeard's Castle</u>, Faber, London, 1977. Variations on this theme do of course occur in the works of Max Weber (his discussion of the rationalisation and dis-enchantment of modern life leading to an 'iron cage' of meaningless existence for the modern individual), and Horkheimer and Adorno (their discussions, especial-ly Adorno's, of a 'totally administered society' and a 'new feudalism').

(63) Here we are aware that Christianity does not corres-pond completely to Borkenau's ideal type of death-defying conduct, having features which are death-denying. As Max Weber indicates, of all the world religions Christianity is one of the most 'rational-ised', and especially in its Protestant variant, demands systematic inner-worldly ascetic, (death-denying) conduct of the individual.

(64) In 'The Image of God or Two Yards of Skin' in J. Benthall and T. Polhemus (eds.), <u>The Body as a Means of Expression</u>, Allen Lane, London, 1975, J. Broadbent refers to the interconnection between the body and the soul which Christianity emphasised up to the 17th century. Here the body was taken as the manifestation

of the soul, as Spenser in his 'An hymn in honour of beauty', 1596, observes: 'For of the soul the body form doth take, For soul is form, and doth the body make.'

(65) U. Stannard, 'The Mask of Beauty', in V. Gornick and B.K. Moran (eds.), Women in a Sexist Society, Signet, New York, p.194.

(66) See for example: Boston Women's Health Book Collective, Our Bodies Ourselves, Penguin, Harmondsworth, 1978; G. Tuckman, A.K. Daniels and J. Benet, Hearth and Home: Images of Women in the Mass Media, Oxford University Press, New York, 1978. Zoe Moss in 'It Hurts to be Alive and Obsolete - The Aging Woman' in R. Morgan (ed.), Sisterhood is Powerful, Vintage Press, New York, 1970, captures this when she says that conventionally the aging woman is a joke, no longer desirable: 'You are still you, you know that ... don't pretend for a minute as you look at me, 43, fat and looking exactly my age, that I do not suffer from the category into which you are forcing me...'

(67) S. Sontag, 'The Double Standard of Aging' in V. Carver and P. Liddiard (eds.), An Aging Population, Hodder and Stoughton, London, 1978.

(68) This is not to deny that in the short run there may be the creation of new forms of sexual inequality. See M.F. Winter and E.R. Robert, 'Male Dominance, Late Capitalism and the Growth of Instrumental Reason', Berkeley Journal of Sociology, 1980.

(69) B. Ehrenrech and D. English, For Her Own Good: 150 Years of Experts' Advice to Women, Pluto Press, London, 1979.

(70) See, for example, G. Sheehy, Passages: Predictable Crises of Adult Life, Corgi, London, 1977; E. Le Shan, The Wonderful Crisi of Middle Age, Warner Books, New York, 1974; R. Reitz, Menopause: A Positive Approach, Harvester Press, London, 1979; R.C. Barnett and G.C. Baruch, 'Women in the Middle Years: A Critique of Research and Theory', Psychology of Women Quarterly, 3, 2, 1978.

(71) R. Williams, Culture and Society 1780-1950, Penguin, Harmondsworth, 1961, p.312.

(72) D. Rosenblatt and E.A. Suchman, 'Social Class and Becoming Ill', in A.S. Shostak and Gombrich (eds.), Blue Collar World, quoted in L. Rainwater, 'The Lower Class, Health, Illness and Medical Institutions', in I. Deutscher and E.J. Thompson (eds.), Among the People, Basic Books, New York, 1968.

(73) Neugarten and Datan, op.cit.

(74) K. Rogers, 'Crises at the Mid Point of Life', New Society, 15 August, 1975.

(75) H. Davis, Beyond Class Images, Croom Helm, London, p.196.

(76) J. Alt, Telos, 28, 1976.

(77) J. Clarke, 'Capital and culture: the post-war working class revisited', in J. Clarke, C. Crichter and R. Johnson (eds.), Working Class Culture, Hutchinson, London, 1979, p.245.

(78) R. Jacoby, 'Narcissism and the Crisis of Capitalism', *Telos*, 44, 1980.
(79) C. Lasch, 'The Narcissistic Society', *New York Review of Books*, 30 September, 1976. See also *Culture and Narcissism*, Norton, New York, 1979.

6 Egalitarianism and Social Inequality in Scotland

DAVID McCRONE, FRANK BECHHOFER AND STEPHEN KENDRICK

The tradition of all the dead generations weighs like a nightmare on the brain of the living. And just when they seem engaged in revolutionising themselves and things, in creating something that has never yet existed, precisely in such periods of revolutionary crisis they anxiously conjure up the spirits of the past to their service and borrow from them names, battle cries and costumes in order to present the new scene of world history in this time-honoured disguise and borrowed language.

Karl Marx, The Eighteenth Brumaire of Louis Bonaparte. (1)

More than most, Scotland is a country of contradiction and paradox. The student of its history, politics and sociology has to cut his way through an undergrowth of myth and legend masquerading as fact. No myth is more prevalent and persistent than that asserting Scotland is a 'more equal' society than England (or Britain) and that Scots are some- how 'more egalitarian' than others in these islands. These others may well question this assumption about their own attitudes and habits, but certainly the assumption prevails north of the border. Like most myths, it is very difficult to pin down, let alone explain, but prevalent it is in the historical, sociological and literary accounts of Scotland.

The historical ones are particularly potent, as they allow the student of Scotland to delve into the past in order to recover what is 'distinctive' about the society. It is usually in the past that the Scot can discover what looks like an 'identity' sufficiently differentiated from the English (or British) one. It is the survival of this history which has ensured the inheritance of old ways and values, although encumbered by new and more alien forms of identity. Thus, the eminent Scottish historian, Gordon Donaldson (2) asserts:

It is true to this day that Scotland is a more egalitarian country than England, but as a result of class consciousness horizontal divisions into classes have become ... more important than vertical divisions into nations.

Historians have been given to lamenting the cultural as well as economic incorporation of Scotland into Britain after the Union of 1707 as Allan Maclaren (3) has pointed out:

> The belief that Scotland was an open society whose fundamental egalitarianism was gradually eroded, in part by contact with its more powerful neighbours is not just a piece of popular nationalism but has penetrated and been propounded by works of academic scholarship.

Historians are not alone in their belief about Scottish egalitarianism. The theme finds expression among literary historians as well. Thus, Kurt Wittig makes it the central motif of his book The Scottish Tradition in Literature and charts its progress from the poems and plays of 14th and 15th century writers such as Barbour, Henryson, and above all, Lyndsay, through Burns and even Walter Scott, to the novelists of the 19th and 20th century, such as Gibbon and Gunn. All make a virtue of the 'common folk'. Wittig (4) describes their common theme as follows:

> The democratic element in Scottish literature is one of its most striking characteristics. 'Democratic' is not really the correct word; it is rather a free manliness, a 'saeva indignatio' against oppression, a violent freedom, sometimes an aggressive spirit of independence and egalitarianism.

Even non-Scots are willing at times to participate in keeping this egalitarian belief alive. Hobsbawm, (5) for example, points to the different historical experience of Wales as well as Scotland, and makes their apparent commitment to political radicalism as expressed first in Liberal then Labour voting, a major feature of his opposition to nationalism and political independence, which would leave England witnout the leavening of these radical and egalitarian influences. Wales and Scotland, apparently, would save the English from the folly of their own political conservatism.

Although the egalitarian myth is, in essence, to be found in the past - in the history, social and literary, of Scotland - it is by no means dead, for history, or rather a reconstructed 'past', is a potent social and political force in contemporary Scotland. (6) Reference to Scotland's 'history' has a legitimatory function, especially in politics, and in politics of a radical and socialist variety. In a perceptive article, Stephen Maxwell, (7) himself a nationalist of a leftward bent, points to the importance of the egalitarian myth for nationalists:

> The idea that Scottish society is egalitarian is central to the myth of Scottish Democracy. In its strong nationalist version, class division is held to be an alien importation from England. In the weaker version, it describes the wider opportunity for social mobility in Scotland as illustrated in 'the lad o' pairts' tradition.

The myth takes a more radical form for socialists:

> ... the myth, that the Scottish working class has an instinct for radical if not revolutionary socialism lacking in its Sassenach counterpart.

It is clear, then, in this brief review of the egalitarian myth that it not only persists but that it lends itself to various interpretations and usages. The myth is often ambiguous and ambivalent, and it is this essential characteristic which helps to explain its persistence. In various social relations and forms of consciousness, it has continued to act as a partial interpreter of social reality and social change.

In this paper, we will attempt to examine the myth of egalitarianism in Scotland, and ask why and in what ways it has proved to be so prevalent and resilient.

EGALITARIANISM AND SOCIAL INEQUALITY

The myth, however, receives little support from available evidence, which points to Scotland being a _more_ not _less_ unequal society than England.

With regard to equality of economic resources and social condition, for example, Scotland fares badly in comparison with other parts of Britain.

Wealth is more unequally distributed in Scotland than in England or in Wales. In 1975, the top one per cent of the population over eighteen owned twenty-seven per cent of all wealth, compared with twenty-three per cent in England and Wales. (8) Scotland cannot compare with the more equal distribution of wealth in Wales, (9) and despite the obvious methodological pitfalls involved in doing this sort of comparison, it seems safe to say that Scotland is more unequal in this respect.

In terms of the distribution of income, the picture is not very different. Whereas the average earnings of manual workers have been above the UK average since 1975, poverty and deprivation are major problems in Scotland. (10) Low pay, unemployment and disability have kept upwards of twenty-five per cent of the population in poverty. This is compounded by the concentration of deprivation (11) in Scotland's towns and cities, particularly in purpose-built council schemes, and reinforced by Scotland's dependence on public sector housing.

With regard to equality of social opportunity and academic achievement, there appears to be little to support the myth. The Aberdeen social mobility study shows a pattern of mobility not very different from that for England and Wales, (12) while Scotland's social and occupational structures are different in degree rather than kind. (13) Recent work also gives the lie to the assumption that Scots have a greater chance of educational advancement. In terms of access to higher education, the position is, if anything, worse. (14)

Certainly, the 'facts' concerning the extent of social inequality in contemporary Scotland offer little support for the egalitarian myth, but, by and large, myths do not depend on 'facts' to sustain them. Strictly speaking, egalitarianism and social inequality are not directly comparable. Egalitarianism refers essentially to a set of social values, a social ethos, a celebration of sacred beliefs; social inequality is a characterisation of the social structure referring specifically to the distribution of resources and opportunities.

In this respect, the co-existence in Scotland of the egalitarian myth with structured social inequality need not be a contradiction, although the apparent anomaly may give impetus to those who judge it to be one.

THE ELEMENTS OF THE MYTH

Myths are notoriously difficult to examine. By their very nature, they are a collection of symbolic elements organised to explain and validate a set of social institutions. In Mitchell's (15) words, myths operate 'to record and present the moral system whereby present attitudes and actions are ordered and validated'.

Myths are guides to the interpretation of social reality, and are not meant to be tested in any rigorous or positivistic way. As guides, myths are of little help in predicting or explaining the precise characteristics of social structure for social structural features are on a different plane. Consequently, the egalitarian myth can operate without these constraints; it is, in essence, ambivalent. Because it is so unencumbered, it lends itself to a variety of ideological uses and interpretations.

Myths differ from ideologies insofar as they provide the raw materials for ideological interpretations of the world. They operate as the reservoirs of beliefs and values which are drawn upon to provide accounts of the social world, and social identities for the believers. We shall see that the Scottish myth can be drawn upon in the composition of quite different political ideologies.

Insofar as myths are drawn from the past, and provide partial interpretations of social reality and social change, they are akin to 'traditions', and like traditions they have an active, contemporary significance. As Raymond Williams (16) puts it:

> ... 'tradition' has been commonly understood as a relatively inert, historicised segment of a social structure: tradition as the surviving past. (However)

what we have to see is not just a 'tradition', but a
selective tradition: an intentionally selective version
of a shaping past and a pre-shaped present, which is
then powerfully operative in the process of social and
cultural definition and identification ...It is a
version of the past which is intended to connect with
and ratify the present. What it offers in practice is
a sense of predisposed continuity.

Myth, like tradition, does have some connection, however
tenuous, with past realities. It does, however, draw
selectively from the past, a process which involves
selective exclusion as well as inclusion. In doing so, myth
becomes a contemporary and an active force, providing, in
most instances, a reservoir of legitimation for belief and
action.

The paper will explore the Scottish myth of egalitarianism, not as some inert and historical force, but as a
living force which is drawn up (selectively) to explain
and to reinforce identity.

In the Scottish myth, the inherent egalitarianism of the
Scots is the central motif. This motif appears in many
different ways at different levels. While there are social
structural factors such as the system of education and
forms of democratic government which are judged to have
contributed to the relatively open and democratic ethos of
Scotland in the 17th century, the myth of egalitarianism
has an asociological, mystical element. It is as if Scots
are judged to be egalitarian by dint of racial characteristics, of deep social values which apply at the level of
the individual in an undifferentiated manner. Man (or at
least Scots-man) is judged to be primordially equal;
inequality is man-made, created by the social structures
he erects or which are erected by others around him.

The ambivalence of the myth can be seen in two common
interpretations. The first, which might be called an
'activist' interpretation, takes the co-existence of man-
made inequality and primordial equality, and argues for an
active resolution of this apparent anomaly in favour of
social equality. A second interpretation, which might be
labelled 'idealist', adopts a more conservative response to
the anomaly. If man is primordially equal, social structural
inequalities do not matter, so nothing needs to be done. In
this way, the egalitarian myth lends itself to conservative
as well as radical interpretations.

An expression of these deeper levels can be seen in at
least two forms in Scots vernacular: the allusion to
common humanity in 'we're a' Jock Tamson's bairns', and in
Burns' poem 'A Man's a Man for a' that'. The former phrase
has no precise origin in literature, whereas Burns' phrase
so struck a chord in his own society that it entered
immediately into the language. (17) 'Jock Tamson's bairns'
has a curious and fascinating set of meanings associated

131

with it. According to David Murison's authoritative _Scottish National Dictionary_, (18) the most common meaning is: 'the human race; common humanity; also with less universal force, a group of people united by a common sentiment, interest or purpose' - innocuous enough, and fitting in well with its frequent usage by Presbyterian ministers to refer to 'God's children'. However, there are meanings which might make them less keen to use it. 'Jock Tamson' can also refer, jocularly, to whisky; more darkly, it has been authoritatively suggested, (19) it is a Scottish version of 'John Thomas', which certainly conveys more force to the 'common humanity' reference. In truth, the explosive mixture of drink and sex might not be at all to the liking of Presbyterian ministers and their flocks!

In the same way that 'we're a' Jock Tamson's bairns' touches upon the essential commonality of humanity, Burns' 'a man's a man for a' that', seems to strip away the differences which are essentially social. In spite of these (the 'a' that'), Burns is saying, people are equal. Burns' message of equality, however, conveys nicely its ambiguity. (20) He is calling, not for a levelling down of riches, but for a proper, that is, _moral_ appreciation of 'the man o' independent mind'. It is 'pith o' sense an' pride o' worth' which matter, not the struttings and starings of 'yon birkie (fellow) ca'd a lord'. The ambiguity of his message is retained to the last stanza 'that man to man the world o'er shall brothers be for a' that' - an appeal to the virtues of fraternity rather than equality. (21)

There are, then, two sets of implications to be derived from this. In the 'idealist' one, the objective facts of social inequality, status and poverty melt into insignif-icance alongside the common humanity (and Scottishness) of people. In the 'activist' one, Burns is making a revolution-ary appeal. In his own time, the French Revolution and the appeals for democracy gave a heady political flavour to such poetry, and in David Craig's opinion, (22) 'the significant Scottish literature of that time _was_ popular, entirely so, and furthermore, the polite public tended to hold aloof from such work'. Of course, Burns may have simply adopted 'a man's a man ...' from the vernacular, but there is no doubt that such works had an immediate popular impact, and found their way into popular parlance, and reinforced the imagery of egalitarianism.

Burns' poetry offers a particularly good example of the ambivalence of the egalitarian message, the more so as he tended to use different languages (Scots and English) to convey the message to different audiences.

Other poets, particularly in England, have found their radical message lost in a welter of bourgeois sentiment. Blake's 'Jerusalem', a most revolutionary hymn, has become a celebration of (bourgeois) England; Wordsworth's praise of the French Revolution has been lost in favour of less threatening poetry about Nature.

Although egalitarianism was in essence a set of social values, a mystical celebration of common humanity, in Scotland it did partially become associated with features of the social structure. Not only was Scotland judged to be 'more equal' than England, reflecting in part the widespread literacy of the Scots in the 18th century, (23) but within Scotland it was claimed there was greater opportunity for the son (usually) of the peasant and proletarian to be upwardly mobile. Using a series of 'ad hominem' arguments, it was not difficult to show that, by dint of discipline and hard work, the child of the poor could make it. The 'lad o' pairts' was, in Murison's phrase, a 'talented youth', often the son of a crofter or peasant who had the intelligence, but not the means to receive further education, often at 'the university'. Translating 'lads o' pairts' to these illustrious establishments was the role of the parish school-teacher, the 'dominie', who acted as a sort of unpaid talent-spotter. Scotland was 'more equal' because, it was argued, the system worked well.

Now, the 'egalitarian' element of the lad o' pairts phenomenon had a precise meaning and specific sociological significance, for it did not assume actual equality. As Allan MacLaren (24) points out:

the egalitarianism so often portrayed is not that emerging from an economic, social or even political equality; it is equality of opportunity which is exemplified. All men are not equal. What is implied is that all men are given an opportunity to be equal. Whatever the values attached to such a belief, if expressed today, it would be termed elitist not egalitarian.

With our modern conceptions of equality, we find it hard to appreciate precisely what such 'opportunity' consisted of. It did not, seemingly, relate to equality of educational outcome or achievement for broad classes or collectivities. It referred in essence to formal opportunity afforded to an able pupil to proceed through the parish school to university. His (rarely her) path was smoothed by the local dominie who would bully, cajole and persuade affluent members of the parish, often the local farmers, to give a bursary to support his lad o' pairts.

In the context of 18th century Scotland, it worked tolerably well, for a small elite was being catered for in a limited number of professions - education, law, the ministry and religion. The failure of a talented lad to make it was rarely an indictment of the system itself because it relied in essence on personal contacts and moral worth. Failure could result from a poorly connected dominie, or the imputed moral laxity of the candidate. Hence the 'lad o' pairts' phenomenon survived for much longer in the face of contrary empirical evidence.

In many respects, egalitarianism was a key element in a conservative ideology which congratulated itself on the openness of Scottish society and its social institutions.

133

Indeed, it has even been employed in recent times to justify the continued existence of fee-paying schools, which afforded the 'lad o' pairts' an educational and social opportunity not given in comprehensives. Egalitarianism could serve some unlikely purposes.

Alongside the 'lad o' pairts' sits a belief in the inherent democracy of Scottish society. In many ways, these were connected because the Kirk, and its secular arm, the parish, lay at the heart of each. Presbyterianism was clearly a more democratic form of church government than Catholicism or Episcopalianism and the doctrine of predestination, the essence of Calvinism, helped to confirm the natural equality of the elect. The hegemony of Presbyterianism in 17th and 18th century Scotland allowed the religion to become a social and political philosophy; 'Calvinism in one country', in Chris Harvie's apposite phrase. (25) Extreme forms of Presbyterianism such as the Covenanters' Movement allowed radical and violent opposition to central government to become respectable. The purist and sectarian Covenanters entered into the myth as an example of principled and high-minded opposition to authority. Radicalism in this form became respectable. The myth was expanded to include the idea that, in Maxwell's (26) words, 'Scottish political opinion never embraced the doctrine of parliamentary sovereignty, preferring the more radical doctrine of popular sovereignty'.

The 'radical' element of the myth found favour with Nationalists and Socialists alike. To Nationalists, Scots are judged to have a healthy respect for 'democracy'; to Socialists, the populist radicalism of Burns is the raw material of the new order. To both, the strength of the Labour Party in Scotland is an indicator of how different Scotland's behaviour is politically, and proof of the fact that Scotland is 'radical' and 'democratic' as well as egalitarian.

To connect these elements of the Scottish myth together is to give them a coherence, a rational organisation which they do not have. Nor does such a myth need to, because the myth is of a self-evident supra (or sub-) rational nature. Instead, it provides a set of pre-ordained assumptions about Scotland, a framework of symbols and motifs which are available to make sense of Scotland and the Scots to themselves and to others.

It is clear, however, that it is a very flexible, ambivalent and multi-stranded myth. It can lend support to the conservative in persuading him that all is well with his world; to the nationalist in providing a vision of a future society, democratic and different; to the socialist, in confirming the radical and socialist predispositions of the Scot. The flexibility of the myth derives from its neutrality; it is radical or conservative depending upon the framing assumptions. However, its egalitarianism is retrospective rather than prospective; it harks back to a

134

previous state of affairs (a retrospective golden age)
rather than proposing a goal (however utopian) to be fought
for. In this respect, it is old rather than new.

The myth is 'old' because it is premised upon the
existence of a hierarchical social order, not a classless
society. As MacLaren (27) says:

> There is some evidence to suggest that the 'Scottish
> Myth' is a product of a former rural paternalism
> rather than an urban industrialism in which class
> identity and economic individualism overruled a de-
> clining concern for communal and parochial obligations.

The myth describes putative conditions in the typical pre-
capitalist and pre-industrial community, rural or urban.
Social identity is one of community, not of class. The
commitment is to the parish, whether secular or religious,
which is comprised of sturdy and self-sustaining individuals. The social hierarchy of the parish is not questioned,
and differences of economic social power are taken for
granted, rather than resented. The myth has it that
material rewards may bring social or psychological dis-
benefits, or at least insists that wealth carries social
duties and obligations. The unalloyed pursuit of profit
offends the moral economy of the community. (28) In this
respect, the political economy of the community is pre-
capitalist insofar as money-making is motivated by avarice
and greed, rather than the emotionally neutral and rational
pursuit of profit. (29) In this context, egalitarianism
indicates the 'equality of the elect', in a spiritual rather
than a material sense, a religious and moral equality borne
of a commitment to the Kirk and to Godliness. The locus of
egalitarianism is the parish, religious and secular, whether
in the country village or the small town.

THE GAIDHEALTACHD AND THE KAILYARD

The persistence of the egalitarian myth in Scotland,
however, does not simply derive from its survival and
embodiment in certain institutions such as the Kirk, Law
and Education. If it did, then it would be a weak rather
than a resilient myth, as these distinctively Scots institutions wane in social importance. The myth persists because
it is embedded in the Scottish identity, an identity
partially formed and re-cast by two socio-literary movements
of the 18th and 19th centuries, the Gaidhealtachd and the
Kailyard. These are, to borrow the term of Raymond Williams,
(30) 'cultural formations', which are

> ... effective movements and tendencies, in intellectual
> and artistic life, which have significant and some-
> times decisive influence on the active development of
> a culture, and which have a variable and often oblique
> relation to formal institutions.

In these formations, the Romantic quest after Gaelic
culture and Highland mythology in the late 18th century,

and the literature and culture of the late 19th century 'Kailyard', egalitarianism was a prominent symbolic element. These cultural formations, two out of many, were crucial in the re-formation of the Scottish identity. In them we can identify different versions of the myth, the idealist and the activist, as well as conservative and oppositional elements discussed above. Gaidhealtachd Romanticism and the Kailyard used imagery derived from defunct social formations to provide meaning in periods of rapid social change.

The late 18th century saw an awakening of interest in 'The Celts', and specifically the Scottish Gaels. The 'discovery' of the so-called Ossian poems with their images of the noble savage fitted the Romantic mood of the day, in Europe and England especially. As Chapman (31) says:

> In assisting at the birth of the Romantic movement, the Ossianic poems were defined in opposition to the English language classical tradition of the 17th and early 18th centuries, and owed their form far more to a reaction against this tradition than they did to the Gaelic verse tradition on which they were based. The reaction against the conventions of style and subject of classical verse took the form in Ossian and later Romantic verse of an assumed affinity with nature, simple and unaffected, a praise of the spontaneous rule of the emotions in human conduct, and later a <u>political radicalism</u> (our emphasis).

Celtic society, which had largely been destroyed some forty or fifty years previously, was given characteristics at the opposite end of the spectrum from the dominant rational society. Highland or Celtic society was defined as the antithesis of Lowland or English society; <u>Gemeinschaftlich</u> rather than <u>Gesellschaftlich</u>. In Chapman's (32) words,

> Gaelic culture has been subjected to literary manipulation such that it is, relative to English, associated with folk-life, the non-rational, the parochial and the spiritual.

This literary tradition can be seen to lend itself to the idealist interpretation of the egalitarian myth, articulating with the Romanticism and Idealism of late 18th and early 19th century literary culture. Dubious dualities between 'Highland' and 'Lowland' culture were built into the social and literary perspective. The Gaidhealtachd took cn a symbolism, especially for Scots, out of all proportion to its actual significance. As Chapman says (33)

> The use throughout Scotland of Highland symbolism is not mere theft, but part of a process whereby the social space that the Highlander occupies is defined.

The Highlands was judged to be more mysterious, more interesting because it was believed to have a different 'culture' and ultimately and paradoxically to be more 'Scottish' because of this. The irony was that whereas the

Lowlands had connived in the destruction of this culture and society, it now sought to use it as a vehicle for its own identity. (34)

It was a noted feature of this Highland way of life that it was judged to be egalitarian, a feature derived from the nexus of obligations and rights residing in the clan system. A sturdy communalism was woven around these social arrangements, and 'equality' was judged to be a feature of the society. It is, once more, impossible to separate out fact from myth, though historians were willing to give it credence in its ideological form. (35) 'Highland philosophy of the equality of all men is nowhere stronger than in the Hebrides.'

Noted Gaelic scholars such as Derrick Thomson have also been willing to give it credence. Thomson attributes the survival of a sturdy Gaelic folk-poetry tradition to the clan system with its reduced 'class differences', and to an 'egalitarian educational system'. (36)

The image which was created and then buried within the Gaelic tradition was of a society based on a form of primitive communism, a Golden Age. The myth of a primitive society was to act as an important ideological and political benchmark for radicals at large. Raymond Williams in The Country and the City (37) points out the potency of myth as memory:

> The persistent and particular version of the Golden Age, a myth functioning as a memory, could then be used by the landless as an aspiration ...'all things under heaven ought to be in common'.

Despite its retrospective nature, this folk-memory could operate in an 'activist' and radical way rather than simply an 'idealist' or conservative way. As C.B. Macpherson (39) has pointed out, the rather conservative political philosophy of the Levellers, based as it was on the concept of freedom derived from individual property ownership, could be harnessed to radical political action. Similarly, the Highland landless in the latter decades of the 19th century were to use much the same justification for action in their battles with the landlords. (39)

If this version of egalitarianism had remained a Highland phenomenon, it is unlikely that it would have had the impact that it did. Instead the 'Gaelic vision' was to be incorporated into the very image of Scotland, and with it, the myth of egalitarianism was reinforced. The Scottish face presented to the outside world was increasingly a Highland face.

The search for the Gaelic vision in Scottish culture occurred in the late 18th century, when the first phase of capitalist industrialisation began to have an impact on Scotland. The economic consequences of the union of the parliaments in 1707 had taken some time to work through; the military and political destruction of the clan system after 1745 was at a sufficiently safe distance to allow a degree of nostalgia for what could never return. The economic and social impact of late 18th century capitalism was altering the face of Scotland, (40) and inducing problems of social and political identity. The incorporation of Scotland into Britain was sufficiently recent to make it susceptible to questioning and re-interpretation.

The 'idealist' bias of the Gaidhealtachd myth grew up in a public sphere with a limited and middle class readership and orientation, and was not without aristocratic and royal associations. And although 'Scotland' was an important subject of 19th century Romanticism, it was by no means the only subject.

The Kailyard, on the other hand, was oriented to a much wider reading public and by no means dependent upon pro-fessional and aristocratic patrons as the earlier wave had been. To a far greater extent it was a popular movement and had a mass readership. (41) It was a peculiarly home-grown product, and characterised in the words of one of its critics as being replete with 'sweet, amusing little stories of bucolic intrigue as seen through windows of the Presby-terian manse'. (42)

The 'kailyard' was so named by an earlier critic, W.H. Millar, a reference to the parochial or 'cabbage-patch' quality of the writing. Of the three major writers, two were Free Church Ministers (S.R. Crockett and J. Watson or 'Ian MacLaren'); the other was J.M. Barrie. The term 'lad o' pairts' has been attributed (43) to MacLaren and is the title of one of his short stories first published in 1894 (44) although it seems probable that the term was in sufficiently common usage for it to be a recognisable reference to its readers.

In his review of this literature, Ian Carter (45) draws a parallel with other writing:

> MacLaren's novels share important features with the parish histories that poured off the presses in such numbers in the 1880s and 1890s. Both rest on an ideology of community - parish life as harmonious - and both tell pawky stories of local characters to demonstrate that sense of shared community.

It was, Carter continues, a community under grave threat at the time of decline and even extinction. The commitment was to the parish and to its folk. It was a literature cele-brating the virtues of the self-contained village, and the cult of homeliness, a cult given a charge by, among others, Burns at his most sentimental. (46)

Although most critics were and continue to be dismissive (47) of its literary and social merit, the Kailyard cele-brated egalitarianism at its most clannish and communal.

138

In Anderson's words, (48)

His (MacLaren's) Drumtochty is an island-world. The
railway (for Hardy the sinister symbol of the town's
influence on the country) is used by MacLaren to
emphasise its isolation and immunity to change.

The virtues of the community were, in MacLaren's own words,
'a sound education, unflagging industry, absolute integrity
and an underlying attachment to Drumtochty'. The type of
egalitarianism and comradeship it fostered was a far-cry
from the Communist International.

The celebration of 'getting-on', of the 'lad o' pairts'
and the virtues of the parish school as a vehicle for
individual mobility was always a tenuous one. In many ways,
democracy and egalitarianism were features of a bygone age,
an age which, as Williams (49) has shown, lies 'just back
...over the last hill'. By the time they were elevated into
fiction, they had already become anachronisms. The social
and economic contexts of the closed communities had
irrevocably altered. Carter (59) believes that the ideology
of the 'lad o' pairts' was a feature of peasant society:

The crofter's son who stayed on the land might hope to
climb some way up the farming ladder. His chances were
not very good after the middle of the 19th century -
it is clear that relatively few peasant farmers made it
in these years into the ranks of the large farmers -
but the ideology of the lad o' pairts asserted the
opposite and moulded the aspirations of peasant
children.

The egalitarianism bred of an attachment to peasant values
and the social organisation of small towns was a nostalgic
one. Scottish fiction could make little sense of the new
urban industrial experience and preferred to wallow in the
homely, rural past with its apparently secure values and
communal virtues. In the words of one critic (51) who
credits the Kailyard with some literary significance:

The Kailyard's importance is that in writing of parochial matters, its authors conjured up at the same
time much of the essential Scottishness of the Scot,
those qualities which in modern times may in large
measure have been eroded by city life and the influence
of easy travel. Eroded but not destroyed.

So the essence of 'Scotland' was located in this image
of small, intimate communities, in much the same way as
the 'Gaelic vision' had provided an image at an earlier
period. Whereas the image of the latter emphasised an
egalitarianism born of primeval communism, that of the
Kailyard envisaged a society of sturdy peasants - democracy
deriving from the ownership of property. There are distinct
echoes of Raymond Williams' (52) Golden Age as he says,

The natural idea is the recreation of a race of small
owners, and this is projected in the island of Utopia
...but in the island paradise it is not quite to be all

things in common. It is to be rather a small-owner republic, with laws to regulate and protect but also to compel labour.

This form of egalitarianism extends to owners of property; those who sell their labour have no a priori claims to democratic participation. It is a far cry from the socialist concept of equality. It is the egalitarianism of the petite bourgeoisie, the 'social credit' mentality translated into a social ideal.

It was a cultural formation well suited to this class and age. Scotland was an industrialised society, occupying a place in the sun of Victorian prosperity. In social and political terms, however, the latter decades of the century brought special anxieties. The mid-century destruction of the unity of the Kirk (in the 1843 Disruption), the removal of the last vestiges of old Scottish administration and the attempts to rework the identity of Scotland as 'North Britain' betrayed an anxiety about national and social identity. In economic terms, industrial capitalism was in the process of reshaping cities and restructuring industries to benefit from the advantages of Victorian imperialism. Mass migration into towns and cities from Ireland, the Highlands and Lowlands, reflected a rate of unprecedented social change. In rural areas, as Carter (53) has pointed out, the penetration of peasant agriculture by agrarian capitalism was undercutting the social and economic organisation which had supported peasant culture and values. In this respect, in both town and country, the Kailyard with its homely celebration of (and panegyric for) virtues of independence, hard work and 'getting on', became a celebration of a doomed culture and way of life. The parish, the community, could no longer be taken as the typical mode of social existence; the industrialised and anonymous city was now dominant. In this new environment, the lad o' pairts was no longer a recognisable model.

In many respects, then, the Scottish myth is rooted in 'reactionary' movements of both the Gaidhealtachd and the Kailyard, a Scottish never-never land, 'Tir Nan Og' - the land of Youth. Celebrating egalitarianism meant celebrating a dying culture which was judged to be truly 'Scottish' in a way that the new urbanised and industrialised culture could never be. To adopt Williams' (54) comments on another society at another time,

> an idealisation, based on a temporary situation and on a deep desire for stability, served to cover and to evade the actual and bitter contradictions of the time.

These cultural formations laid down the bases of a Scottish identity which has survived long after the literary movements have lost relevance. The selective images presented had entered into social consciousness as prime embodiments of social identity. These images and ideas could then be mobilised and put to use by different interests, especially when such interests may have had no immediately available vocabulary. In this respect, the myth may function not simply as a folk-memory - a 're-presentation' rather than a recall of the past - but as the embodiment of future aspirations. In a real sense, these aspirations are unattainable, because the Utopian dream of the myth can never be realised. It remains, in the activist interpretation, primarily a stimulus for action.·

Raymond Williams has pointed out that in Britain, and especially England, the ideas and images of 'country' and 'city' retain great force. However, their sociological importance lies in their ideological dualism rather than as accurate reflections of social reality, historical or contemporary. The potency of the dualism, he argues, (55) is because,

> The contrast between country and city is one of the major forms in which we become conscious of a central part of our experience and of the crises of all society.

In other words, the persistence of these ideas indicates some social need to which they are addressed. They are ideological devices to make sense of our social worlds - of what is persisting and what is changing. The terms themselves are secondary to the meaning attributed to them.

> People have often said 'the city' when they meant capitalism or bureaucracy or centralised power, while 'the country' ... has at times meant everything from independence to deprivation.

And more tellingly, (56)

> It is significant that the common image of the 'country' is now an image of the past, and the common image of 'the city' an image of the future. That leaves, if we isolate them, an undefined present. The pull of the idea of the country is towards old ways, human ways, natural ways. The pull of the idea of the city is towards progress, modernisation, development.

Given the generality of these images, they are as appropriate as ideological tools in Scotland as they are in England, but they operate perhaps in a different way. Williams points out that the literature of Scotland, Ireland and Wales also relies on 'country' themes, but that built into these accounts are sub-nationalist ideas. Perhaps the phenomenon of the 'English' absentee-landlord helps to convey a surviving national as well as community sense. In these countries, he suggests (57)

> Different versions of community have persisted longer, nourished by and nourishing specific national feelings. It is not so much a peasantry, it is a subordinated and relatively isolated rural community, which is conscious, in old and new ways, of its hard but independent life.

The Scottish self-image of egalitarianism can be seen by the Scots over against its polar opposite, English hierarchy and aristocratic status structures. The egal-

141

itarian myth defines the boundary of 'Scottishness' in social and ideological terms; but its roots are in the mythical past.

As such, the sub-nationalist character of egalitarianism is kept alive by external forces as well. Like many societies whose prime export has been people, Scotland is chained to the image generated in and by the diaspora of emigrants, few of whom ever re-settle in the home country. The reality dimmed by time and memory is translated into a potent image of the home country, an image which is so beguiling to many in the home country that it becomes incorporated into the self-image. This 'maladie du pays' has had a distorting effect on much of Scottish literature, as Craig (58) argues. The nostalgia for a homely, essentially rural past, 'produced the full Kailyard and "Canadian Boat Song" nostalgia, fixated on the auld hame, the wee hoose and the whaups crying on the moor'. Now, this nostalgia generated by emigrants was not of itself sufficient to keep the myth alive, but it did make it more difficult to jettison at home.

The myth was partly sustained because it provided a comforting and supportive ideology in a world of social and cultural alienation. The loss of political independence, the depredations of capitalist industrialisation and urbanisation, the lack of full-blown nationalism allowed the myth to operate as a soothing balm 'to cover the actual and bitter contradictions of the time' (Williams). It allowed the Scots to retain an elemental identity in a changing world, and it permitted them to console themselves about the world, but not necessarily to change it. At one level, why bother? It was somehow 'natural', not man-made, and over against England, the dominant partner in the real world, Scotland had the consolation of feeling itself morally and culturally superior. In this respect, Scottish consciousness had retreated to an entirely ideological level, thereby producing a fantasy world in which 'a man's a man for a' that'; an ideological theme which, in its idealist form judges material circumstances as irrelevant.

Now this is a handy ideological weapon for the ruling elites, for it is in essence a conservative one. It also fitted well into the Weltanschauung of Scotland's petite and local bourgeoisie, being an ideology of independent and petty capital. It was a conservative force for inaction, even when it entered the realms of political ideology. The myth could also be mobilised as a distinguishing cultural and even political feature, and it is not surprising that political ideologies have helped to sustain it in existence. To radicals, of a nationalist or socialist persuasion, the natural egalitarianism of the Scots is seen as a potential which can be tapped in terms of political action, as rationale for radicalism. In the mobilisation of the myth, use can also be made of what is apparently contradictory, namely, the plain existence of so much 'real' inequality. Faced with objective inequalities generated by social structural circumstances, the radical approach finds it particularly offensive given the 'natural' egalitarianism of the Scots.

The apparent paradox of egalitarianism and social inequality can be reconciled. For the socialist, the Scottish working class is 'more working-class', proletarian, radical because it is more oppressed in 'objective' terms. (60) There is no more seductive pre-revolutionary Utopia than a working class which is 'naturally' more egalitarian (because it is Scottish), and objectively more oppressed. The nationalist version is a variant of this. Instead of the working class, 'the Scottish people' are oppressed. Thus, in this form, there is no more seductive pre-independence Utopia than a 'naturally' egalitarian people which is objectively oppressed.

At this level, there is no incompatability in combining the leftist and nationalist versions, and this has been done in literature (the work of both MacDiarmid and Gibbon tries to combine them) and in politics (witness the attempts at new political formations like the Scottish Labour Party, now defunct, and the leftist wing within the SNP - the 79 Group).

There is, of course, nothing illegitimate in these ideological and political ventures. Indeed, radical social and political movements have often delved into the past to recreate radical retrospects which purport to show how the organic society, the moral economy, has been distorted by industrialism and capitalism, that by looking forward the clock can be turned back. (61) What is illegitimate is substituting myth for a social explanation of events and circumstances.

The myth of egalitarianism can also figure prominently in historical and political analysis. It has become, for example, a crucial assumption in the analysis of Clydeside in the first two decades of this century. Without wanting to understate the real social and political significance of these events, one wants to warn against the ease with which the 'folk-memory' of the Clyde becomes inserted into the Scottish mythology. It is also rather dangerous to assume uncritically that Labour domination in Scotland in any significant sense implies the radical and socialist nature of the working class in Scotland. (62) Myth masquerading as analysis is a dangerous obstacle to the sociologist in Scotland. The significance of myth has to be understood in its ideological role, as something to be explained, and not as an organising or causal variable.

The myth of egalitarianism is a flexible and ambivalent one. In its assumption about the primordial equality of the Scot, it can lend itself to radical and conservative interpretations. It is this ambivalence which makes it a rather formidable but dangerous weapon for those who would change society and eradicate man-made social

143

inequality. Its use in literature and history has a definite non-socialist character - it refers to the individualism of the petty property owner, it is the equality and democracy o of the 'elect' - it is the equality of the Kirkyard and the Kailyard. In incorporating the myth into their analysis, socialists may be in danger of building in unwarranted and misleading assumptions. The Scottish myth may be an ideological comfort, but it is by no means an altogether appropriate weapon for changing society.

NOTES AND REFERENCES

We wish to acknowledge the contribution of the SSRC who financed the project 'A Sociographic Account of the Modern Scottish Social Structure' (HR 6948). We are also grateful to many colleagues who have read and commented on the paper. We are very aware that there are many aspects of the myth that we cannot do justice to here, but we are pleased to acknowledge that some of these aspects, notably religion, education and political culture are being studied by others better qualified than ourselves.

(1) K. Marx, 'The Eighteenth Brumaire of Louis Bonaparte' excerpt in L. Feuer Marx and Engels: basic writings in politics and philosophy, New York: Doubleday, 1959, p.320.
(2) G. Donaldson, Scotland: The Shaping of a Nation, London: David and Charles, 1974, p.117.
(3) Allan MacLaren (ed.), Social Class in Scotland, Edinburgh: John Donald, 1976, p.2. MacLaren refers to the work of G. Davie, The Democratic Intellect: Scotland and her Universities in the 19th Century, Edinburgh University Press, 1961; and L.J. Saunders, Scottish Democracy, 1815-1840, Edinburgh: Oliver and Boyd, 1950.
(4) K. Wittig, The Scottish Tradition in Literature, Connecticut, USA: Greenwood Press, 1958, p.95.
(5) E. Hobsbawn, Industry and Empire, Harmondsworth: Penguin Books, 1969, Chapter 16; for a sustained attack on political separatism, see E. Hobsbawm, 'Some Reflections on the Break-up of Britain', New Left Review, September/October 1977.
(6) M. Ash, The Strange Death of Scottish History, Edinburgh: The Ramsay Head Press, 1980. 'The time that Scotland was ceasing to be distinctively and confidently herself was also the period when there grew an increasing emphasis on the emotional trappings of the Scottish past ... its symbols are the bonnie Scotland of the bens and glens and misty shieling, the Jacobites, Mary Queen of Scots, tartan mania and the raising of historical statuary' p.10.
(7) S. Maxwell, 'Can Scotland's Political Myths be broken?' Q, 19th November 1976, p.5.
(8) Royal Commission on the Distribution of Income and Wealth Report No.1, 1975, p.123; A. Harrison, 'The Distribution of Personal Wealth in Scotland' Research

<u>Monograph</u> No.1, Fraser of Allander Institute, Glasgow, 1975.

(9) J. Revell and C. Tomkins, 'Personal Wealth and Finance in Wales', Cardiff: Welsh Council, 1974, quoted in G. Rees and T.L. Rees (eds.) <u>Poverty and Social Inequality in Wales</u>, London: Croom Helm, 1980, p.46.

(10) G. Norris, <u>Poverty: the Facts on Scotland</u>, Child Poverty Action Group, London, October 1977; and I. Levitt, 'Poverty in Scotland' in G. Brown (ed.) <u>The Red Paper on Scotland</u>, Edinburgh: EUSPB, 1975.

(11) S. Holterman 'Areas of urban deprivation in Great Britain; an analysis of 1971 census data', <u>Social Trends</u>, 1975. For a more detailed account see Department of Environment, 'Census indicators of Urban Deprivation', Working Note No.6 CIUD (74) 6, London, Feb. 1975: Ann ^K. Millar 'A study of multiply deprived households in Scotland', Edinburgh: Central Research Unit, Scottish Office, 1980.

(12) G. Payne, G. Ford and C. Robertson 'Changes in Occupational Mobility in Scotland', <u>Scottish Journal of Sociology</u> 1, 1, 1976; for comparative purposes see J. Goldthorpe, <u>Social Mobility and Class Structure in Modern Britain</u>, Oxford: Clarendon Press, 1980, pp.44-5 and pp.289-90.

(13) T. Jones, 'Occupational transition in advanced industrial societies - A Reply', <u>Sociological Review</u> 25, 1976; R. Parry, 'Territorial dimension in United Kingdom Public Employment', <u>Studies in Public Policy</u>, No.65, Centre for the Study of Public Policy, University of Strathclyde, Glasgow, 1980.

(14) D. Hutchinson and A. McPherson, 'Competing Inequalities: The Sex and Social Class Structure of First Year Scottish University Population, 1962-1972', <u>Sociology</u> 10, 1, 1976. For a comprehensive analysis, see J. Gray, A.F. McPherson and D. Raffe, <u>Reconstructions of Secondary Education: theory, myth and practice in Scotland since the war</u>, London: Routledge and Kegan Paul, forthcoming.

(15) C.D. Mitchell, <u>A Dictionary of Sociology</u>, London: Routledge and Kegan Paul, 1968, p.122.

(16) R. Williams, <u>Marxism and Literature</u>, Oxford University Press, 1977, p.115.

(17) D. Craig, <u>Scottish Literature and the Scottish People</u>, <u>1680-1830</u>, London: Chatto and Windus, 1961, Chapter 4.

(18) W. Grant and D. Murison (eds.) <u>Scottish National Dictionary</u>, Edinburgh: The Scottish National Dictionary Association Ltd., 1974, vol.V, p.337.

(19) Personal communication from Hamish Henderson, School of Scottish Studies, University of Edinburgh.

(20) D. Daiches (ed.) <u>The Selected Poems of Robert Burns</u>, London: Fontana, 1980, pp.141-2.

(21) Burns' Ayrshire in the late 18th century had a social structure replete with small farmers and 'bonnet lairds' who must have provided the social ideal of 'independent men' for Burns.

(22) D. Craig, <u>op.cit.</u>, p.111; although 'polite' society was keen to lionise other aspects of Burns' work.

(23) T.C. Smout, A History of the Scottish People, 1560-1830, London: Collins, 1969, Chapter XVIII.
(24) A. MacLaren, op.cit., p.2.
(25) C. Harvie, Scotland and Nationalism: Scottish Society and Scottish Politics, 1707-1977, London: Allen and Unwin, 1977, p.28.
(26) S. Maxwell, op.cit., p.5.
(27) A. MacLaren, op.cit., p.9.
(28) Two novels which set out to chart the decline of such communities caused by the over-pursuit of profit, make this abundantly clear: see George Douglas Brown, The House with the Green Shutters, 1901 and J. Macdougall Hay Gillespie, 1914. These novels 'celebrated' the end of the old parish.
(29) The distinction is central in M. Weber, The Protestant Ethic and the Spirit of Capitalism, London: Unwin University Books, 1974, p.56.
(30) R. Williams, 1977, op.cit., p.117.
(31) M. Chapman, 'What Science is saying about the Celts', Journal of the Anthropological Society of Oxford, vol.8,2, 1977, p.85.
(32) M. Chapman, The Gaelic Vision in Scottish Culture, London: Croom Helm, 1978, p.131.
(33) loc.cit.
(34) J. Hunter, The Making of the Crofting Community, Edinburgh, John Donald, 1976.
(35) Caird and Moisley, 'Leadership and Innovation in the Crofting Communities of the Outer Hebrides', Sociological Review 9, 1961, p.21.
(36) C. Wittig, op.cit., p.197.
(37) R. Williams, The Country and the City, London: Chatto and Windus, 1973, p.43.
(38) C.B. MacPherson, The Political Theory of Possessive Individualism, Oxford University Press, 1962, Ch.III.
(39) J. Hunter, op.cit., Chapter 8.
(40) T.C. Smout, op.cit. B. Lenman, An Economic History of Modern Scotland, London: Batsford, 1977, Chapter 5.
(41) I. Carter, 1976.
(42) Quoted in E. Anderson 'The Kailyard Revisited' in I. Campbell, Nineteenth Century Scottish Fiction, Manchester: Carcanet New Press, 1979.
(43) W. Grant and D. Murison, op.cit., vol.VII, p.15.
(44) Ian MacLaren, Beside the Bonny Brier Bush, Edinburgh: The Albyn Press, 1977, pp.5-13.
(45) I. Carter, 'Kailyard: the literature of decline in 19th century Scotland', Scottish Journal of Sociology, 1,1, 1976.
(46) 'To make a happy fireside klime to weans and wife, that's the true pathos and sublime of human life'. Quoted in Anderson, op.cit., p.144.
(47) At best, says David Daiches, the Kailyard 'is generally agreed to be something one shakes one's head over', Anderson, op.cit., p.13.
(48) E. Anderson, op.cit., p.139.
(49) R. Williams, 1973, op.cit., p.9.
(50) I. Carter, Farm Life in North-East Scotland, 1840-1914, Edinburgh: John Donald, 1979, p.94.

(51) E. Anderson, op.cit., p.146.
(52) R. Williams, 1973, op.cit., p.44.
(53) I. Carter, 1979.
(54) R. Williams, 1973, op.cit., p.45.
(55) ibid., p.289.
(56) ibid., p.296.
(57) ibid., p.269.
(58) D. Craig, op.cit., p.148.
(59) ibid., p.288. A flavour of the 'Canadian boat song' can be had from the following extract:

> From the dim shieling on the misty island,
> Mountains divide us and a world of seas,
> But still our hearts are true, our hearts are
>   Highland,
> And we in dreams behold the Hebrides.
> Tall are these mountains, and these woods are
>   grand,
> But we are exiled from our fathers' land.

(60) See a recently formed, taken-for-granted assumption that 'Scotland was "more working-class and its population ... less skilled, vis a vis England, than at any time since the First World War"', T. Dickson et al., Scottish Capitalism, London: Lawrence and Wishart, 1980, p.296.
(61) R. Williams, 1973, op.cit., Chapter 4.
(62) The major assumption in, for example, James D. Young, The Rousing of the Scottish Working Class, London: Croom Helm, 1979.

7 Inequality of Access to Political Television: The Case of the General Election of 1979

ALAN CLARKE, IAN TAYLOR AND JUSTIN WREN-LEWIS

INTRODUCTION

This paper is one of several we have produced, and will continue to produce, on the General Election of 1979. (1) In this particular paper, we want to examine the structure of the 'television election' (2) in somewhat more detail and somewhat more critically than the officially accredited commentators have yet succeeded in doing. (3) We have what we believe to be the largest and most carefully coded collection of data in the country recording the 1979 Election on national television (in the form of over one hundred videocassettes). From the day before the official opening of the Election campaign (April 8) to the closing of the polling booths on 3 May, the three television channels transmitted 263 programmes containing election material on their national networks, (4) and we have been able to record and code 217 of these programmes - 83 per cent of the total. The completed coding sheets record the details of the basic narrative structure of each programme, the issues covered and the details of the individuals who were 'accessed' to deal with them.

The paper operates within some practical limitations. In particular, we have not had the resources or time to do any analysis on the coverage of the national, local and foreign newspapers, or, in what we think is an increasingly significant element in the election coverage, national and local radio. (5) The overwhelming support given the Tory Party and Margaret Thatcher by the popular press has been widely commented on elsewhere, (6) but the role of Election Call (the popular phone-in chaired by Robin Day at 9 am. each week-day morning during the Election) has not been examined although there is some evidence to suggest that this programme was influential in setting up the issues for the day, even if not to the same degree as the official party press conferences. (7)

All of this does require close analysis, particularly because we do believe that there is a given form or structure to general election coverage in each of the mass media, and these forms are relatively 'permanent'. That is to say, forms of election coverage of the kind observed in the 1979 Election are likely to structure the coverage given the 1984 Election, or any earlier election. Students of the media, and particularly socialists involved in political practice, must do much more work in understanding these forms, in order to identify points of intervention at which alternative frameworks can be given primacy. The work displayed in this paper is on television alone, which may be justified as the most important medium which people in general use in forming opinions at the moment of elections. There is certainly widespread evidence that people feel that television is more real, impartial and personal in its reportage than are newspapers and even the (unseen) professional journalists on the radio. (8)

A final cautionary point is essential before we turn to the substance of this paper. The corner stone of the Tory victory was the very significant electoral foothold in traditionally Labour-voting constituencies that the Conservatives gained, as Margaret Thatcher had predicted they would. (9)

Kellner's examination of the popular vote in May 1979 revealed that 37 per cent of skilled and semi-skilled workers voted Tory as against only 28 per cent in 1974, and that 41 per cent of the 18-24-year-old age group cast their vote to the Tories in 1979 as against only 24 per cent five years before. (10) It is in no way our intention to indict television journalists, in any simple-minded fashion, for this victory. In fact, at the end of the campaign, on 3 May, the Tory lead had been reduced to 7.2 per cent of the popular vote where an early opinion poll (published on 8 April, the day before the official start of the campaign) had given them a lead of 21 per cent. Although this poll, the Observer newspaper's 'Research Services' Poll, was higher in its estimation of the Tory lead than most, a straightforward interpretation of television's influence would suggest that the election coverage was favourable to Labour and actually helped Mr Callaghan.

The television coverage of the campaign cannot, however, be seen in isolation, as a self-contained, self-generating 'event'. The campaign was one moment in a longer process, as was clearly understood by the Conservatives' preparation for the election-that-never-was in 1978 - preparation which informed their campaign in 1979. Our attention is directed to the political and ideological work undertaken by the parties in the period between the elections of 1974 and that of 1979, much of which was done 'publicly' on and through television, profoundly affecting the framework within which the election itself was to be televised. The framework which was created - elaborating the already established framework within which television news and current affairs programmes routinely report political issues - acted reflexively onto the television election itself. To say this does not in itself explain the Conservative victory, but it does identify the terms within which the

150

1979 Election was presented and the issues defined. It also therefore identifies the framework within which Labour Party politicians and their various supporters had to work in presenting their particular political arguments.

We will call this framework a 'discursive formation', a term which can be understood in the following senses. Its totality is a complex structure of words and images, produced via a variety of television practices, in a range of different programmes and formats. The verbal and visual discourses which made up the television election drew in part on an established and relatively unchanging set of conventions that are present in television's representation of politics generally. These conventions help to structure the way in which they become 'issues' for partisan arguments between the parties or topics for in-depth analysis, and a range of other representational questions. But these discursive conventions do not carry over directly into the form in which elections are presented on television. The 1979 television election, for example, was much more historically specific and immediate in its concerns than is the general form of routine political television: it was a television election structured around the immediacy and urgency of 'the British crisis'. Nonetheless, the structure of television's presentations did continue to draw on many of the discursive conventions of political television: the discursive formation contained both a general and a specific element. Overall, however, we will argue that the specific discursive formation constructed in April and May 1979 was one which allowed the Thatcherite programme a dominant position, whilst also excluding a range of other parliamentary and non-parliamentary political analyses and perspectives.

The specifics of the discursive formation in use in the 1979 Election were a product, in our view, much more of the so-called 'winter of discontent' than of the election campaign in itself. We should recall that in June 1978, some eleven months before the Conservative election victory, Labour and Conservative parties were given equal support by nearly all public opinion polls. Labour then lost its lead until November (largely, according to the Nuffield Study, because of the Conservative campaign on the theme 'Labour Isn't Working', handled by their new advertising agents, Saatchi and Saatchi). But in November 1978, prior to the first confrontations with public sector workers, there was a (small) Labour lead (of 1 to 2 per cent) in the polls. The significance of the following 'winter of discontent' in creating an ideological space for Thatcherism to undercut the Callaghan Government's appeal for popular support for consensual and corporatist themes was clearly overwhelming: in those three months, the polls were to register a minimal swing of 22 per cent to the Tories. It was no surprise, then, that the whole of the second Party Election Broadcast put out by the Conservatives on 23 April, was focussed entirely around the 'winter of discontent'. It was also no surprise, especially for our argument, that the mixture of

151

images in this Party Election Broadcast (of dustbins and
garbage bags in Leicester Square, empty supermarket
shelves, undug graves, closed airports, etc.) were taken
directly from television coverage of the winter events which
has since been widely criticised as sensational and
selective. All of these scenes did undoubtedly occur, but
they were exceptional rather than the rule. The shots of
dustbins and garbage bags were all taken in Leicester
Square, but from different angles, apparantely 'spanning'
vast expanses of rubbish. There were few such concentrations
of unofficial rubbish dumps elsewhere in London, and hardly
any elsewhere in the country. It is tempting to speculate
that collective or individual instincts or memories of
television camera crews were at work here, since it was only
in 1975 that the strike of Glasgow Corporation lorry drivers
had been turned, via television coverage, into a strike by
rubbish collectors, reported almost exclusively in terms of
the alleged danger to public health. (11) It is also true,
we should add, that (some) supermarket shelves _were_ emptied,
but this resulted as much from panic buying as from strike
action - panic inspired to a large extent by the sensational
news stories.

So the 'winter of discontent' was a complex and powerful
moment of ideological movement in popular political sentiment. It was all put extremely well by Jeremy Seabrook:

> Long before there was any question of the withdrawal of
> labour of a whole Mayhew sub-class of occupations we
> scarcely know exist - the ratcatchers and draincleaners
> and gravediggers - we were in the midst of something
> more fundamental than mere industrial dispute. It was
> breakdown Britain; Britain wrecked, strangled and
> reduced to the breadline; a threat to our whole way of
> life. (Seabrook, 1979, p.151)

And in what is the only piece to have really attempted to
understand the virulence of mass media reaction and the
anger and frustration of certain kinds of 'Britons' to the
possibility of a strike amongst low-paid public sector
workers, Seabrook noted how:

> We had reminders every day of our own vulnerability.
> There was a sense of discomfort and shame as if it was
> discovered that the serving classes still exist, even
> though they may have deserted their former private
> masters and mistresses 40 years ago. Because it was
> brought home to us that blood and vomit are the daily
> concern of thousands of working people, we had to be
> reassured that this was all they were fit for - a
> contemporary version of knowing their station in life.
> Se we were allowed to be present while they used sick
> children as counters in their demand for more money,
> while they ceased answering mercy calls, declared their
> readiness to leave the sick and injured to suffer, the
> old to perish. The language took on a heightened, almost
> biblical quality. It was as though the press had come
> upon its vocation. It was writing scripture. (_Ibid._)

The 'winter' condensed anxieties about class and about bourgeois social order as such; and it was to become both an active and passive ingredient in the television campaign articulated by the Tories in April 1979. As important as the visual reminders of the discontent were, the 'political space' thus created provided the ground for further work which developed from these already established, 'taken-for-granted' interpretations, especially in respect of an attack on the trade unions' alleged immunity from law.

The 'winter of discontent' was primarily important, then, in creating the possibility for legitimising the Thatcher leadership's claims to speak for 'the people' generally, and its aggressive attacks on trade unions as enemies of the 'national interest' and the 'community'. This was to become the opportunity that the Conservatives had been seeking since 1975 for creating the conditions in Britain for an electoral victory by a leadership of the radical Right, and as such it drew on a great deal of work already done – for instance at the time of the Grunwick dispute – and established the basis for much more. What was achieved in this work was the shifting of the discursive formation to the right with the acceptance of the Right's terms of debate and their proposed 'authoritarian' solutions. (12) The effectiveness of this shift was helped by the poverty of social democratic politics in 1979. This was, in part, a product of the Labour Government's failure to maintain a 'corporatist' strategy in the face of the deepening problems of the British economy. Callaghan's delicate and opportunistic attempts to forge a variety of parliamentary alliances became increasingly precarious and it eventually was clear that the Government could not deliver on its political and economic pledges – to the Liberals, the SNP, Plaid Cymru, and, with the imposition of the 5 per cent pay norm, to the unions. The Treasury's refusal to meet the costs of such arrangements undermined the pragmatism of the Callaghan administration and left the Labour Party with arguments about the benefits of continuity in Government, and the diplomatic experience and responsibility of the ministerial team as a whole. (13) So the exhaustion of the social democratic 'repertoire' contributed in itself to the fact that the General Election of 1979 was fought on a terrain advantageous to the Right.

Despite this exhaustion of social democratic politics and the unrelenting rhetoric of the Right and the popular media on Labour's 'winter of discontent', there was, as we have indicated, a considerable swing to Labour in the election period, on all the various opinion polls. It may therefore seem churlish to indict television for helping Thatcher to power, but we shall argue that the medium did this in two connected respects. Firstly, we shall argue that the articulation of the 'discursive formation' by television gave priority to the Tories' rhetorical calls for social discipline and all their related ideological themes. Partly, the emphasis given the rhetoric of the Right is explicable in terms of journalists' conceptions of the

newsworthy, and partly, also, it clearly derived from the
earlier ideological work undertaken in and through
television and the media by the Right, from 1977 onwards
but highlighted in the 'winter of discontent'.

But secondly we shall show in a moment that television
coverage of the 1979 Election involved a minimal degree of
popular participation. Thus, the discursive formation,
which was already in place as a result of ideological work
of journalists and politicians in a period between
Elections, could not be penetrated, revised or questioned
during the television election itself.

ANALYSIS OF THE DATA

In this section of the paper, television coverage of the
1979 General Election will be broken down into a series of
tables illustrating the details of accessing. (14) Apart
from curtailing misguided conjecture, these data provide a
commentary on the logic of the television election, as well
as providing a basis for analysis of some of the problems
of that logic.

Access of spokesmen assumes a variety of forms: they may
be quoted, filmed, interviewed on film or interviewed in a
studio (either independently or as part of a discussion).
The most common form of access for politicians during the
General Election was what we shall call 'visual quotations'
— brief film clips of speeches on the hustings or at the
Parties' morning news conferences. It would be misleading
to accord too much significance to these general categories
out of their precise context. A short quotation, though it
may take up less air time, is not necessarily less
authoritative than, say, an interview or a clip of filmed
speech. (15) We shall see, later, that frequent, recurrent
access on particular issues (of the kind given trade unions
to speak about trade union law, for example) does not by
itself (by virtue of frequency) accord spokesmen the power
to frame an issue in an influential fashion. So the figures
we present in these tables cannot be read de-contextually.

Formal balance: the Parliamentary Parties

The BBC and ITN, on the whole, concentrated their election
output around visual quotations gathered from the three
main Parties' morning press conferences or from following
politicians round the hustings, and supplemented these with
a brief selection of verbal quotations. The studio
interview and inter-party discussions were mainly used on
current affairs programmes, like Panorama.

Whatever else, Table 1 must be acknowledged as a tribute
to the success of television's political balancing act.
The requirements of balance that exist in the Prescribing
Memoranda of the BBC and the rules governing impartiality
under the Television Act of 1954 were exhaustively

fulfilled. Indeed, our research has entirely confirmed Trevor Pateman's impressions of the first General Election of 1974, namely that:

> these requirements (were) fulfilled in practice to the general satisfaction of the three major parties, but sometimes at least in a tediously mechanical way which sacrifices other values for which television organisations supposedly stand. (Pateman, 1974, p.10)

The overwhelming presence of the three main parties is an integral part of the logic of election television.

Both main party leaders notched up appearances on 61 per cent of the recorded programmes, whilst Labour politicians pipped their Conservative counterparts by a mere 1 per cent. (16) Television editors are aware that the output of election programming is constantly monitored by the major parties, with the amount of access granted to each party's spokesmen being counted and stop-watched on videotaped recordings of each programme. It is apparent that the sensitivity of the editors themselves, and the 'policing' of election television by the parties, taken together, are amazingly successful in the production of what the parties would consider to be proper (quantitative) balance. Whilst the massive coverage given to the Conservative, Labour and Liberal Parties is of no great surprise, the success of Mrs Thatcher, Mr Callaghan and Mr Steel in receiving considerably more attention than all their respective party spokesmen put together, indicates very clearly what has been called the 'presidential' character of the election. (17)

The notions of balance governing political broadcasting require that we compare, on the one hand, the columns marked Thatcher, Callaghan and Steel, and the columns marked Conservative, Labour and Liberal on the other. The massive 'imbalance' revealed when comparing the first three columns with the last three - so that, for example, the Conservative Leader is accessed nine times more frequently than the Conservative Deputy Leader (and Home Secretary) - is not considered relevant to the achievement of political balance by television. The logic here is fairly clear: once formally balanced party political accessing is achieved, all other distinctions are considered politically inconsequential.

This point is emphasised by Table 2, which records the number of occasions in which party politicians and party leaders were filmed 'campaigning in the country'. This kind of film appearance (usually of an event pre-arranged by the parties for the camera) is usually presented in 'non-political' fashion, with a light-hearted commentary by the presenter. Examples of these include Mrs Thatcher's famous calf-holding escapade, Jim Callaghan's jovial appearance at a party worker's 21st birthday celebration ('many happy returns for May 3rd!) and Sir Keith Joseph's tentative

155

probe into a Jobcentre. From television's point of view, the easy tone and emphasis on individual personalities in these films dilute the routine fare of electioneering and, above all, they make 'good television'. Television's awareness that 'the uphill intellectual work of following arguments and grasping policies' is not popularly appreciated by the viewing public (Wober, 1979, p.1), cannot be underestimated. The 'campaign film' sustains a crude political symbolism (Maggie versus Jim signifies Conservative versus Labour Party) and, via the dramatic exposition of personality, gives the television election a narrative coherence. The focus on individual politicians allows the narrative to develop around unities (the person) rather than having to elaborate the complex character of the political alternatives on offer. Voting Conservative because you like the way Mrs Thatcher looks (as one woman interviewed on Campaign '79 on the 30th April indicated she would) is actually a legitimate interpretation of 'the dramatisation of politics' attempted by television during elections. (Wober, ibid .). Table 2 indicates just how large a part campaign films played in the 1979 General Election, and further confirms the importance of the three Party leaders as the chief protagonists in this conflict, both Thatcher and Callaghan appearing in this form in approximately a quarter of all recorded programmes. (18) Once again, from a party political point of view 'balance' was generally successfully maintained, whereas the forms of imbalance - thought to be politically inconsequential - are revealed to be even greater than in Table 1. Mrs Thatcher appeared on campaign film nearly six times more frequently than the rest of her party's spokesmen put together, and Mr Callaghan was also accessed in this way to nearly the same disproportionate extent.

During elections, then, the party leaders are primary definers par excellence; (19) their power as political symbols and personalities framing the election remains entirely unchallenged, and indeed is magnified by the chosen practices of television professionals covering elections.

It is also clear from our research that those given primary access to political television in the past do not lose their position immediately on withdrawing from the front line of party politics. This is demonstrated by the presence of Heath, Wilson and Thorpe within the coverage, all three having relinquished their positions as party leader since the 1974 election, but nonetheless retaining an importance in the television election.

The coverage given these ex-leaders (and in particular Heath and Wilson) alerts us to the existence of a 'political' realm quite independent of the realm of issues and confrontations between the parties, and also analytically separable from the realm occupied by the individual personalities currently occupying the leaderships of the parliamentary parties. This is a realm in which individuals

are given access not because of their contemporary
significance as party leaders or as controversial, note-
worthy individuals, but because of the positions they used
to occupy as political figures in positions of authority.
The access given these figures in the 1979 Election was
considerable: Edward Heath appeared on more programmes than
any other Conservative politician after Thatcher, whilst
Labour's former leader was given more appearances than
prominent Cabinet Ministers (such as the Deputy Prime
Minister, (20) the Foreign Secretary and the Industry
Secretary). It is interesting, however, that the access
which was given Wilson and Heath was initially offered
within a very particular format. Heath was initially
examined by television on his notoriously problematic
relationship to his successor as Tory leader although later
he succeeded in using the opportunity presented in order to
speak for Tory policies generally. Wilson was interrogated
on his wife, Mary's statement that she would 'vote for a
woman', a story which was exhausted when Wilson
explained that this was a statement of principle rather
than intent. So the fact that Heath and Wilson were given
access to the television election in 1979 is largely to
be accounted for in terms of a 'rule' that allows or even
encourages a particular kind of personal consultation
with ex-leaders of the parties (and especially ex-Prime
Ministers) on particular details of the election
campaign. Outside of election times, this television
practice - of turning to recently 'authoritative' individuals for their views - is frequently used to elicit
comments from 'responsible' people on contemporary
political developments, such as when Wilson or Callaghan
are given access to 'comment' on initiatives taken to
democratise the Labour Party.

The practice - of accessing familiar, responsible leaders
of Government and the state for their comments - is no
conspiracy of television and the primary definers working
collaboratively together. It may, as we have seen, involve
a persistent, and even embarrassing interrogation of primary definers by television. But it does serve the function
of providing a familiar 'sense' to a general election, by
inserting previously well known political personalities into
the uncertainties of a general election contest. It suggests
the essential continuity of responsible British government
and indeed underlines the importance of assessing new
candidates and new political movements or policies through
the perspectives of the authoritative and experienced
individual.

The coverage given Jeremy Thorpe's attempt to retain his
seat in North Devon in the aftermath of his murder trial
must in part have derived from Thorpe's position as an ex-
leader of a parliamentary party (although a similar level of
coverage would probably have been given any MP who attempted
re-election in such circumstances). But the coverage must
also have been influenced by television's love of any 'non-
political', personalised way of reporting the political

parties, as well as by the easy susceptibility of the media generally to simplified morality plays. Thorpe's struggle for re-election had all the elements of any such play, and the story remained open, as all good plots of this kind should, until the final act, when the voters of Devon North sealed his fate.

Looking at the Tables 3 to 5 as a whole, we can also see that although the spread of politicians receiving slightly less access than Steel was decidedly uneven, both Labour and Conservative Parties were given a more or less equal allocation of politicians accessed on five or more programmes. This serves once again to emphasise two key features of the coverage: its use of already 'well-established' party political personalities and also the fixed parameters of formal balance. 'What is to be done' in television elections can therefore only be done within existing party political parameters, that is within television's definition of what is political.

Formal balance: the limits and beyond

The rules governing access of all parties to Party Political Broadcasts in general are based on the Aide Memoire agreed between the BBC and the political parties in 1949, which was later revised, privately, by the Conservative Party, the Labour Party and the BBC on 3 April 1969. (Dearlove, 1974, p.42). An elusive body known as the Committee on Party Political Broadcasting, consisting, usually, of representatives of the three main parties, the BBC and the IBA, meets annually to allocate the number of political broadcasts on television and radio to be given the parties for that year. In practice, Labour and Conservative always receive equal time, the Liberals also receiving a generous amount of time (in 1979, as in 1974, three-fifths of the time given to Labour and Conservatives). For other political parties to be allocated time (one five-minute broadcast on radio and TV), they must put up fifty candidates nationally. In 1979, this qualified the National Front, the Workers Revolutionary Party and the Ecology Party in the UK as a whole, but, as in 1974, the SNP was allocated time to broadcast in Scotland as a whole (three ten-minute broadcasts as against one ten-minute broadcast in 1974), and Plaid Cymru in Wales (one broadcast of ten minutes).

As we have seen with the three main parties, the criteria in use for regulating balance extend beyond the allocation of Party Political Broadcasts, which constitute a comparatively insignificant part of election broadcasting (there were 16 Party Political Broadcasts during the 1979 campaign), (21) to include all forms of access to air time during campaigns. In practice, our statistics suggest that minor parties receive a proportion of access to air time roughly corresponding to their vote in the previous General Election. (22) Inevitably, this does not amount to very much. The largest minor party (after the Liberals), the SNP, received just less than one-twelfth of one of the

158

major parties' share of the programmes in 1979.

It is worth pointing out that the SNP returned 11 MPs in October 1974, just two less than the Liberals, yet Liberals received eight times as much TV access in the country as a whole. Similarly, in 1979, in what was its worst election performance since 1966, the Plaid Cymru received 8.1 per cent of all Welsh votes, which was still only marginally short of the Liberal vote of 10.6 per cent. (23) The under-accessing of all minor parties and the over-accessing of the Liberals (in relation to their respective electoral bases) is an instance of the continuing imbalance and inequality of political television in Britain.

The Liberals' space within the structure of election television is long established - indeed, we should not forget that the Liberals <u>were</u> one of the two major parties until the advent of the first Labour Government in the 1920s: to redefine the Liberals as a minor party would subvert that structure. A minor party, on the other hand, is <u>by definition</u> marginal to what television sees as the main arena of political (i.e. parliamentary) activity. The minor party is located in advance within a 'minority' position; unable to break free from this structure within the auspices of a television election. For the Ecology Party, or any other minor party, to develop as a political force, they must do so <u>outside</u> the television arena.

In 1979, however, the logic structuring minor party representation was seriously problematised by the events surrounding the campaign meetings and marches of the National Front. Clashes at Leicester and Southall made headline news, while every National Front election meeting following Southall became newsworthy in anticipation of further trouble. As a result, the National Front were able to break free - in an extremely limited way - of the formal restrictions to gain more access than any other minor party. In some programmes, it could be argued, television resolved this problem by 'balancing' its coverage of the far Right, giving access to groups like the Anti Nazi League and the Indian Workers Association, who would not normally have any access to election television. (24) This signals an important stage in our argument, the stage beyond the limits of formal balance.

The accessing of non-politicians - the positioning of definitions

Balancing the access given non-politicians is not subject to any concrete forms of control in the sense we have discussed so far. If minor parties gained comparatively little access to election television, where did this leave the rest of the population (including those trying to pursue non-parliamentary forms of political activity)? The answer, by and large, is simple - on the other side of the TV screen. There were, nonetheless, as shown in Table 7, certain privileged groups who did gain access, even to a greater extent than the minor parties - trade unionists, police, judiciary and certain other experts and journalists.

Journalists and experts are definers with a specific function in the discursive formation. They are not always given the specific power to define a discourse - their function is to inform and elaborate a particular discourse from a position of specialised knowledge. The experts and journalists are limited to certain kinds of television space from which they can inform issues and debates: programmes reserved for 'analysis' like Weekend World, Panorama and Campaign Diary and segments of programmes (like Nationwide) which have other overt or apparent functions. Placed within this format, journalists like Andrew Alexander of the Daily Mail, David Wood of The Times and Ian Aitken of the Guardian could comment, for example, on the 'style' of the campaign from an apparently non-political position of authority. (25)

If journalists and experts are near the top of the hierarchy of definers, their counterparts at the bottom are what journalists themselves call 'vox pops' - 'ordinary people' who are accessed in such a way as to give them no power to redefine the terms of the election. They, too, have specific spaces allocated them during general elections; they occupy a realm beyond the real business of politicians and issues, the realm of 'the voter'. Television's use of clips of ordinary people tends to adopt a lighthearted tone: the people in Chelmsford waiting in the rain for the Liberal battlebus, the confrontation between a Labour woman and Margaret Thatcher in Newcastle, the man who had staked £30,000 on a Conservative victory, and the Devon man who reprimanded John Tyndall ('it's Plymouth rates you're screwing up'). (26) They are not so much definers as defined. The only programmes during the election to give an apparently more influential form of accessing to people in general were the Granada 500 slots, and Nationwide's On the Spot, from a position in a studio audience or via live relay questioning of politicians. These programmes were, nonetheless, heavily structured, and there was little space to develop, or go beyond, the operative limits of the discursive formation.

More important than either of these categories were the police and the judiciary. Whilst journalists, experts and 'vox pop' were an integral part of this television election (as in February 1974), the police and judiciary were accessed, in the 1979 election, to sharpen certain issues in the already elaborated field of 'law and order'. The access they received was far in excess of any coverage received in any previous post-war election.

Sir Robert Mark and Lord Denning were also used as definers in response to the Conservatives' articulation of the issue of trade unions and the law. Sir Melford Stevenson was massively accessed to inform the law and order question in general, and, after Southall, the public order

160

issue in particular. In these instances, the relation between 'issue' and 'definer' was unproblematic for television. (27) But when an issue became too complex to be handled coherently within this structure, the frame was broadened out. The death of Blair Peach during the demonstration at Southall was just such an instance - it gave space to people not normally accessed <u>during election coverage</u>, i.e. anti-racist demonstrators and members of the Asian community (who in fact comprise the bulk of the 'Other' category in Table 7). (28)

The relationship between an issue and its definers can be understood further by examining the largest single accessed group - the trade unionists. On the face of it, this group was accorded considerable time and opportunity in which to impose its definitions upon issues (especially in comparison with the minimal opportunities granted businessmen): trade unionists were filmed making speeches, they were inter-viewed, quoted and they took part in studio discussions. Yet, we would argue, their power to define was extremely limited.

During the 1979 election any reference to trade unions was <u>by definition</u> to a <u>problem</u> - a problem which, partly as a result of the ideological work of the Conservative leader-ship, self-evidently consisted of several connected parts. The trade unions were discussed exclusively in terms of their contributions to inflation and Britain's economic problems, to their alleged immunity from the law, their role in secondary picketing and in demonstrations and strikes, and even (following Margaret Thatcher) the resemblance between the demands made by unions and those made by 'muggers'. So the access given trade unionists to television programmes, in such an election context, never allowed the trade unionists the power to define the terms of their participation, but was nearly always framed in such a way as to present trade unionists as symbols of the 'trade union problem'.

Before examining this in more detail in relation to the 'issues', it is worth noting an instance where trade unionists' <u>formal</u> status did allow them to occupy an authoritative position. Normally, trade unionists were accessed on issues concerning themselves (countering Lord Denning's statement in Canada, for example, that trade unions were 'above the law'), or as spokesmen for the Labour Movement. However, on ITN's early evening news bulletin on 25 April, we were told by Leonard Parkin that:

> The TUC have called for a new law on racial incitement to prevent a repetition of the Southall riot on Monday. The TUC say they can't accept that under the guise of protecting freedom of speech the NF can be allowed to spread, what they call pernicious doctrines that spread tension and fear amongst coloured and white citizens alike.

Albeit for a brief moment, the TUC were allowed to speak

upon issues _in general_ - their views were considered important enough to give them access on issues which do not apparently concern them. But this was an exception. (29) _Overall_, our research affirms the existence of a relatively impenetrable logic which accords persons the right to speak during television election _and_ the frame within which they can speak.

The issues: what they are and how they work

Table 8 records the main issues of the 1979 General Election as articulated on television, whilst Tables 9 to 14 list the politicians given access on those issues. (30) These statistics provide a basis for understanding what the 1979 election campaign was about, but they cannot be fully understood without some further explanation: the way in which these problems were formulated remains to be investigated.

The first point to be made is this: an 'issue' is not an isolated unit of meaning - its meanings refer to different contexts. (31) By this, we do not simply mean that one party may be on the defensive on another party's issue (as Labour were on the Tory electoral promise of tax cuts), but that the different constructions of the 'discourse' makes what appears to be a unitary category multi-referential.

A straightforward example of this is the inflation issue. Table 8 shows that inflation was the most important question for Labour, and equal fourth for the Tory Party. The Conservative Party articulated their attack on Labour's record on inflation via their women politicians, Margaret Thatcher and Sally Oppenheim (remarkably, our statistics recorded only one programme that did _not_ feature Thatcher or Oppenheim as the Tory spokesperson on this issue). Inflation became a women's issue, the concern of the housewife worried about prices in the shops, a discourse that Thatcher and Oppenheim, as women, were able to inform from a position 'in the know'.

For the Labour Party, inflation was merely a component in a discourse which ran: co-operation with the Trade Unions = wage restraint/planned economy = low inflation. As Table 8 shows, this provided the logic behind Labour's three biggest issues. Thus, authoritative spokesmen attempted always to locate the problem of inflation into the overall economic strategy, this work being done almost exclusively by Jim Callaghan, Denis Healey, John Silkin and Roy Hattersley.

The Labour Party's reliance upon this logic, with its emphasis on diplomacy and statesmanship, was severely jeopardised by the importance of the Trade Unions in the formula. As we have argued, the work done during the 'winter of discontent', with its negative images of trade union action, substantially constructed the discourses

162

informing the election itself. Despite the considerable work done by Jim Callaghan on trade union issues (his first and third most important issues), stressing 'co-operation not confrontation' and evoking long-forgotten images of the miners' strike of 1973-4 (an image which the 'winter of discontent' neatly replaced), they were fighting at a considerable disadvantage. The Tory Party, on the other hand, were able to turn the union issue to their own advantage by positioning it upon an already established terrain, constructed with reference to the 'winter of discontent', and arguing for an extension of law to curtail certain forms of union action.

The Right's condensation of ideological work on 'unions and the law' was clearly explicated in a speech made by the Conservative Party leader on 19 April 1979 in Birmingham. Referring to Labour's 'soft' approach to the trade unions and on 'law and order', she argued that:

> in their muddled but different ways the vandals on the picket lines and the muggers in our streets have got the same confused message - 'we want our demands met, or else' and 'get out of our way, give us your handbag, or else' ... the path Labour delegates were charting ... was the path to social disintegration and decay, the path to a pitiless society in which ruthless might rules and the weak go to the wall. Across that path we will place a barrier of steel.

What was being offered was a discourse establishing the signifying chain: striker = mugger = disintegration and decay (all as expressions of the weakness of law). Within these discursive parameters, a legal solution to the 'trade union problem' not only fits 'naturally', but assumes a paramount importance for the law-abiding citizen. It is within such a context that the work done by the media, both on television and in the press, during the 'winter of discontent' had most purchase. Connections which might previously have been incoherent (in particular, between street crime and union picket-lines) were now taken up and affirmed by politicians of the Right and by journalists, as commonsensical relations.

Furthermore, the space was cleared to access the police and judiciary as non-political primary definers (the forces of law and order battling against 'ruthless might'), on the issue of trade unionism, as both Lord Denning and Sir Robert Mark were during the election period. These law and order spokesmen allowed the development of the discourse sustaining the union law issue (striker = mugger, etc.). A structure had been put in place by the Tory Right and by television professionals, which by its nature required that television give access to the judiciary and the police, who were able (by virtue of their 'knowledge') to inform and to elaborate the gravity of the problem of the threat(s) postulated to 'law and order'.

163

Inevitably, with such formidable opposition, the Labour Party was put on the defensive. The framing of the 'winter of discontent' by the discourse of the Right (Conservative politicians echoed by the forces of law and order) provided the 'evidence' to subvert the Labour strategy, evidence which, as we have argued, trade unionists themselves were powerless to counteract. Thus (as shown on Table 8) the Labour Party was forced to acknowledge the 'weight' of the Conservatives' case, in a way that was not reciprocated; by the end of the campaign, union law had become Labour's fourth biggest issue. On a day when Mrs Thatcher had referred to a 'government by picket', Jim Callaghan issued one of his many replies:

> You'll remember the last Conservative Government brought in legislation, whose aim, it said, was to improve industrial relations. It failed. On the contrary, not only did it not improve industrial relations, it worsened them, and twice as many days were lost in strikes during the period of the Conservative Government as when the Acts were in operation, than in the days of the Labour Government when the Acts had been repealed. Now surely, there's a lesson there somewhere ...There are twelve million working men and women in trade unions today. They're not extremists. It's wrong to tar them all with the same brush ... (News at Ten, ITN, 25 April)

Having acknowledged that trade unions are a problem, Callaghan attempts to inform the union law discourse with 'facts', forming a counter logic (to the Tory position) so weak that all that can be said is: 'there's a lesson there somewhere'. Quite where this lesson is to be located or understood is left hanging in the air. Furthermore, the mugger = striker logic is not negated but compromised: 'it's wrong to tar them all with the same brush'. By implication, therefore, it must be right to label some of them as 'extremists', a key word within the Tory law and order discourse.

A straightforward reading of our statistics shows that trade unions represented, in one form or another, the most cogent problem facing the incoming British Government (and, therefore, the logic runs, the British electorate), in a way that issues concerning women (a theme prioritised by foreign journalists, in relation to Mrs Thatcher), immigration, housing, defence or foreign affairs were not. What these crucial absences indicate, we would suggest, is that the discursive formation constructed in dialogue between the main political parties and the practices of television professionals and in dominance at the moment of the 1979 election, was massively inadequate in interrogating and displaying the real character of the Thatcher programme (whilst inexhaustible in its interrogation of the Labour alternative). (32) Moreover, the formation was unresponsive to political and social interests who were attempting to raise alternative conceptions of 'the issues'

164

to those dominant in Parliament. Furthermore, the discourses operating within this 'discursive formation', we would argue, were defined and informed, by their very nature, more powerfully by the Right than the Left.

SOME CONCLUSIONS

We want to emphasise two particular points by way of conclusion.

Firstly, we want to try to fill in what we mean by the 'discursive formation'. It should be evident by now (contrary to the accounts in Harrison and Pilsworth) that the 'issues' identified (as in Tables 8 to 14) are not merely lists of distinct empirical issues which happen to have been raised, and then given access by an essentially 'pluralistic' television medium. Rather they are artificial-ly categorised expressions of the way in which certain powerful discursive themes and campaigns were pursued by politicians (and other primary definers) and also given access to television. In this latter respect, television professionals were extremely active 'mediators': they put into use conventions they had helped to create as to what constitutes the proper form of electioneering on television. They observed, with great application, the formal require-ments in election law governing 'balance' and informal understanding about the 'proportional' access of different parties whilst informally using the professional sense which all journalists claim to have in order to decide on what should count as 'news'. Out of this process of collaboration between journalists, behaving (usually) with impeccable professionalism and fastidious formal neutrality, and the parliamentary parties, was constructed a television election of the kind we have tried to describe, in which the rhetoric of the radical Right was enormously more influential than that of the social democratic Left.

We have tried to show that the existence of a formation of discourse advantaging the radical Right was made possible by the events of the winter of discontent and by the ideological work put into those events by the Tory leadership. But our point is also that the routine professional practices of journalists as specifically adapted for general election work played a crucial role in the reproduction of this dominant discursive understanding as to what the election was about. From the preferred use of certain politicians for access, to the preference for accessing 'the public' or 'electors' only during walkabouts by these same politicians, the conventions of general election television worked to reproduce and extend the already established definitions of 'political issues' created by the party leaderships, and reproduced by tele-vision news editors. The discursive formation was not merely a product of professional conventions, however, in the sense of being constructed unreflexively out of practical pro-fessional routines. It did involve, as does all journalism,

the attempt to identify the relevant items of 'news',
mediated through the particular definition of what constituted relevant and newsworthy material for the election,
and that was informed by the discursive formation.

Now, in part, these decisions seem to be almost direct
reproductions of the existing parliamentary situation: that
is, a lot of election news coverage was about 'the economy'.
As has been argued elsewhere, election coverage of the
economy, like political television's coverage of economic
questions in between the last two elections, one-sidedly
reproduced an ideological chain which identified inflation
(rather than unemployment) as the central issue in the
British economy, and linked inflation, causally, to the
wage-push that allegedly results from trade-union
'militancy' (cf. Glasgow University Media Group, 1980).

Similarly, whilst the apparently unexpected events at
Southall (and especially the death of Blair Peach) did have
a disturbing effect on the discursive formation, they did
not prevent television journalists from reproducing, via
the definitions of massively accessed politicians, an
entirely distorted interpretation of the events as the
determining frame within which the television audience was
asked to work to understand them. On the day after Southall,
24 April, Margaret Thatcher was widely reported as having
'condemned' the previous evening's events. These must be
dealt with, she was quoted as saying, by 'the full might
and power of the law'. But as subsequent investigations
have entirely confirmed, (33) the worst violence in
Southall began after the arrival of massive police re-
inforcements, many of whom were uninhibited in the use of
the 'might and power of the law'. In other words, 'the full
might and power of the law', if it refers to anything,
refers to forces that were already in Southall, in the shape
of 2,750 truncheon-wielding policemen. In this sense,
Thatcher's statement is utterly incomprehensible. In the
context of her speech on the 19 April (see above), however,
it fits neatly into a pre-established framework informed
by certain primary definitions. Consequently, the viewer's
signified images of the events at Southall were subject to
a reading which completely mis-represented the real
character of those events.

So the tragic events at Southall (and at Leicester) -
although 'unexpected' news for journalists - were worked
upon to inform and confirm the discursive formation
established by the Right. In her interview with Denis Tuohy
(TV Eye, 24 April) Mrs Thatcher elaborated the 'connections'
established by the discursive formation still further.
Answering a question about striking hospital workers during
the 'winter of discontent', she referred to the 'great
destroyers': 'you have seen those destructive elements
yesterday on the television' she said, linking the Southall
'riot' with the 'winter of discontent'. 'This', she claimed,
'is the most important point you've (Tuohy) raised ...One
of the problems today is that we have a few, a comparatively

people ... who wish to destroy the kind of free society we have ...Many of those people are in the unions.'

Denis Tuohy, to his credit (within the limits of a half-hour interview), attempted to interrupt and to question the links made by this inexorable logic. No one else did. The problem is that Tuohy <u>was</u> in fact extremely 'unprofessional' in his behaviour towards Margaret Thatcher (he did interrupt her and attempt to interrogate her, and he did try to unpack the logic of the discourse which politicians of the Right and professional journalists had helped to construct in the wake of the winter of 1978-9). He distanced himself from the kind of professional journalism that had arisen, as a specific adaptation, to the crisis in the British economy. Even as the exception he was <u>not</u> able to break the logic of the discursive formation, wielded as it was with coercive authority and with vivid references to the chaotic alternative by Margaret Thatcher. The more typical procedure during the 1979 election, even in self-designated 'in-depth' programmes like <u>Weekend World</u>, was to reproduce the assumptions of the Right (for example, on the question of the unions) as the determinant assumptions on which discussion and/or analysis ought to proceed. On 8 April, Brian Walden, as presenter of a <u>Weekend World</u> special, set up the terms of the debate in the following way:

> There's now fairly general feeling that the unions have a lot to do with what's wrong with Britain. They're blamed for slowing down Britain's economic growth by enforcing restrictive practices and overmanning. They're said to be infringing individual liberty by abusing the closed shop. They're accused of disrupting our lives with irresponsible industrial action. Above all, they're thought to be stoking up inflation and unemployment by demanding pay rises far above what the nation can afford. Politicians know they've got to be able to convince the voters they can handle the unions.'

Here, Walden <u>apparently</u> distances himself from the 'fairly general view' which is stated, by displacing the authorship of this feeling from the first person (plural or singular) onto 'the voters': the unions are 'blamed' 'fairly generally', 'tney're said to', 'they're accused of', 'they're thought to'. But he then reiterates a characteristically right-wing view of the voters as a unified mass held together by a concern for 'the nation' and what 'the nation can afford'. This discursive representation of the unions set against the nation (the people) then becomes the frame within which the 'in-depth' analysis (sic) proceeds for the remaining 55 minutes of the programme.

We have not attempted in this paper to examine all the processes that are involved in the general and specific reproduction and reconstruction of this discursive formation: to weigh the relative importance of specific conventions about election and political television against

the ongoing production of a commonsense definition of
politics that is the stuff of 'everyday' television in
Britain (cf. Brunsdon and Morley, 1978). Nor have we tried
to produce any formal model as to how these conventions
about election television result from a mix of technical
considerations (for example, the technical problem of
accessing people in the street to television discussion),
legal considerations (in the Representation of the People
Act and elsewhere) and the less tangible agreements and
understandings of politicians and journalists governing
proper rules of debate and proper forms of access. All that
we can say for the moment is that the 1979 Election was
fought within a set of conventions (governing all these
questions) which had an extremely predictable and permanent
appearance to them, and which will undoubtedly be in use in
future elections. Further, it was also the case, in 1979,
that these conventions proved to be extremely weak in
generating a television journalism capable of interrogating
(rather than merely reproducing) the 'newsworthy' advance
of the radical Right.

The second point we want to make about this 'discursive
formation' is that it had contingent effects (as indicated
earlier) in silencing certain issues (by excluding them
from the 'real' or the 'serious' business of the election)
and also in massively underaccessing important alternative
political and social movements in the country. In their
influential article analysing a Panorama programme during
the 1974 Election, Stuart Hall, Lidia Curti and Ian Connell
argued that:

> The media, in Current Affairs television, do not
> represent in a biassed way (ideologically) the structure
> of political power and its dominant mode of operation:
> the media accurately reflect and represent the pre-
> vailing structure and mode of power. (Hall, Curti and
> Connell, 1976, p.92)

Television certainly does do this, as we have confirmed,
by reproducing a definition of the political issues at
elections that accurately reflects the existing balance of
parliamentary power, and then by accessing narrow groups of
significant primary definers to elaborate these dominant
definitions.

But further on in their article, Hall, Curti and Connell
argue that the work which goes into television discourse
reflects 'the field of the political class struggle in its
contradictory state' (ibid., p.93). Television coverage of
the 1979 Election did not produce 'the political class
struggle in its contradictory state'. It produced a series
of programmes that overwhelmingly accorded the quality of
newsworthiness to Margaret Thatcher (though not to
Thatcherism, properly analysed), and also many programmes,
like the BBC and ITN specials on law and order, were almost
entirely framed in terms of the Right (cf. Clarke and
Taylor, 1980). It was silent on women's issues and the

problems of the black community in Britain; and it was silent on a range of questions (like the real character of 'monetarism', Conservative defence policy and the ideological divisions within the Conservative Party) which are now obvious to the view. Moreover, as we saw earlier in the paper, the coverage given minor parties was often in the form of a token report (in particular, the nationalist parties were unable to win air time corresponding to their level of electoral support).

So we think that there are certain formal features of existing television journalistic practices, especially in regard to political television, and specifically in respect of election television, which makes these television productions extremely difficult to democratise, and thereby to open to 'the people'. What is also clear is that merely to call for democratisation of access to political and election television is to leave unanswered the problem of the continuing inequality in the power to define the primary political problems facing the people as a whole.

NOTES

(1) These papers can be consulted in Clarke 1980, Clarke and Taylor 1980 and Clarke, Taylor and Wren-Lewis 1981. We were fortunate in being given a small grant in March 1979 by the Social Science Research Council (HR/6545/2) and other supplementary grants from the SSRC (August 1979) and the University of Sheffield Research Fund (Grant 508, December 1979). The ostensible purpose of these grants was to enable us to collect as much of the mass media's coverage of the election, concentrating particularly on the television coverage.
   Our initial concern was with the way in which the Conservatives declared their intention to make 'law and order' an issue in the election. This was first revealed in 1978 in a report leaked to the Guardian (21 October 1978) and led us to consider how the problematising of the law and order would be handled by a visual medium. Hence our main research concern was with the kind of camera shots, captions and programme structures used to bring crime and 'law and order' to the television screen. For our detailed work on two individual programmes, see Clarke and Taylor 1980 and Clarke, Taylor and Wren-Lewis 1981.
(2) The notion of a 'television election' is from Pateman who argued, in our view absolutely correctly:

   television can only cover an election when the campaign has an existence independent of the presence of television. Today, it does not possess such an independence ... we do not have television coverage of an election: we have a television election. (Pateman, 1974, p.2)

(3) We are thinking particularly here of the pieces by

169

Harrison (1980) and Pilsworth (1980).

(4) The majority of the 263 programmes were news bulletins (eight a day every weekday). But the 'population' of General Election programmes also included BBC and ITA's regular current affairs programming (Nationwide, Panorama, World in Action, TV Eye and Weekend World), the Money Programme and programmes designed specifically for the General Election (Campaign '79), appended to Tonight; Hustings, appended to News Night) and the sixteen Party Political Broadcasts.

(5) We have over thirty hours of taped material from these radio shows (and especially Robin Day's Election Call) awaiting coding and analysis. We also have a sample of North American newspaper coverage, and full files of national newspaper coverage in this country, and some local English, Welsh and Scottish newspapers for the period.

(6) See Baistow 1979, Foot 1979a and 1979b.

(7) There is, indeed, support for the view amongst informed MPs, like Austin Mitchell, that the election as a form is entirely constructed within the various media (from Election Call in the morning to the lunchtime coverage of the parties' morning press conference and then onto the evening news and late night news and Hustings programmes). Canvassers on people's doorsteps in this sense interrupted what for most people was the 'real' election.

(8) Evidence of this widely repeated view can be found in Bad News, especially ch.1. More recently, however, the BBC's own Audience Research Department appears to have detected some loss of uncritical support for television's coverage of politics and current affairs. Peter Fiddick's reading of this report revealed that some 22 per cent of BBC television's audience detected a bias, particularly on news bulletins; and three times more people thought this bias was to the Right rather than to the Left. (Peter Fiddick, 'Why Love for Auntie is Cooling' Guardian, 16 April 1980)

(9) For example, in her interview with Denis Tuohy on TV Eye, 24 April 1979, and also at the conference of Conservative trade unionists at Wembley Conference Centre on Sunday, 29 April.

(10) Peter Kellner (1979). Given that these two groups comprise a very high proportion of the total population, these were indeed the important 'swings' of electoral support which increased the Conservative vote by nearly a third on its total in November 1974 (13,697,753 as compared to 10,464,817) and close to the number of votes cast in Macmillan's victory in 1959 at the high point of the 'age of affluence' (13,749,830).

(11) This connection had been forged by shots 'spanning' expanses of garbage bags and rubbish (which were filmed at tips some miles outside the city). For an illuminating description of television coverage of this strike, see Bad News vol.1, pp.244-56. The Leicester Square shots have probably been even more powerful

170

visual carriers of ideological messages than were the shots taken at the Glasgow dumps.

(12) The character and advance of this 'authoritarian populism' has been discussed, with more insight than we could muster, in Hall 1979, 1980.

(13) The agreements struck with the IMF (to initiate reductions in public expenditure on social services), in particular, focussed attention on the limitations of existing social democratic policies.

(14) These tables are the compilation of the 217 completed coding sheets mentioned earlier. These sheets were annotated by six coders, working independently, whilst viewing the 217 individual programmes recorded. These sheets were mainly constructed as a checklist on the individuals given access (and their political or organisational affiliation), and the issues which were given either 'significant' discussion or a passing mention. The sheets were later cross-checked by the three authors of this paper.

(15) On the evening of the Southall demonstration, for example, 10 days before polling day, Sir David McNee was quoted describing the evening's events as 'unprovoked attacks upon the police'. This quotation was used on all the evening news programmes, but on BBC-1 and BBC-2 it was juxtaposed with the 'facts': '18 policemen were injured, 4 of them seriously, 1 stabbed.' In this context, a brief quotation was given the authority to define the events (at Southall) and then the definition was grounded in a statistical truth. An interview with McNee with an introduction like: 'Tonight, Sir David McNee gave the police's view of the day's events' would not have carried such authority. Indeed, the more clearly defined the source, the less 'objective' or 'neutral' the words would seem. It is for this reason that any decontextualised discussion of statistics on types of formal access could only lead to loose conjecture.

(16) Our figures differ from those in Pilsworth because they are compiled on a different basis. (Cf. Pilsworth, 1980, pp.209, 210) Pilsworth gives the number of times that party leaders were 'quoted' on an (untotalled) number of BBC-1, ITN and Radio 4 news bulletins. Our figures are for any kind of access (from direct interview to quote) on all kinds of election-related programmes on national networks. His second table, on party shares of election news coverage, is not really clearly explained, especially in terms of its construction by his research; but his figures are obviously intended to indicate the share of total party-political discussion obtained by each party. Our own figures on the access of politicians from the different parties merely total the number of individual 'accessing' occasions, for each party as a percentage of all programmes.

(17) Harrison and Pilsworth both observe that the concentration on party leaders was even greater in 1979 than in October 1974. (Harrison, 1980; Pilsworth, 1980).

(18) Adam Raphael and Geoffrey Wansell observed at the time that whilst few of News at Ten's nine million viewers 'would ... remember one word of what Mrs Thatcher said 24 hours later (what would) remain was an impression of how she looked.' (The Observer, 22 April, 1979.) The phenomena of 'impact' and 'recall' cannot be attributed solely to the high density of campaign films shown on election television, but these films do strongly reinforce and develop the perception of politics as a conflict between a small number of personalities.

(19) We are not here implying that Party leaders are the origin or source of general election discourse. The creation of the framework of election television is an ongoing accomplishment of a variety of groups who are given the power, by television, to define the terms of the General Election. The leaders of the parliamentary parties are accessed to this debate as a matter of course.

(20) The heavy access given Denis Healey (on 12 per cent of all programmes) was, of course, in itself something of a mistaken conception of the balance of forces within the Labour Party, and Michael Foot's election to the party leadership in 1980 was in no way anticipated by the access given him (in only 3.5 per cent of programmes).

(21) The sixteen Party Election Broadcasts (of 5 and 10 minute lengths) on national (UK) television during the 1979 Election were as follows:

Conservative Party	5	(50 minutes)
Labour Party	5	(50 minutes)
Liberal Party	3	(30 minutes)
National Front	1	(5 minutes)
Workers Revolutionary Party	1	(5 minutes)
Ecology Party	1	(5 minutes)

(22) This was not, however, the only consideration governing the access of formal parties. One of the most important questions is existing Election law. Section 9 of the Representation of the People Act requires that if one candidate 'takes part in' a broadcast report on a constituency, then either all other candidates must take part, or they must sign a waiver giving their agreement for the others to take part in their absence. This legal requirement often poses severe problems for the television journalists attempting to do stories on constituencies where minor parties are standing, since there are frequently 'joke' candidates and candidates who will refuse to stand down or sign a waiver. As a result, minor parties, such as the Socialist Workers' Party on the Left, a variety of special interest group candidates, and a variety of Far Right groups are denied access to which they are formally entitled. These formal constraints may not be so important however as the informal professional understandings which journalists use to determine the extent to which they should be given

serious examination, which seem to revolve around, as we have suggested, the size of the individual minor party's existing electoral vote. The result of these legal and informal constraints, however, is what Harrison calls 'alibi' broadcasting, where merely token coverage is given. So for example the only explanation given of Communist Party policy during the 1979 Election ran as follows:

> The Communist Party, which intends to field about 40 candidates, published its Manifesto which looks for a socialist society based on the common ownership of the means of production, distribution and exchange. It calls for an end to VAT in favour of a tax on luxuries, a freeze on prices, a 35-hour week, and a withdrawal from NATO. (ITN News, 5.45 pm, 10 April)

(23) The logic of producing a proportionality between a party's performance in the previous General Election and the amount of current television time is actually formalised in the All Party Committee rules for allocation of Party Political Broadcasts during non-election periods. (Pateman, 1974, p.14.) It was subsequent to the 1970 General Election, when they received 11.5 per cent of the Welsh vote, that Plaid Cymru were allocated a further five minutes' party political broadcast time a year (to give them ten minutes altogether). But, as Pateman points out, the All Party Committee did not extend this principle to the three major parties as the Liberals only secured 6.8 per cent of the Welsh vote in 1970 but still received 30 minutes of time per year (ibid., p.15).

(24) The coverage of the National Front during the election was heavily framed by the presentation of it as a legally constituted political party (see the Newsnight reconstruction of Southall on 29 April). This was undercut by the widely reported condemnation of their 'extremist' policies by all the leading politicians of the major parties. Against this, it is worth remembering that the NF was also nearly always presented as the victim of violence perpetrated by the extreme Left (cf. Clarke and Wren-Lewis, 1981).

(25) The accessing of other journalists and experts occurs largely around the periphery of election broadcasting, with their appearance being confined to the serious programming of current affairs. This may remove them from the mainstream of prime-time news programming but, in fact, it also serves to reinforce the authority with which they speak as it is imbued with the importance of the programme on which they are speaking.

(26) The examples are taken from the following programmes:
1. the Chelmsford Wets   (ITN 5.45 pm. 23 April)
2. the Tory 30,000 bet   (ITN 1.00 pm. 3 May)
3. the Plymouth man   (ITN 5.45 pm. 24 April)

(27) The accessing may have been unproblematic for

television but it certainly was a problem for practical politicians of a liberal or left persuasion, and also for conventional analysis of television as a pluralist medium. Accounts of this kind could not explain why a group such as 'New Approaches to Crime' which was set up by leading figures in the social work and caring professions, specifically to counter the Right's interpretation of the crime and delinquency issue, was never called upon to state its case. The coverage was, therefore, seriously problematic in denying access even to figures who had only recently been highly authoritative in defining 'consensual' views on crime as a matter for expert intervention, individual treatment etc.

(28) In fact, the Southall accessing looks remarkably like the standard format used at the scenes of serious crimes such as murder, with the interviewing of local people, eye witnesses and people who knew the victim. The implication of this form was eventually rejected, as television remained silent on the causes of the death of Blair Peach. (Cf. Clarke and Wren-Lewis, 1982)

(29) This example of the way in which the 'unexpected news' of Southall was covered points to both the importance of Southall in disrupting the <u>routine</u> framing of the election coverage <u>and</u> also to the way authoritative sources come to be routinely accessed once their position has been established. Hence it was the TUC who were reported on racial incitement and not (then) the Commission for Racial Equality, who would superficially have seemed a more logical group to access on this point, but who had (and still have) no position in the structure of access to political television. In different context, Molotch and Lester examined the ways in which 'accidental' (unanticipated) news can momentarily disturb the routine use by the television media of a small number of primary definers who are normally deemed to be authoritative in their interpretation of events. (Their subject was a massive spillage of oil onto the beaches of suburban Santa Barbara, California.) (Molotch and Lester, 1974, 1976) But the disruption of routine accessing of primary definers, in the Southall and Santa Barbara cases, was only short-lived, and within days modified authoritative definitions had been re-established, and the credibility of police chiefs and local Californian oil company senior executives reaffirmed.

(30) We recognise that Tables 8 to 14 contain all the ambiguities of apparently unitary categories and that Table 8 by itself, if unexplained, merely reproduces these categories.

(31) This is the major problem with the tables of content presented in both Harrison (1980) and Pilsworth (1980). For them, content appears to be presented in discrete categories which are readily recognisable. The inherent problems of content analysis are increased by the overlaying of this content with explicit and implicit political meanings. In our view, any analysis which

fails to take account of the specific context of the content will be inadequate.

(32) We have already argued in the text of this paper that the character of the television election was one of critique of the failings of social democracy (on the economy and on law and order, in particular). Additionally, one of the other issues in the election, frequently raised against the Labour Party, was the presence of an 'extremist' Left within its ranks. This was usually presented in the form of news items about individuals (like Lord Wilson of Langdale, Lord George Brown and others) who had left the Party because of its alleged shift to the left. There were at least fifteen 'red-baiting' stories of this kind during the election period. There were no equivalent stories about the entry of the extreme Right into the Conservative Party, although such 'entryism' has been widely reported on in the informed political press. It is also interesting to note, in Table 3, the relative frequency of the access given Reginald Prentice, the ex-Labour Minister turned Tory, who was interviewed on 12 separate election programmes and using this opportunity largely to attack the left inside the Labour Party.

The 'effects' of these red-baiting stories on audiences are unclear, but their effects on the 'discursive formation' in use in the election period was to place the Labour Party on the defensive in the face of an already 'established' problem ('extremism' within the Party). It also had the effect of silencing any serious examination by television of analyses of the British crisis undertaken from any political position further left than the centre of the Labour Party.

(33) This was actually indicated in the mid-evening news bulletins which reported that the violence was increasing after the arrival of the police reserves. But no emphasis was placed on this fact, which was, in any case, negated by the emphasis placed on the injuries sustained by the police. Again a failure to question the primary definers' definition of the 'unexpected news' led to a partial and superficial (not to say misleading) version of the events being worked up and eventually established quite firmly (as in Newsnight on 29 April).

REFERENCES

Baistow, T, (1979), 'The Making of Margaret Thatcher', _Guardian_ (30 April).

Brunsdon, Charlotte and Morley, David, (1980), _Everyday Television: 'Nationwide'_, BFI Television Monograph no.10, London: British Film Institute.

Butler, David and Kavanagh, Dennis, (1980), _The British General Election of 1980_, London: Macmillan.

Clarke, Alan, (1980), 'The Response of the Media', in _Southall 23 April 1979: A Report of the Unofficial Committee of Enquiry_, London: National Council for Civil Liberties.

Clarke, Alan and Taylor, Ian, (1980), 'Vandals, Pickets and Muggers: Television Coverage of Law and Order in the 1979 Election', _Screen Education_ no.36 (Autumn) pp.99-111.

Clarke, Alan, Taylor, Ian and Wren-Lewis, Justin, (1981), 'Law and Order, Television and the General Election of 1979', University of Sheffield, Centre for Criminological and Socio-Legal Studies, Law and Order Project, Paper no.1.

Clarke, Alan and Wren-Lewis, Justin, (1982), 'Reading the Riot Act', Open University Working Paper (forthcoming).

Dearlove, John, (1974), 'The BBC and the Politicians', _Index 1_ (reprinted in Pateman (1974) Appendix 2).

Foot, P, (1979a, b), 'Fleet Street and the Elections', _New Statesman_ (20 April, 4 May).

Glasgow University Media Group, (1976), _Bad News_, London: Routledge and Kegan Paul.

Glasgow University Media Group, (1980), _More Bad News_, London: Routledge and Kegan Paul.

Hall, Stuart, (1979), 'The Great Moving Right Show', _Marxism Today_ (January).

Hall, Stuart, (1980), 'Thatcherism: a New Stage?', _Marxism Today_ (February).

Hall, Stuart, Connell, Ian and Curti, Lidia, (1976), 'The 'Unity' of Current Affairs Television', _Cultural Studies_ no.9 (Spring) pp.51-94.

Hall, Stuart, Crichter, Chas., Jefferson, Tony, Clarke, John and Roberts, Brian, (1978), _Policing the Crisis: Mugging, the State and Law and Order_, London: Macmillan.

Harrison, Martin, (1980), 'Television News Coverage of the 1979 General Election', Paper to Political Studies Association Conference, University of Newcastle upon Tyne, 16-18 April.

Kellner, Peter (1979), 'Not a Defeat: a Disaster', _New Statesman_ (18 May) pp.704-6.

Kumar, Krishan, (1975), 'Holding the Middle Ground: the BBC, the public and the professional broadcaster' _Sociology_, no.9 (3), (September), reprinted in J. Curran, M. Gurevitch and J. Woolacott (eds.), _Mass Communication and Society_, London: Edward Arnold, 1977.

Molotch, Harvey and Lester, Marilyn, (1974), 'News as Purposive Bheaviour: on the Strategic Use of Routine Events, Accidents and Scandals', _American Sociological Review_, no.39.

Molotch, Harvey and Lester, Marilyn, (1976) 'Accidental

News: the Great Oil Spill as Local Occurrence and
National Event', _American Journal of Sociology_, no.81 (2)
pp.235-60.
NCCL, (1980), _Southall 23 April 1979: The Report of the
Unofficial Enquiry_, London: NCCL.
Pateman, Trevor, (1974), 'Television and the February 1974
General Election', British Film Institute Television
Monograph no.3, London: British Film Institute.
Pilsworth, Michael, (1980), 'Balanced Broadcasting', in
Butler and Kavanagh, _op.cit._
Seabrook, Jeremy, (1979), 'Winter of Resentment', _New
Society_, 19 April, pp.151-2.
Wober, J.M, (1979), 'The May 1979 General Election: Viewers'
Attitudes towards Television Coverage', IBA Audience
Research Department Special Report, London: Independent
Broadcasting Authority.

ACKNOWLEDGEMENTS

We would like to thank Les Hargreaves, Karen Jones, Barry
Smart and Alan O'Shea for some very helpful comments on the
original version of this paper, Rosemary Duncan and Peter
Morley of the Cartographic Drawing Office, Department of
Geography, University of Sheffield, for producing the
tables, and Vera Marsh for her usual efficiency and speed
in the typing of various versions of this paper.

TABLE 1

PROPORTION OF ELECTION PROGRAMMES GIVING PARTY LEADERS/POLITICIANS ACCESS

TABLE 2

PROPORTION OF ELECTION PROGRAMMES FEATURING CAMPAIGN FILMS

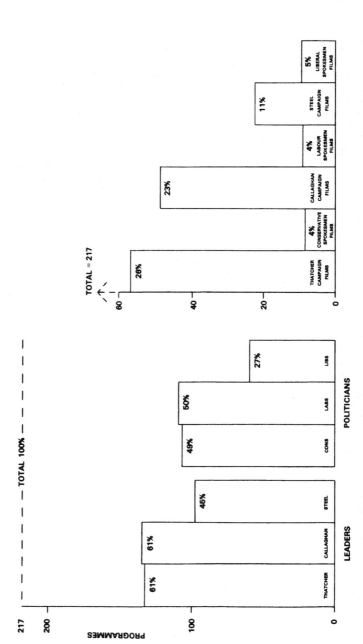

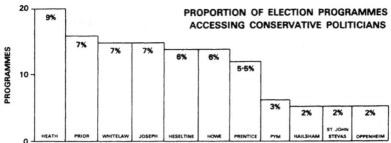

TABLE 3

PROPORTION OF ELECTION PROGRAMMES ACCESSING CONSERVATIVE POLITICIANS

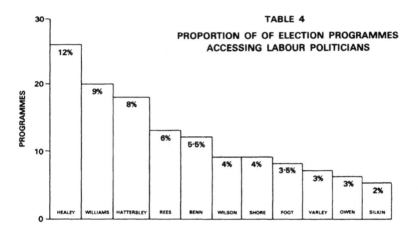

TABLE 4

PROPORTION OF OF ELECTION PROGRAMMES ACCESSING LABOUR POLITICIANS

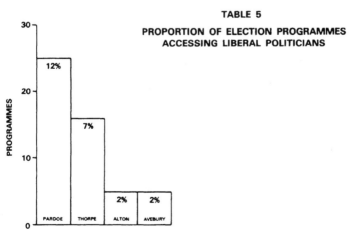

TABLE 5

PROPORTION OF ELECTION PROGRAMMES ACCESSING LIBERAL POLITICIANS

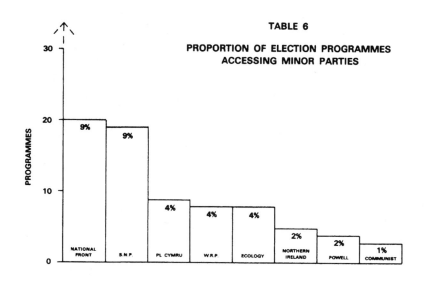

TABLE 6

PROPORTION OF ELECTION PROGRAMMES ACCESSING MINOR PARTIES

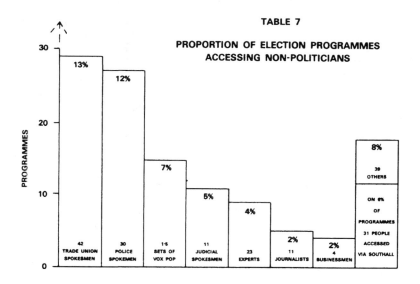

TABLE 7

PROPORTION OF ELECTION PROGRAMMES ACCESSING NON-POLITICIANS

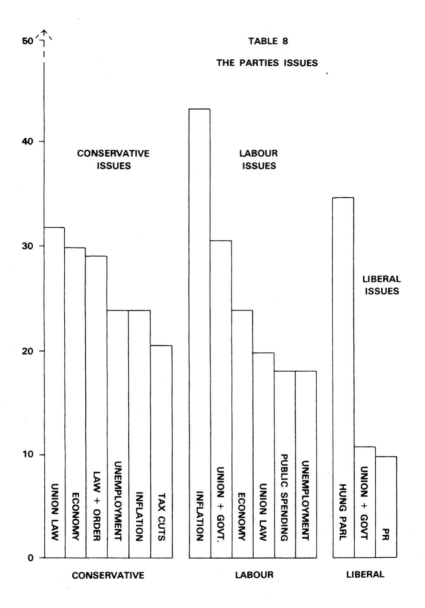

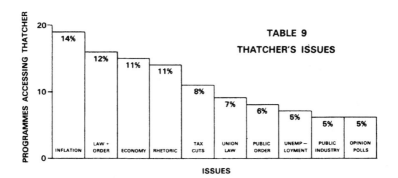

TABLE 9
THATCHER'S ISSUES

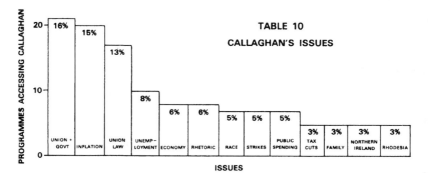

TABLE 10
CALLAGHAN'S ISSUES

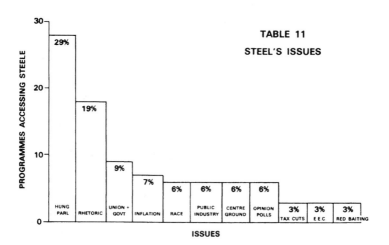

TABLE 11
STEEL'S ISSUES

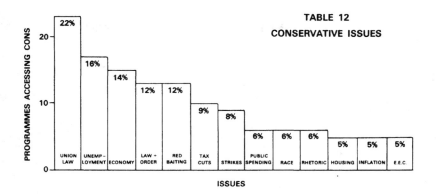

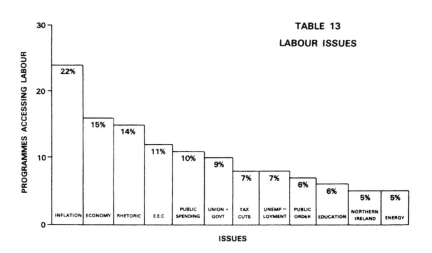

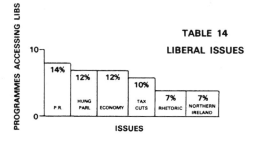

8 Classes, Class Fractions and Monetarism
KEVIN BONNETT

INTRODUCTION

This chapter is a preliminary product of a current research project on economic policy, class interests and forms of state. Over the past few years a diverse body of literature has grown up around the concept of corporatism, broadly suggesting that the modern configuration of political and economic forces demands some form of 'social democratic compromise', above all in economic policy. State intervention, incomes policies and especially 'social contracts' imply a politicisation of economic problems and, usually, an attempt at a 'consensus' solution. On the face of it, monetarist policies, especially in their Thatcherist guise, actively reverse this trend. The politics of quasi-voluntary compromise are being abandoned for the politics of coercive deflation throughout the Western bloc. One basic question, therefore, is whether the new politics is merely a reflection of a changed world, or whether the basic dimensions of this world persist sufficiently to doom the monetarists to failure.

Firstly, though, I'll make the usual disclaimers. My focus is on economic policy and interests, rather than on broader aspects of the revival of the Right. I certainly would not deny that monetarist policies are only one central element in a broader attempt at political and ideological realignment by Thatcher, Barre, Reagan, Fraser and the rest (cf. Hall, 1979, 1980). One of the major points of strain and weakness in monetarism is that it often purports to be a new, purely technical solution to pressing problems while in fact it not only connects with wider right-wing ideologies, but crucially depends on those conceptions of society for its basic propositions. In so far as the world is recognised to be divergent from these conditions, political initiatives are necessary (cf. Gamble, 1980, Jones, 1980). Hayek's call for an onslaught on trade unions is only one example. This means that the effectiveness of monetarist policies depends not only upon their own coherence and validity but also upon their ability to destroy or transform the political and ideological compromises of the post-war period. If the key to this is, as Andrew Gamble says, 'taking credit for the recession' then we need to know whether the recession will recast social forces as much as it recasts domestic industry.

CLASSES AND INTERESTS

If we assume that monetarism is a _political_ solution to a crisis with political, ideological and economic dimensions, we can move on to raise some questions about the social origins of the phenomenon. The starting point for this must be the relationship between economic policies and independent economic interests outside the state. Putting it crudely, how is it possible for the Party of capital to treat a chronic complaint (inflation) in a way which produces seizure and crisis in all sectors of manufacturing industry. Even if we accept that short-term costs may bring long-term benefits, it is not strikingly obvious that contemporary western policies can be easily read off from the interests or 'needs' of domestic manufacturing capital. A number of obvious responses can be made to this. Firstly, one may suggest that western economies do need restructuring to raise the average rate of profit and shake out restrictive practices and retrograde enterprises. The Thatcher government says very similar things. Secondly, one must accept that 'capital' and 'manufacturing industry' are not identical and therefore current policies may simply reflect the long-term dominance (in Britain at least) of financial capital over industrial capital. There is no guarantee, however, that this economic dominance is automatically translated into a broader _hegemony_ for financial capital - that is, where the City succeeds in presenting its favoured policies as being in the general interest, so that the state adopts and implements these policies. It could be argued that monetarism constitutes a distinctive ideological initiative which attempts to secure such a hegemony for City interests at the broadest level of social and economic policy. This theme, however, meets all the familiar problems in the location of ideologies in relation to classes and fractions. We can immediately identify various versions of such a 'hegemony thesis'.

The simplest version of this would simply say that monetarist policies produce effects such as high interest rates and a strong pound which directly aid the profits of City institutions; if these benefits involve huge costs for industry then this is simply further evidence for City dominance.

This argument cannot be lightly dismissed. There is a great deal of evidence (referred to shortly) which demonstrates the highly unequal relationship between financial and industrial capital, and I will later try to show the vital role of City institutions and their representatives in the securing of monetarism as the dominant policy. One might wish to go on to argue that the real effects of monetarist policies demonstrate this hegemony of finance and prove that sectional interests lie behind

186

policies which claim to serve all fractions of capital. One might have either an instrumentalist, an economistic, or a more complex structural interpretation of this, thus:

(1) the City actively cooked up their ideology for their own immediate benefit, and cynically presented it as serving the general interest, or:

(2) the economic structure of dependence and dominance between fractions of capital determined the outcome regardless of the sincerely held theories / ideologies of anyone involved, or:

(3) the economic structure does not automatically reproduce the dominance of financial capital, but instead legal, political and practical conditions have to be secured and defended through the state. Thus the continued autonomy of City activities depends upon ideological and political initiatives to preserve existing parameters of state policy or to initiate new policies. This means that existing economic structures are potentially open to change through the struggles around the state to secure hegemony for particular ideologies linked to particular groups.

From (3), one hypothesis worth pursuing is that the monetarist rejection of concern for the 'supply side' or 'real' economic variables in favour of purely monetary indicators somehow articulates with the City's sole concern with capital in the money form. That is, the real performance of firms is of less concern to them than variations in interest rates, exchange rates and share values (assuming, of course, that movements in these money variables are not directly determined by the 'real' economy of production and consumption). This reversal of priorities is clear in the radically changed analysis of 'Britain's economic problem'. Throughout the sixties it was obvious to all that government policy and economic growth were heavily constrained by the exchange rate and the balance of payments - but the prevailing assumption was that these constraints were the effects of problems on the supply side such as low productivity and weakness of products in export markets. Now the prevailing view is that nothing can come right in production until inflation is squeezed out, and that this inflation is not caused by cost-push factors originating in industrial costs or the labour market. The monetary climate must be stabilised to allow, in due course, spontaneous wealth-creation by industry, unsullied by any direct state contact.

Hence, one hypothesis could be that the rise of monetarism, its content and its effects all have a natural affinity to financial capital and thus reflect and demonstrate City hegemony. However, in order to evaluate this we need to explore further the notions of 'dominance' and 'hegemony' of a class fraction.

It is clearly very dangerous to assume that any economic policy can be explained by the 'needs' of this or that

187

fraction of capital, let alone by the 'needs of capital' in general. Except in the most tautologous sense ('capitalism persists, therefore the state must be aiding or not much hindering this persistence') I would not wish to assume any guarantees that the state will serve the interests of any particular fraction of capital. Instead, it might be more appropriate to attempt to identify the consequences if the state were to fail to serve the interests of a particular class or fraction. This consideration of consequences would relate to a number of aspects. Firstly, we might identify the active political, economic and ideological strategies adopted by such a fraction to either influence policy or impose unpalatable consequences. This relates to a wide range of phenomena ranging from formally instituted interest groups to publicity campaigns, to investment strikes, to the closure or export of plant and capital. Since this might initially be conceived as the 'conscious' exercise of economic power we could therefore take as our data the perceptions of their own interests actually generated by these institutional actors. The construction of these perceptions could itself be a topic for research as an ideological process, for example, the establishment of a wide-ranging monetarist frame of analysis for conceptualising economic problems and solutions was effective in shaping the perceptions of different groups.

Secondly, we might wish to analyse consequences in terms of those generated by the overlapping system of economic relations such as foreign exchange markets, markets for goods and labour, or patterns of investment. In very different terms, the classic economic accounts of Smith and Marx would both identify systematic unintended outcomes from the isolated decisions of actors. In this there are apparently uncontrolled system constraints which generate real consequences for state economic policy. The practical methods by which the policy makers attempt to anticipate both these levels of consequence (reaction by the powerful and system-generated outcomes) are themselves problematic and imperfect. The indicators by which success or failure are judged are especially problematic during the monetarist episode, hence the debates over the definition of the money supply.

Needless to say, these analytical distinctions cannot be rigidly sustained, because the 'planes' of consequence interlock at the level of decision-making in real economic institutions. The broadest system consequences (world recession for example) have to be manifested at the level of concrete decisions to invest, destock or sell sterling. It is clear that in the current economic climate the range of options open to an institution are extremely tightly constrained; even for ICI the strong exchange rate generated through the exchange markets becomes an uncontrolled factor limiting exports. The 'perceptions' of, say, the ICI Board have significance only in affecting choices in relation to these external constraints, moreover, the nature of these perceptions of their interests is primarily determined by their interpretation of the nature of these constraints. If we are concerned with the ways in which economic institutions attempt to exercise their economic power, and also try to influence state policy, then the ideological and theoretical basis of these calculations can be regarded as variable.

The implication of this is that the relationship of ideologies and practices to 'objectively analysable' economic interests is problematic and indirect, but <u>not</u> indeterminate. The problem of actually specifying the nature of this relationship unfortunately seems far from resolution in current debates on ideology and hegemony. The application of discourse theory (Laclau, 1979, Mouffe, 1980) seems to carry real dangers of losing sight of the material structures which provide the contexts and conditions for the production and reception of ideologies (cf. Hall et al, 1980). While the danger of crude reductionism is real enough, one escape route may be given by clarifying our conception of how classes or fractions are actually constituted, in a way that distinguishes between (i) an objective structure of economic relationships (analysable by the observer) which consists of classes and fractions placed in relation to the circuit of capital, and (ii) the political effectivity of such classes through political and ideological organisation and initiatives. Quite clearly, there will be scope for disagreements between observers over accounts of the objective structure of relations at any point, but any notion that these accounts are purely arbitrary seems dangerously destructive. Equally, theories, ideologies and doctrines seldom present themselves as narrowly class-based but instead claim to represent the 'truth' or the 'general interest'. Hence one cannot escape paying attention to the origins and the intended effects of ideas in order to locate them in social relations.

(i) Accounts of objective economic relations

At one extreme, the classic concept of <u>finance capital</u>, in Hilferding's sense, appears to deny the possibility of distinguishing the interests of banking/credit/money capital from those of large industry. Since the large-scale enterprise is itself a primarily financial entity (and not necessarily committed to any particular productive activity for its profit) it is argued that an effective merging takes place. This might be direct, or through interlocking directorships and mutual financial dependence. As the largest enterprises turn to external funds, a symbiosis occurs. It is usual to argue that all this applied well enough to bank-dominated Germany or USA in the early decades of this century, but that the giant financial empires crumbled in favour of a more diverse structure of relationships (cf. Kotz, 1978, Hussein, 1976). In Britain, Scott argues, it had never existed at all (Scott, 1979, ch.4). However, the postwar growth of monopolies, oligopolies and multinationals has led to the view that a more 'equal' merger of financial and industrial capital is occurring.

Thus, it has been argued that 'both Britain and the USA are moving from entrepreneurial capital to finance capital, though they are moving at different rates and have followed different routes' (ibid. p.91). Soref agrees, and adopts Zeitlin's view that 'the interests of financial capital rise above those of bank and industrial capital' (Soref, 1980).

An orthodox conclusion drawn from this (though not by these authors) is the state monopoly capitalism theory that the state is necessarily tied to this overwhelmingly powerful bloc of capital. This further integration is necessitated by the need for close functional coordination between the monopolies and the state, and facilitated by interchange and fusion of personnel (cf. Jessop, 1980). The 'monolithic' quality of this view of the state seems to leave little space for the conflicts and confusions which surround actual economic policies. In addition, empirical evidence suggests that we should be cautious about assuming the predominance of this fraction of capital in Britain. Important work has confirmed the view that a long-established gulf persisted between the City and manufacturing industry in Britain (Longstreth, 1979, Lisle-Williams, 1981). An orientation to trade financing and capital export left aside the needs of domestic manufacturers, who invested on the basis of personal profits or local finance. As Lisle-Williams usefully shows, the postwar period has seen a substantial intensification of the relations between banks (Lisle-Williams, 1981b) and the merchant banks, while retaining their wide range of autonomous financial activities, now generally provide financial advice and services including management of mergers and takeovers. The traditional role of the clearers in providing overdrafts has only just begun to broaden and gain flexibility. The Bank of England has also come to reflect these changes and takes an active role in finance for large firms - especially in the current rescue operations for major employers hit by recession (cf. Lisle-Williams, 1981a). These developments, together with the increasing interlocking and interchange of directorships provide empirical indications of new partial merger in key areas of capital. But the dominance of this is not proven: the clearers are closely involved in other financial operations including foreign exchange and Eurodollar transactions whose outcome may not help industry, and there is clearly potential strain over lending policies and interest rates. The continuing debate over finance for industry is a clear indication of this strain. More generally, the City is involved in a range of investment and finance operations in property, commodities, foreign capital and, above all, government debt, which have independent effects on the climate for trade and investment. The special autonomy for these transactions in London strengthens the independent importance of the financial institutions in Britain.

One final qualification should be made: it may be necessary to distinguish between the interests of the largest firms, locked together with the banks, and the rest of medium-to-large industry which enjoys less support or is less worthy to borrow. The recession may be hitting these harder. It is also important to distinguish between 'independent' firms and subsidiaries or dependents of large multinationals - the latter position may provide protection, or greater weakness as the parent firm rationalises.

(ii) The political effectivity of class fractions

Whatever the outcome of debates over the current real pattern of economic structure, this structure has to be linked to political conflicts and outcomes by some process and radically different accounts may be given of the degree of determinism involved. It could be argued that no political effects whatever will emerge without specific organisations being formed to pursue group interests, and that professed ideology and organisational acumen are key variables in the mechanics of representation. An opposed interpretation might claim that ideological or political <u>effects and outcomes</u> are fairly directly predetermined by the relationships of domination and dependence which exist within the economic structure. A comparison of the work of Moran and Clarke provides a good contrast between these two approaches (Moran, 1980, 1981, Clarke, 1978).

Mike Moran has produced very illuminating accounts of the relationship of the City to pressure group activity and demonstrated the extent to which explicit organisation in interest groups has been necessary. As he puts it: 'to know that financiers caught the pressure group habit late, that they find it difficult to unite in a single organis- ation and that the manner of their incorporation into the policy process is changing, is still to know nothing directly of their power.' (Moran, 1981, p.26.) Moran goes on to suggest that evidence of personal and institutional links between the City, Bank of England and governments provides no conclusive evidence of actual control or influence. Studies of decisions which explore effective control come up against the classic problems of represent- ativeness, as well as the continuous change in these relationships. Thirdly, Moran discusses the view that the City has managed to manipulate the <u>outcomes</u> of policy to secure their interests. He rejects this on two grounds: firstly, he questions whether City interests really have prevailed, given physical credit controls and low interest rates over past decades, and secondly, he denies the view that economic policy <u>strategy</u> was determined by the City. That is, the long term commitment to sterling strength and to open capital markets (cf. Strange, 1971) 'was not the result of manipulation by the City or the Bank; it pervaded the political elite, sustained by a commitment to the system established at Bretton Woods and by the belief that great power status required the pursuit of appropriate currency policies' (Moran, 1981, pp.31-2).

Moran rejects the view that these were 'City policies'

because industry did not object, and these company directors were unlikely to be suffering from false consciousness. Moran does not ask whether the long-term consequences for domestic manufacturing were fully understood by the sections of industry which favoured low cost food and raw materials, easy markets in the sterling area and easy capital export. Put more directly, he does not ask what structural constraints there might have been on policy, nor whether the economic structure determined the long-term, unintended/unanticipated effects of policies which had different consequences for different parts of capital. The routine institutional practices of, say, foreign exchange markets are not immutable, and the state may be able to change their mode of operation, but until that occurs the constraints on policy from such things as sterling crises and crises of confidence cannot be wished away. Moran adopts a sophisticated instrumentalist approach but he does not escape from the model of the state as all-powerful agent moved by deliberate external influence. This level of analysis needs to be articulated with structural context, constraints and outcomes. Despite this, he does demonstrate in a very illuminating way that groups or classes have no direct political existence or efficacy without successful organisational efforts to establish the distinct identity of the group and its interests.

In direct opposition to instrumentalist approaches to economic policy (in this instance directed against accounts of the South African state) Clarke attempts to develop more rigorous usage of the concept 'fractions of capital' (Clarke, 1978). The pursuit of their own interests by individual capitals must be distinguished from capital-in-general, the collective embodiment of capital's interests. If groupings within this are to be distinguished, Clarke insists that this should not be ad hoc or on the basis of their income (e.g. mining capital versus farming capital) but grounded in the relations of production. Real fractions of capital are located in different moments of the circuit of capital:

> The 'particular form' of capital refers to the special-
> ised 'functions' in the circuit of capital which at a
> certain period of capitalist development give rise to
> specialised capitals: productive capital, bank capital,
> commercial capital, landed capital... (ibid, p.57)

However, on particular issues groups might come together to form 'capitalist interest groups'. What is the difference and why does it matter? For Clarke, the answer is that the current limits on the production of surplus value set the limits on the state: it cannot intervene in ways which disrupt valorisation. On the other hand, where capital-in-general 'fails to impose itself' on capital via competition, the state has to intervene. Thus the key to state intervention is found by identifying the representative of capital-in-general, and thus turns out to be the Central Bank. Money is capital in its most elemental form, and so the semi-independent Central Bank embodies the general interest of capital. Hence, presumably, domination by finance is to be expected: 'Domination of capital-in-general over state is not direct but is mediated through capital's domination of all social relations.' (ibid, p.64.)

All this seems to be a seriously unsatisfactory answer to the problem of specifying the structural conditions for the dominance of financial capital. Clarke's analysis seems to combine a metaphysical economic reductionism with a notion of structural guarantees of success in the state's economic role. Once again, we do not seem to be helped to articulate different levels of structure and practice.

In a short critique of Clarke, Solomos defends a Poulantzian conception of class analysis (Solomos, 1979). Production relations are an insufficient component of class relations, he argues, for classes exist in a 'definite articulation of economic, political and ideological factors'. Moreover, the political stances adopted by classes (their 'class positions') cannot be immediately explained by relations of production. To this might be added the Poulantzian concept of hegemony in the power bloc. In his early work, at least, Poulantzas uses the concept of hegemony to refer to (i) the way in which the interests of the dominant classes comes to be defined as the national/ general interest, and to (ii) the position of direzione or leadership of one among the dominant classes and fractions in the power bloc.

As John Urry points out, this gives a very problematic place for politics and ideology in its effects on agents' actions: 'the political and the ideological operate both to determine structurally basic social classes and their objective interests, and at the same time to produce class positions divergent from such objective class determin- ations.' (Urry, 1981, p.16.) This makes the status of 'class struggle' highly problematic in Poulantzas, with no solution to the problem of linking 'real' structures and outcomes with actual class practices (let alone those not class- based). If we are to take at all seriously Poulantzas' claim that the power bloc is a 'complex contradictory unity in dominance' and that class struggle is always present, then we need to stress that different fractions/groups may engage in 'hegemonic projects' to secure a position of ideological or political dominance. However, this is seriously complicated by Poulantzas' cautions that those in charge of the state may not be those whose interests are served. While this is perfectly justifiable, it does not mean that we need to articulate analysis of active political and ideological initiatives with a structural analysis which adequately explains the unintended outcomes.

This leads us to the unremarkable conclusion that there is no currently available solution to the problem of relating ideology, political practices, and 'objective' structures of social relations. As the contributions to Hall make clear, abstracted formalistic discourse theories provide an inadequate alternative to the simple determinism of the base-superstructure metaphor since complex social structures must provide the conditions for the generation and reception of ideologies (Hall et al, 1980). At the same time, these ideologies and accounts-of-the-world are actively constructed and proseletysed by social groups and their leaders; this mediates and potentially transforms the link between structural social relations and the practices of groups and individuals. Equally though, the imposition and institutionalisation of routinised practices and relationships, and the unanticipated consequences of practices, both point to the real significance and effectiveness of social structures. Perhaps these should be conceptualised as interlocking 'layers' of structures of varying degrees of generality and scope, with reciprocal effects generated by changes at any level.

Efforts to implement ideologies into practices therefore will collide with a recalcitrant complex reality of structures and structural effects which will generate political crises and responses. The account of the rise of monetarism in the rest of this paper attempts to portray some of the conditions for the rise of a new ideology and the effects of the clash between the policies and economic and political structures.

THE RISE OF MONETARISM IN BRITAIN

The advance of monetarism as a theoretical innovation in British economics has never been divorced from policy prescriptions. Only a very tentative and heuristic distinction can be made between 'technical monetarism' (as a purely practical technique for reducing inflation) and 'monetarist politics' which has to confront the problems of securing the social and political conditions necessary for monetarist prescriptions to work. It is difficult to sustain such a division because all monetarism embodies propositions about economic systems and processes and must therefore either assume, for example, that openly competitive markets for labour already exist, or that political intervention will create the conducive structural conditions (such as the weakening of trade unions). Thatcherite monetarism must be seen, therefore, as a broad response to economic, political and academic crises which revives and recasts many of the traditional themes of classical liberalism concerning economic processes and the role of the state. Key elements therefore include active withdrawal from state involvement in firms' planning and investment, and an attempt to diminish the overall spending and scope of the state which also implies the 'recommodification' (return to the market) of collectively-provided services. Public expenditure cuts therefore rest on 'technical' justifications (such as the supposed 'crowding out' of investment) and on the desire to recreate a competitive 'supply side' of private enterprises paying less tax for less collective services. It can be readily seen that

monetarist politics rapidly confronts political organisational barriers to this process, so that the task of
creating an economy where classical market forces work
freely comes to a rapid halt. The 'technical' prescriptions
of monetarism thus fail not only because of their own
internal incoherences, but also because the practical
institutional conditions for success (e.g. means to measure
and control the money supply) simply do not exist. The
failure of Thatcherite policies has so far been due to the
confrontation with economic reality, rather than due to
concerted political resistance from any quarter.

The characteristics of monetarism

Thompson has asked pertinently whether monetarist policies
are really qualitatively distinct (Thompson, 1981). They
clearly are in terms of their theoretical base, and their
commitment to attack directly only the inflation component
of stagflation. Stabilisation of money by recession in order
to set the climate for spontaneous industrial recovery is a
strategy far removed from the fine-tuning for growth of
Keynesian stop-go fiscal management. The development of the
latter, from stop-go to more direct sectoral intervention
and prices and incomes policies, shows a concern with the
'supply side' and with cost-push inflation which is
radically rejected by Thatcherite monetarism. It is impossible to isolate monetarism as a purely 'technical' theory
of inflation; it contains implicit propositions about the
structure of real economy ('markets rule') and explicitly
embraces traditional economic liberalism. However, the
'technical' elements of monetarist policy appeared in
British policy well before the full-blown world-view of
Thatcher, and because the instruments of policy have never
been 'purely' monetarist (cf. arguments over monetary base
control) there is a degree of continuity.

Mayer offered an ideal type of the elements of monetarist
belief (Mayer, 1978). I will not elaborate all of them:

(i) Quantity theory of money. The identity $MV = PT$, i.e.

$$\text{money stock} \times \frac{\text{velocity of}}{\text{circulation}} = \frac{\text{price}}{\text{level}} \times \frac{\text{no. of}}{\text{transactions}}$$

is their starting point. On the basis of highly contested
correlations they link rises in M to rises in P, i.e. money
stock rises are the immediate cause of price inflation.
Causal status for this correlation is claimed through
statistical evidence for <u>lags</u> (normally two years, but now,
according to Peter Jay, three to five years!) which show
temporal precedence for the money growth. All of this is
what allows Mrs Thatcher to claim that monetarism is not
theory but <u>fact</u>. Others disagree.

(ii) Monetarist model of transmission process. The theory
that money is a market commodity like any other, and this
determines interest rates and affects wage and price
adjustments, thus linking money growth to inflation.

(iii) Belief in the inherent stability of the private market sector. It is self stabilising in a sound monetary environment.

(iv) Not concerned with institutional analysis of sectors or bargaining arrangements. The market is stronger.

(v) Focus on general price level which is given 'naturally' unless money growth creates inflation in nominal values. Governments must not tinker with relative prices.

(vi) Small econometric models: no sectoral detail is needed.

(vii) Use of reserve base as monetary indicator: 'high powered money'.

(viii) Money stock is target for policy.

(ix) Money stock growth is tied rigidly to the real level of output.

(x) Inflation is a greater priority than unemployment.

(xi) Hostility to government intervention is the real economy, or in credit and interest rates.

This list gives only a very schematic indication, and takes no account of the doctrine's many varieties. This simplification serves to emphasise the underlying coherence of monetarism as a world-view and not just a trendy new policy instrument. The symbolic moment for this reversal of previous assumptions came not with Thatcher but in 1976 with Callaghan's speech at the Labour Party Conference:

> The cosy world which we were told would go on for ever where full employment could be guaranteed by a stroke of the Chancellor's pen has gone. We used to think that you could just spend your way out of recession and increase employment by cutting taxes and boosting Government spending. I tell you in all candour that that option no longer exists and insofar as it ever did it worked by injecting inflation into the economy followed by higher levels of unemployment as the next step. This is the history of the last twenty years.

Thus when Mrs Thatcher talks of twenty years of failure, and equates reflation with inflation, she merely repeats the new 'truths' established in the mid-seventies. The postwar social democratic compromise founded on active governmental pursuit of growth, full employment, stable prices and trade balance had crumbled away. The Labour government tried to incorporate the unions in the Social Contract while simultaneously changing to monetarist goals, public expenditure cuts, and cuts in real wages. The surprise is that such voluntary compliance survived in a stagnant economy as long as it did; certainly the anti-interventionism and anti-corporatism of Thatcher fitted better with the collapse of the postwar compromise.

196

This is not to suggest that there are no differences between the economic regimes of Healey/Callaghan and Howe/Thatcher, for although it is true that from 1976 onwards Labour abandoned all aims of reflating to cut unemployment, they never committed themselves to a deliberately engendered slump. The Thatcherite strategy involves exacerbation of the general recession conditions for a number of purposes: firstly, as prescribed by monetarism, curbing money supply growth involves costs in output (though accounts of the time-scale vary); secondly, recession speeds the restructuring of capital in a 'natural' way without any direction, subsidy or planning by the state; and thirdly slump will weaken union bargaining power, and supposedly recast the balance of economic power. All this constitutes a 'political monetarism' which was never adopted by the 1974-9 administration or by the authorities in that period; however it is also true to say that Callaghan's speech of 1976 signals a decisive abandonment of counter-cyclical intervention in favour of deflation. Given the deeper presuppositions behind monetarism concerning economic structures, it is interesting to ask whether the Labour combination of 'technical' monetarism and social contract can ever be sustainable. The answer may be that incomes policies and other forms of incorporation are much less stable than in societies like West Germany, and so deflationary policies will undermine them even further. Other societies may have more chance of sustaining technical monetarist policies within a framework of economic class compromise. Of interest here is David Cobham's suggestion that 'technical' monetarism can be separated from broader economic liberalism. The tight monetary control he advocates - to avoid sterling crises - is an unusual version of Alternative Economic Strategy (Cobham, 1981).

A decisive element in the British situation is the inability of Conservative governments to generate either a pro-corporatist ideology or a successful corporatist practice. The experience of the Heath government broke the credibility of two opposed tendencies within Conservative policy. Firstly, the attempt to implement a simple laissez-faire approach in the 'Selsdon Man' period exposed the economic consequences (in the 'lame-duck' industries) and by confrontation (the miners) both failed dismally. The economy could not be made free for competition and enterprise by these means; a new route to vigorous capitalism was needed, and monetarist theory came to offer just such a neutral, technical solution. Specific policy proposals and explanatory propositions came to replace the vague faith in laissez-faire. Monetarist theory in pure form even magically removed the problem of union power by declaring it to be irrelevant the explanation of inflation, since change in the general price level is solely explicable by money supply growth.

The adoption of monetarism by key Tories in the mid-seventies therefore gave the much older tradition of economic liberalism a much tougher and resilient intellectual

197

basis with much clearer policy prescriptions.

If this tradition was transformed, the managerialist 'one-nation' Tory tendency was profoundly discredited. The celebrated Heath U-turn attempted to throw Tory policy into the mainstream of corporatist compromise. The 1972 Industry Act provided the means for economic intervention on a grand scale, and the attempts to secure incomes policies led to extensive incorporation of union leaders in the formation and implementation of economic policy. Barber's 'dash for growth' may be seen as the last flourish of counter-cyclical expansionism, with his substantial tax cuts and increases in state expenditure. This growth bubble burst so quickly into unproductive investment and inflation that irretrievable damage was done to the credibility of macro fiscal policy as a means to economic recovery. Some alter-native had to be found. This crisis for neo-Keynesian policies extended further still. The pursuit of economic growth and full employment had developed two crucial effects (cf. Jessop, 1980a). Firstly, there was a continuous pressure to move beyond macro fiscal measures to sectoral intervention, either to ease the impact of decline or to sponsor leading sectors. Since the British economy could not 'spontaneously' generate growth comparable to competing economies, the solution lay in direct coordination and intervention. At the same time, the pursuit of full employ-ment meant a strengthening of union power hence creating a degree of dependence on their cooperation in policy implementation. Even for the managerialist and 'wet' ele-ments within the Conservative Party and its supporters, the prospect of <u>unsuccessful</u> compromise with the unions and failure to achieve policy goals such as wage restraint was disturbing. The Heath government seemed forced onto the road of social-democratic intervention and class compromise without having the capacity to secure them successfully, and without having any real basis of ideological support among those economic groups who looked to the conservative government as their representative. With the loss of the 1974 elections Heath came to be regarded as having abandoned the principles of his supporters in favour of policies which still failed to avoid inflationary crisis and acute political conflict. The field was open for a new doctrine which could offer a solution to inflation without expanding the economic role of the state or increasing dependence on union cooperation. Monetarism came to offer a solution to the crises in economic and social policy afflicting the Conservatives which was entirely compatible with the existing ideology of economic liberalism lurking within the Party and prevalent among its key supporters. But monetarism was more than just a handily-available doctrine; it was a sophisticated academic theory linked to detailed policy prescriptions as well as to wider conserv-ative political philosophy. We need to know why monetarism triumphed and filled the policy vacuum, rather than any more innovative or original alternative.

That question is echoed within academic discourse. It is

clear that Keynesian theory and neo-Keynesian policy applications were severely strained by the need to account for inflation. It is not that they had no answers, but that Keynesian policy has always been oriented to growth and employment; anti-inflation policies (e.g. those of Lord Kaldor) have to involve physical controls on incomes and often prices. To the extent that this political strategy succeeds it would be wrong to say that the Keynesians have 'no answer' to inflation. However the severe strains set up by such policies involve direct issues of power concerning the relationships between union leaders and Labour or Tory governments, and between union leaders and their members. In no sense can this be a 'technical' or 'purely economic' solution to inflation. It is for this reason, perhaps, that an apparently defunct doctrine from the lumber-room of economic theory came to be resuscitated. Once again, the question is why monetarism and not some other, perhaps new, alternative to Keynesianism? Perhaps a prime reason is the rigid distinction made by monetarists between the auto-nomous real economy and the world of inflation in nominal values. Governments can, indeed must, withdraw from these problematic interventions and compromises in order to deal with what is really in their power: the rate of growth of money supply. No reference is needed to any social force outside the state, the policy is squarely within the competence of government and is a purely technical operation.

More prosaically, monetarism had never actually died. In the United States especially, 'monetary economics' was not so down-graded as it was in Britain after the 1959 Radcliffe Report. Here, money supply was seen as 'not a critical factor', the concern was for the general level of demand, via fiscal and credit policy. Both the Treasury and NIESR regarded money factors as very minor, and did not build them into their models, claiming empirical backing for this judgement. Thus nothing was heard of the money supply until the IMF intervention of 1967.

The deflationist and monetarist inclinations of the IMF were long-established and the Jenkins Chancellorship of 1968-9 conformed to their expectations with trade balance and a move to budget surplus on public expenditure. Con-currently, the academic debates began in earnest in the late sixties, including within the Bank of England, who had to pay attention to IMF concern for money supply growth. The policies were broadly rejected, but statistics on M3 did appear as early as autumn 1970. This was mere back-ground, however, for the whole thrust of Barber's (and the authorities') regime was to loosen credit and taxes. After a substantial delay, and under the pressure of a bank crisis it became general to define the crisis as excess monetary growth, accompanying a fearful inflation rate. By 1975, the monetary creed with its ready-made framework of inflation-theory was making a real impact: in 1971-2, Laidler and Parkin at Manchester had become converted and in October 1973, a band of British professors advocated a monetarist

199

alternative to the wreckage of Barber's boom. Academic developments found a bridge to political policy-formation through Sir Keith Joseph who announced his conversion to monetarism at Preston in autumn 1974, arguing against 'government deficit financing, or printing money' and that 'monetary control is the pre-essential for everything else we need and want to do' (Joseph, 1976). Within six months Margaret Thatcher had succeeded Heath as Conservative leader, on most criteria an unlikely victory. Her success demonstrated the depth of crisis in the Tory Party and their desperate need for a radical alternative to Heath's path of compromise, but it was also a victory for a particular doctrine which had been actively promoted by proselytes.

The campaign for hegemony

Since Keynesian and social-democratic/corporatist ortho-doxies were in crisis, we might regard the situation as one where 'hegemonic projects' could be mounted to change the whole conceptual framework for policy. It is not possible to see a sudden break, but one can see deliberate, explicit campaigns mounted to achieve this. It is harder to identify the instigators of these campaigns, and one cannot jump to the conclusion that it was also a campaign for hegemony in the second sense - to gain dominance for one fraction of the dominant classes. Perhaps a tentative indication can be drawn from the character of the media involved. Firstly, although industry representatives supported a pragmatic economic liberalism and backed anti-inflation policy, it is not clear that they espoused and promoted monetarism per se. The impetus came much more from Sam Brittan in the Financial Times, from Robin Pringle's The Banker, and from City economists (mainly in stockbroking firms) such as Tim Congdon, George Pepper and G.E. Wood (e.g. Congdon, 1978). Major converts to the monetarist creed were also William Rees-Mogg and Peter Jay, editor and economic editor of The Times, though it is less easy to identify this organ with the aspirations of City capital. Even with the others, one might wish to know the extent to which they lead or reflect the opinions of their natural constituency. They clearly combine both roles and have a considerable relative autonomy in doing so.

Perhaps more telling is the fact that the people writing opinion-leading journalism were also those constructing the intelligence and analysis for key City institutions. The seventies saw within the City a big expansion of forecasting and the formalisation of economic judgements in bulletins. In recruiting the specialised corps of economists to do this, we may assume that the institutions picked those with a particular concern for monetary expertise. While this is by no means identical with monetarism, many of them do seem strongly influenced by Chicago economics and economic liberalism (e.g. via the Institute for Economic Affairs). Sam Brittan, of course, has demonstrated with great per-ception the political implications of Keynesian intervention and corporatist compromise (Brittan, 1977). On both

200

political and economic grounds, these commentators advocated the abandonment of the previously hallowed goals of holding down unemployment, and steadying the pound and interest rates. This certainly became an open campaign for a new conservatism, though often presented as simply a more rational policy alternative. Perhaps the main impact of this campaign was to help erode resistance to the implications of this policy alternative, which had been clearly recognised earlier on. For example, the Governor of the Bank of England had, in 1971, rejected money supply control as too costly: 'It cannot be emphasised too strongly or too often that attacking a severe inflation simply by holding down the growth of the money supply means reducing real activity.' Similarly, Anthony Barber rejected restriction of the money supply 'unless, of course, we were prepared to accept a massive increase in unemployment, bankrupties and stagnation.' By 1975-6 it seemed that this was what the authorities were beginning to be prepared to accept. The media and the internationally-oriented economists of the City played an important role in publicising the trend to monetary restrictions imposed in other Western economies after the oil price rise (e.g. the US Senate imposed a Friedmanite money growth rule). This, of course, implied criticism of the new Labour policies which continued expansion. As the accelerating weakness of sterling and continuing inflation increased their impact on the Labour government, the pressure grew for the adoption of 'technical' monetarist measures to constrain the money supply, together with policies to curtail growth in public expenditure. Thus Labour's attempt to swim against the monetarist tide met its familiar barrier: sterling crisis followed by externally imposed conservative economic policies. The fateful events of 1976 had certainly key features: the US authorities were determined to bring the UK economy to heel and avoid any danger of Left government (cf. Fay and Young, 1976); the IMF was committed to monetarist policies; Healey was willing to use the IMF stick to beat the Left into submission to cuts and deflation; the Treasury was split between the overseas divisions commitment to deflationary monetary policy and the domestic sections' resistance, while the new Governor of the Bank of England was decidedly deflationist. Thus the Labour government could claim to have been chicaned once more by external forces in the shape of the sterling markets and the IMF.

This claim is not totally disingenuous since the adoption of 'technical monetarism' was not the result of a thoroughgoing theoretical conversion within the government or the Treasury. At the same time, the real victory of monetarism was to establish policies of deflation and money supply control as 'inevitable' if inflation was to be controlled. We could describe monetarism as the hegemonic ideology once (i) anti-inflation policy was defined as being in the general interest, (ii) these policies were given top priority and (iii) monetarist prescriptions were defined as the sole cure for inflation. Just as Labour never really accepted the third stage (the Social Contract was the main plank of inflation control) they never came close to integrating broader monetarist propositions into any existing social democratic ideology. Thus the full development of monetarist hegemony only came with the ideologically committed 'political monetarism' of Thatcher.

MONETARISM AND CLASS INTERESTS

We cannot assume that the rise of a new ideology to hegemony indicates directly a change in the relative power of economic groups. Even though the monetarist concerns for sound money, a strengthened exchange rate, free capital movement and 'realistic' interest rates have some clear benefits for financial capital, it is not the case that City interests were failing to be served before the rise of monetarism. Perhaps the difference is that previously the economic dominance of financial capital helped to undermine or constrain the social democratic/corporatist policies which were defined as being in the 'general interest'. Even if that ideology was broadly hegemonic, its dominance was constrained by commitments to sustain autonomous City activity. Within that limit, a neo-Keynesian corporatist hegemony had ruled theory and policy. As we have seen, this Whitehall-Cambridge 'establishment orthodoxy' came under direct ideological attack through key media by an alliance of City economists, right-wing conservatives, and academics dissatisfied with current theoretical orthodoxies. A right-radicalism was generated in opposition to the combination of mandarin economic management and corporatist compromises with the unions. Severe external shocks and obvious failure of internal policy in the early seventies meant this campaign for a new theoretical and doctrinal hegemony was hammering on an open door. The foundation for this lay in the continued economic dominance of the City despite their distance from political theory and ideology. As Strange and many others have emphasised, the policies for reconstruction of the real economy were massively constrained by the commitments to sustaining sterling as a world trading currency and to maintaining freedom of capital movements for the City and for multinational corporations (Strange, 1971). The City was able to reestablish its world leadership in financial operations and sustain its almost 'off-shore island' position, and multinationals were able to invest and move funds in the sterling area. Thus at the level of policies actually implemented, and their effects, the City and large companies (quasi-finance capital) had their interest served. At the same time, the domestic operations of the manufacturers would not, presumably, have been harmed if governments had been more successful in industrial reconstruction and growth. Keynesian policies <u>attempted</u> to serve domestic industry, often at some cost to financial capital through credit control, but their degree of effectiveness was limited, especially by their coexistence with more general policy strategy on sterling. This could hardly be seen as evidence for the dominance of large and medium industry over other fractions of capital by securing effective benefit from policy. At the level of compromise between politicians and class-representative organisations, the sixties and seventies saw the growth of corporatist attempts at compromise between the economic powers of organised labour and the employers. To the extent that any fraction of capital achieved general ideological hegemony, large exporting manufacturers came closest to being identified with the 'national interest'. This had significance in so far as it was a dimension of the Keynesian orientation to growth and full employment. At the same time, though, the value of the pound and the state of the balance of payments (to the minutest variation) came to be accepted as critical indicators of economic health and stability. Once established as such, everything depends upon the economic agents who create the market conditions. Runs on the pound, gilts strikes and so on are aggregate effects of the judgements of agents in economic institutions; their actions depend upon the economic theories and frames of political judgement that they employ. The routine practices of these agents lock into the institutional activities of the Bank of England and Treasury who have to anticipate the reactions of the markets in order to sell gilts, make policy, or attempt double-bluffs to outmanoeuvre the markets. The history of British policy is one where political and ideological compromises and initiatives are bounded or undermined by the state's dependence on the judgements of the markets. The consequences of ignoring these market responses show their economic dominance. The British state has locked into the international financial community in a manner which makes it **dependent** upon institutions over which it has minimal control. If the markets consider policy changes inadequate, the sterling crisis will continue until external agencies such as the IMF intervene, by invitation, and impose restabilisation according to their economic doctrines. In this sense, financial capital has an economic hegemony within the state which is not dependent upon professed political strategy or ideology. The financial constraint coexisted with corporatist policies in this manner through much of the sixties and seventies. From 1974 onwards, however, monetary criteria of economic health gradually became more pressing: it was generally felt that excess monetary growth took place in 1972/3 and the Treasury instituted internal money growth targets. Official policy thus became an ad hoc mixture of money control, incomes policy, and welfare expansion until 1976, when the public expenditure cuts began. These changes seem to have been a response to the perceived need for new policies for new circumstances, and the campaign for monetarist hegemony began to have serious impact. It is not clear that any rapid conversion took place in the Treasury (cf. Keegan, 1979, pp.94-6) but the arrival of Gordan Richardson as Governor of the Bank of England helped to swing the balance.

In addition, monetarist theory was not only becoming effective at the level of political discourse, but also permeated the economic decisions made in the City, and thus forced itself on the Treasury. As Sir Douglas Wass said in

1978, 'market behaviour has become a significant input in policy making', and this market behaviour was based on economic judgements founded on monetarist theories of inflation, using monetary measures as indicators. The huge increase in pressure from the financial markets in 1976 brought the Bank of England and its monetary targets to the fore and shifted power partly away from the Treasury. The judgements of the City locked into state decision-making in a new and pressing way as control of money growth and cuts in PSBR effectively became demands from the City. The dependence of the state upon sterling markets and gilts sales thus forced policy in the favoured direction. Thus the rise of monetarism as theory and doctrine had effects at a number of levels - the 'change of ideas' leading to 'change of policy' should not be underestimated, considering Thatcher's degree of commitment - but the change in the framework of economic analysis led to a change in economic calculation and behaviour. This is magnified to a tremendous degree when the government publishes money and PSBR targets, as in the Howe Medium Term Financial Strategy. Policy is completely boxed in because immediately visible indicators of success are unambiguously defined. Markets can constantly measure the performance of the government by these measures, and react accordingly. The publication of targets was a wilful surrender of freedom of movement by the state, exactly as prescribed by monetarists. It has been suggested that this Medium Term Financial Strategy is an attempt to create a new 'framework of discipline' to replace the defunct gold standard and fixed exchange rates (Longstreth, 1979, Currie and Smith, 1980). Moreover, as increasing unemployment and crises in nationalised industries put pressure on public expenditure, the only way to sustain the targets was to increase taxation, hence the measures in the spring 1981 budget. The self imposed constraints of the targets are thus mediated through the judgements of the markets, in that deviation from the MTFS carries the danger of 'gilt strikes' or movements out of sterling. As a result the Thatcher government was pressed to meet recession induced public expenditure expansion with responses which exacerbate the slump. This raises the spectre of a financial crisis overlaying industrial crisis, a prospect brought a little closer by the Reagan policies of credit restriction which hoisted US interest rates and weakened the pound against the dollar in June 1981. That development illustrates the extent to which monetarist policies of high-cost credit accompanying a falling inflation trend must favour financial interests, and when a neighbouring economy implements this still further, capital will shift. The removal of exchange controls slightly eased such movements.

Broadly, then, monetarist policies can be regarded as 'in the interests of' financial capital in a number of ways. High interest rates, especially when sustained above the rate of inflation, are of simple direct benefit. This, together with the maintenance of sterling strength, encourages the movement of OPEC and other Eurodollar funds into London, creating profits and helping to generate demand for financial services. Less directly, an almost circular process occurs where (i) monetarist theories of inflation and their policy prescriptions are accepted in the City, (ii) forecasters and analysts adopt these theories to generate forecasts and judgements, hence 'confidence' depends upon the implementation of such policies, then (iii) where the policies are adopted, confidence follows and a favourable climate for financial activity is created. Such confidence must remain fragile, though, because of the great openness of the British economy and the ever increasing importance of massive flows of highly mobile funds. As soon as external conditions change, as in June 1981, movements will occur, and the effects on sterling are beyond the control of the authorities. It became clear in the mid-seventies that intervention in the foreign exchange markets was both ineffective and extremely costly. In a world financial system characterised by instability and lack of coordination Britain's dependence on financial capital, and its hegemony over policy, could prove very dangerous (cf. Calleo and Strange, 1981, Pillay, 1981).

So far this picture of City benefit is somewhat one-dimensional. It must be acknowledged that some sectors were hit hard by the strong pound. Lloyds Insurance, for example, has suffered the same loss of competitiveness as British manufacturers. More importantly, as the earlier discussion showed, there is a significant degree of interpenetration between City and industry which coexists with the other autonomous financial dealings. The pension funds and insurance companies are locked into manufacturing as major shareholders, while corporations are the clearers' main debtors. Although the latter are paying high interest on crisis loans, they must still survive if the banks are to retrieve their funds. This interdependence has markedly increased over the last decade and the 1980-81 relaxation of lending criteria (under Bank of England leadership) is a logical development. As a result, we must not over-emphasise the extent to which industry's loss is the City's gain under Thatcherite policies. It is by no means inconceivable that City opinion could move behind a controlled reflation.

The devastating consequences for industry of continued Thatcherite policy need hardly be detailed. Broadly, the pattern can be characterised as one where international developments damaging to British production were sharply exacerbated by government policy. The weakness of the dollar pushed funds towards other currencies and sterling's oil currency status, together with predictions of falling inflation, held an attraction which was reinforced by British interest rate policies. As a result British exporters experienced a loss of competitiveness between 1976 and 1980 which has been variously calculated from 30 to 50 per cent, and is on any account several times worse than the effects of return to the gold standard in 1925 (Currie and Smith, 1981, p.5). Lower export production and cheaper imports pushed up unemployment while fiscal policies further dampened domestic consumption. The unevenness of public expenditure cuts created great disparity in the effects on industries and regions with the Celtic fringe being joined in recession by previously thriving areas like the West Midlands.

With all these effects, it is plausible to argue that Thatcherite monetarism fails to serve the economic interests of most sections of industry and that one facilitating factor for this is the inability of manufacturers to secure a coherent and viable policy line which could serve as the basis for a bid for hegemony. This relates to the general issue of the impotence of resistance to Thatcher from industry and labour.

Work on the Confederation of British Industry makes clear the barriers involved in generating and articulating a coherent 'business interest' which can influence state policy and retain the support of members (Grant and Marsh, 1977, 1981). The cleavages within the organisation (between sizes of corporation, between individual competitors, between state dependent firms and those not) have real effects on the ability of the organisation to mobilise any sort of 'hegemonic project' where a collective industrial interest can be argued and then presented as being in the national interest. The result is continuous reversion to 'lowest common denominator' commitments to higher profits and less state intervention. The general lip service to a simple economic liberalism leaves them ill equipped to generate a critique of monetarist policy, or to demand a programme of state aided regeneration. While their strategic economic position means that state policies cannot avoid taking account of needs for profit and investment, this economic centrality is not translated into political and ideological hegemony in any direct sense. Grant argues that Conservative governments are _less_ open to CBI influence than Labour, due to the close Tory relationship to the City and the tendency for senior Conservatives to adopt the role of _defining_ the interests of industry rather than seeking guidance from industry's corporate representatives (Grant, 1981). Such observations can only be confirmed by the inadequacy of Sir Terence Beckett's 'bare-knuckled fight' against Thatcher policies. The CBI's alternative Budget package (CBI, 1981) may be regarded as remarkable for its direct demands for mild reflation, but this was vitiated by the usual demands for tax cuts for industry, and diluted by _fifty_ 'main action points'. Once again, the CBI was having to be all things to all its members and no clear alternative strategy was generated. Thus despite occasional angry noises, no concerted political resistance has been generated by industrialists.

This failure of political crisis to accompany economic crisis is even more notable in the response of organised workers. Immediate causes for worker acquiescence are readily found in the fear of unemployment or short-time working, and in the perceived consequences of wage pressure on weak firms. With serious unemployment power is likely to shift away from the shop-floor, and the limits to union strength are exposed by the inability to reverse decisions on redundancies, plant closures or liquidations. At the same time, it is questionable how far the basis for union strength has actually been eroded. Present circumstances provide opportunities for rationalisation, work reorganisation and higher productivity, but it is hard to know how long changed work arrangements will last when (or if) orders and employment recover. Although some strongly unionised sectors (such as steel) have suffered badly it is difficult to see any long term transformation in union power being effected by the recession.

Despite this lack of overt conflict there have clearly been limitations on the implementation of monetarist politics, even if they have been self-imposed within the government itself. There has been no all-out assault on the nationalised sector to recommodify or liquidate it; British Leyland could not be allowed to collapse. Encouragement to private health and education, and effective cuts in transfer payments have had a relatively marginal effect, though straightforward cuts have sliced deeper. The inertia of existing structures, and the real organisational resistance to radical restructuring of institutions are emphasised in Government Policy Initiatives 1979-80 (RIPA, 1981). The complex structure of state involvement with most areas of social life cannot be wished away to match the images of economic liberals, and the sponsoring departments will fight vigorously to protect their domains. Moreover the presence of 'wets' within the government encouraged calculation of the possible political consequences of particular cuts: the basic framework of the welfare state was thus weakened but not demolished. If internal government dissent has been more significant than external resistance, an important condition for its success is the failure of monetarist policies on their own criteria. If inflation climbs, and money supply apparently rockets, and public expenditure creeps upward, then the resistance to further doses of the same policy will be stiffened. The critical reports from the House of Commons Treasury and Civil Service Committee provide a fascinating insight into debates over theory and its application. Not least interesting are the weak defences of monetarist policy from Treasury officials (e.g. HC 1980-81, 163 II) in contrast to representatives from the Bank of England. All these reports expose the vituperative debates amongst economists and politicians over the efficacy of monetarist policy, and thus give some clues to the failure of Thatcherism to achieve its own stated objectives on money supply and inflation. While it is outside the scope of this paper to deal with this issue adequately, some of the key problems can be summarised:

(i) The complete failure to achieve a rapid change in inflationary expectation by the publication of targets (thus undermining the pronouncements of Rational Expectations theorists such as Professor Minford).

(ii) The failure to deal with inflexibility in the determination of wages (note Hayek's strictures on the need to demolish union power directly, rather than relying only on unemployment).

(iii) The inability to define money in any reliable manner to facilitate control. The constant argument over appropriate indicators undermines the supposed statistical support for the status of money supply growth as the preceding cause of inflation (cf. Thompson, 1981).

(iv) The related inability to specify any adequate means to control the growth of money, as in the debates over monetary base control (cf. Cmnd. 7858, Monetary Control) where the Treasury and Bank of England failed to specify any viable means.

(v) The inadequate account of monetary policy in an economy with large-scale open financial markets, and thus the failure to incorporate exchange rate variation as a controllable object of policy (cf. HC 163 II, Bank of England evidence).

(vi) The reliance on the spontaneous operation of the market to reconstruct British industry in a rational manner and to encourage spontaneous recovery, without state subsidy, planning or coordination.

In all these respects, monetarist politics either collapse through their own incoherence, or else collide with a real world of institutionalised economic structures which uncooperatively fail to conform to monetarist propositions. In addition, the manner to which general Thatcherite policies were partly moderated demonstrates the importance of struggles within the state (among politicians and officials) over policy and its consequences. These struggles may take place on behalf of particular group interests but the terms of the debate will be dictated by the dominant theories and ideologies which prevail, as well as by calculations of practical effects. The significance of a particular group or class fraction may thus be measured in three respects: firstly, their practical importance in the structure of social relations, i.e. what costs ensue from their interests not being served; secondly, the importance of sanctions which they may employ in resistance; thirdly, the degree to which the particular group or fraction has secured hegemony, so that debates, policies and choices are conducted in a framework of discourse conducive to their particular interests. The generation, implementation and modification of policy therefore take place in relation to the perception of real structurally-determined outcomes, and to the framework of ideology and theory which provides the frame for the construction of these perceptions.

Overall, this paper has suggested that whatever the relationship between monetarism and class interests, in Britain 'technical' monetarism developed into a full-blown 'monetarist politics' through a combination of economic dominance and temporary hegemony for financial capital. It may be that 'technical' monetarism is a more widespread and more durable variant; as yet we do not know whether the Thatcher episode will result in a long term dominance for a more diluted monetarism, or instead lead to the construction of alternative policy innovations in response to the British political and economic impasse.

REFERENCES

Brittan, S, (1977), <u>The Economic Contradictions of Democracy</u>, Temple Smith, London.

Calleo, D. and Strange, S, (1981), <u>Money in the World Economy</u>, mimeo, LSE.

Clarke, S, (1978), 'Capital, Fractions of Capital and the State', <u>Capital and Class</u>, 5.

Cobham, D, (1981), 'Comments', <u>Socialist Economic Review</u>, 1.

Confederation of British Industry, (1981), <u>The Will to Win - Britain Must Mean Business</u>, London.

Congdon, T, (1978), <u>Monetarism</u>, Centre for Policy Studies, London.

Currie, D. and Smith, R, (1981), 'Economic Trends and Crisis in the UK Economy', <u>Socialist Economic Review</u>, 1.

Cutler, A. et al, (1977, 1978), <u>Marx's Capital and Capitalism Today</u>, vols.1 and 2, RKP, London.

Fay, S. and Young, H, (1976), 'The Day the Pound Nearly Died', <u>Sunday Times</u>, May 14, 21, 28.

Gamble, A, (1980), 'Thatcher - make or break', <u>Marxism Today</u>, February.

Grant, W. and Marsh, D, (1977), <u>The CBI</u>, Hodder and Stoughton, London.

Grant, W, (1981), <u>Representing Capital: the first fifteen years of the CBI</u>, mimeo, Dept. of Politics, University of Warwick.

Hall, S, (1979), 'The Great Moving Right Show', <u>Marxism Today</u>, January.

Hall, S, (1980), 'Thatcherism - a new stage?', <u>Marxism Today</u>, February.

Hall, S. et al, (1980), <u>Culture, Media and Language</u>, Hutchinson, London.

Holloway, J. and Picciotto, S, (1978), <u>State and Capital</u>, Edward Arnold, London.

Hussein, A, (1976), 'Hilferding's Finance Capital', <u>CSE Bulletin</u>, V, 1(13).

Jessop, R, (1980), <u>State Monopoly Capitalism: a review</u>, mimeo.

Jessop, R, (1980a), 'The Transformation of the State in Postwar Britain', in R. Scase (ed), (1980), <u>The State in Western Europe</u>, Croom Helm, London.

Jessop, R, (1982), <u>The Capitalist State: Marxist Theories and Methods</u>, Martin Robertson, London.

Jones, P, (1980), 'The Thatcher Experiment', <u>Politics and Power</u>, 2.

Joseph, K, (1976), <u>Stranded on the Middle Ground?</u>, Centre for Policy Studies, London.

Keegan, V. and Pennant-Rea, R, (1979), <u>Who Runs the Economy?</u>, Temple Smith, London.

Laclau, E, (1979), <u>Politics and Ideology in Marxist Theory</u>, New Left Books, London.

Lisle-Williams, M, (1981a), <u>Continuities in the English Financial Elite</u>, mimeo, Nuffield College, Oxford.

Lisle-Williams, M, (1981b), <u>The Social and Economic Significance of British Merchant Banks</u>, mimeo, Nuffield College, Oxford.

Longstreth, F, (1979), 'The City, Industry and the State',

in C. Crouch (ed), State and Economy in Contemporary Capitalism, Croom Helm, London.

Mayer, T, (1978), The Structure of Monetarism, Norton.

Moran, M, (1980), The unmaking of policy: implementing competition and credit control, mimeo, Dept. of Government, University of Manchester.

Moran, M, (1981), Finance capital and pressure group politics, mimeo, Dept. of Government, University of Manchester.

Mouffe, C, (ed), (1980), Gramsci and Marxist Theory, Routledge Kegan and Paul, London.

Pepper, G.T. and Wood, G.E, (1976), Too Much Money...?, IEA, London.

Poulantzas, N, (1973), Political Power and Social Classes, NLB, London.

Poulantzas, N, (1978), State, Power, Socialism, NLB, London.

Scott, J, (1979), Corporations, Classes and Capitalism, Hutchinson, London.

Solomos, J, (1979), 'The Marxist Theory of the State and the Problems of Fractions', Capital and Class, 7.

Soref, M, (1980), 'The Finance Capitalists', in M. Zeitlin, (ed), Class Conflict and the State, Winthrop.

Strange, S, (1971), Sterling and British Policy, OUP, London.

Thompson, G.F, (1977), 'The relationship between the financial and industrial sectors in the UK economy', Economy and Society, 6.

Thompson, G.F, (1981), 'Monetarism and Ideology', Economy and Society, February.

Urry, J, (1981), The Anatomy of Capitalist Societies, Macmillan, London.

House of Commons, (1980-81), Third Report, Treasury and Civil Service Committee, HC 163-I, II, III.

ACKNOWLEDGEMENTS

I would like to acknowledge ideas and stimulation gained from Bob Jessop, Essex University 'Problems of Marxism' seminar, and BSA State and Economy Study Group.

9 Moral Economy and the Welfare State

ROGER A. CLOWARD AND FRANCES FOX PIVEN

INTRODUCTION

For some years now, European and American intellectuals commenting on the expansion of the welfare state have been sounding the alarm. Democracy is endangered, Brittan tells us, by the 'excessive expectations ... generated by the democratic aspects of the system' which force politicians to incite an inherently incompetent electorate to want and demand more (Brittan, 1975, p.130). Or Crozier announces that European political systems are 'overloaded' with participants and demands, with the result that the feeling spreads that democracies have become ungovernable (Crozier, 1975, p.12). Or Huntington contemplates the American situation with gloom and notes the 'dramatic renewal of the democratic spirit', the surge in participation and demands for equality that results, and warns of the 'danger of overloading the system' (Huntington, 1975, pp.59, 112). Or Daniel Bell expresses concern that '"unrestrained appetite" has moved from the economic realm to the polity, so that economic expectations have been converted into a range of entitlements' (Bell, 1978, p.23, emphasis in the original).

The message is clear. Demands for equality do not surge from the top of society. They surge from the bottom. It is the less well off among the citizenry who have become too clamorous, who want too much. Huntington even hints at the necessity of returning to an old solution when he advises that 'there are potentially desirable limits to the indefinite extension of political democracy' (Huntington, op. cit., p.115).

Intellectuals, whatever else they may be, are the bell-weathers of the actual political currents of their time. It is not surprising to find a striking congruency between erudite opinion and the several-year-long rhetorical assault on federal spending in the United States, especially in such businesss organs as Business Week, The Wall Street Journal and Fortune Magazine.(1) The business rhetoric is more concrete than the language of conservative intellectuals. It consists of the familiar argument that the American competitive position in a world economy is being undermined, and that new capital investment is being discouraged by the drag of high taxes to finance social welfare expenditures. It is, in other words, capital that is 'overloaded', and it is the poor who must be limited. Businessmen are worried. After attending a series of meetings of the Conference Board (a major corporate forum) in 1974, Silk and Vogel reported that business feels as if it's being 'engulfed by a rising tide of entitlement'. There is 'concern in the nation's boardrooms' that 'democracy in America is working too well - that is the problem' (Dickson and Noble, 1981, pp.275-6).

Predictably, the business-oriented administration in Washington that took office in 1981 immediately set about slashing billions of dollars from federal social spending, singling out especially programs that reach the poor in areas of health, housing, food stamps and income mainten- ance. Meanwhile the administration not only left most business subsidies intact, but legislated massive tax cuts for big business and upper income households, and sharply increased capital-intensive defense expenditures as well.

Our object is to discuss this assault on social expend- iture in the United States in the context of a broader discussion of the significance of social welfare in the American political economy. We do not feel prepared to discuss the parallels that do or do not obtain between the United States and England, the press conviction that Mr Reagan is our Mrs Thatcher notwithstanding. Our argument is about the United States. And in the United States, we believe, social welfare has come to play a central role in economy and polity, influencing the dynamics of the labour market, corroding traditional mechanisms for price stabil- isation, altering the distribution of income shares, and changing the configuration of political conflict. We will argue, in a word, that the concerted attack on social wel- fare is an attack on developments that have altered the basic outlines of American economic and political instit- utions. And we will conclude that the outcome of the inevitable conflict over social welfare spending is central to the future course of the American political economy.

THE EMERGENCE OF A POLITICAL ECONOMY

In the past, the Left has looked mainly to worker struggles against capital as the motor of change and progress. It is a model inherited from nineteenth century Marxism. But capitalist societies have changed. One change is the enormously enlarged role of the state in the economy generally, and not only in the distribution of income through benefit programmes. Developments deeply embedded in the dynamics of the capitalist economy itself, ultimately generated pressure on the state for steadily increasing economic intervention. This intervention in turn has led to the emergence of new institutional relations between state and society, and new ideas about the role of the state in society which, taken together, suggest that the arena for group and class conflict has shifted from the workplace to the state. Moreover, these developments also suggest the possibility that the institutional and ideological consequences of state intervention in the economy may render the state increasingly vulnerable to popular demands.

To appreciate this possibility, we need both to consider the range of steadily expanding economic interventions by government, which go far beyond the funding of benefit programmes, and to consider how that expansion came about. The Depression of the 1930s is a good place to begin, for it signalled, both in the United States and in Western Europe, the collapse of the 'unregulated free market' (Polanyi, 1957). Of course, the unregulated free market never existed, even in the United States where the development of capitalism was unfettered by a pre-existing central state. From its mercantile beginnings in the post-revolutionary period, American capital depended crucially on the legal and military support of the state, on laws governing contracts and currency, and on a standing army and navy to protect land speculators and shipping interests. In the nineteenth century, an emerging industrial capitalism turned to government for a variety of supports for investment and demand: exemplified on the municipal level by utility contracts, interest-free capital and traction franchises, and on the national level, by war contracts and free land for railroad rights-of-way. And government on all levels provided the legal authority and military force which enabled employers to resist unionisation. Still, these arrangements, crucial though they were, did not loom so large in relation to the much larger terrain in which the economy seemed to operate unfettered.

The Depression altered that pattern. Economic collapse stimulated insistent demands from industrial, financial, commercial and agricultural interest groups for government subsidies and protectionism, and government policies to raise aggregate demand. The Reconstruction Finance Corporation under Hoover made capital available in the form of federal loans; the New Deal's National Industrial Recovery Act lent government authority to industry-wide compacts to fix production levels and prices; and public works programmes funded by the federal government were turned to building the highways, airports and bridges that business and industry wanted. A little later, in 1934, the Securities and Exchange Commission was established to stabilise financial markets. Sweeping tariffs were enacted to protect American manufacturers. And the Interest Oil and Gas Compact 'fixed prices for a generation' in the high-technology industries (Ferguson and Rogers, 1979).

But the interventions of government during the Depression were not solely a reflection of the demands of capital. During this period, the framework of the benefit programmes was created, most importantly through the passage of the Social Security Act of 1935 which established the national pension programme (Old Age Survivors and Dependants

Insurance), the unemployment insurance programme, and the categorical public assistance programmes. In much of Western Europe, similar programmes had existed since the nineteenth century. But in the United States, with its vigorous laissez-faire ideology, the legislation was a major innovation, anticipated only by the short-lived Federal Emergency Relief Act of 1933 (FERA). And both the FERA and the Social Security Act were forced by popular insurgency, by the mass protests which followed the economic collapse of 1929, a collapse which eventually left one-third of the workforce unemployed, and resulted in sharp wage cuts and speed-ups for those still working. One expression of popular discontent was a national protest movement among the unemployed, on a scale heretofore unknown in American history, perhaps because the scale, penetration and transparency of the economic disaster represented by the Great Depression were greater than ever before in American history. Another expression of popular discontent was the rise of a strike movement among industrial workers. And still another was the protest among the aged known as the Townsend Movement. As Roosevelt confronted the 1936 election, a combination of economic uncertainty, popular protest, and the rise of presidential contenders such as Huey Long, led him to put forward the several measures included in the Social Security Act.

Historically, wars have always been the occasion for state expansion into the economy and society, and the Second World War was no exception. It was even more significant that federal intervention continued after the war, mainly in the form of policies to subsidise investment and maintain aggregate demand. The instruments of political economy took form in subsidies to the construction industry, military spending. highway grants and, somewhat later, investment tax credits. Wolfe and Gold argue that this pattern reflected a distorted form of Keynesian economic management, and attribute this distortion to the political alliance that supported government intervention - an alliance between liberal Keynesians in government and business groups like the Committee for Economic Development. That coalition, they argue, was based on an agreement that limited government's role to the management of aggregate demand, explicitly barring more direct intervention in economic planning. Moreover, capitalists obtained much more from this alliance than government measures to stimulate domestic economic growth, measures which benefited both state and capital. They also obtained tax and tariff policies favourable to American overseas investors, and were able to use measures such as the Bretton Woods Agreement and the International Monetary Fund to facilitate overseas expansion, all of which promoted the internationalisation of American capital and ultimately destabilised the domestic economy, which was not to the ultimate benefit of the state.(2)

Such perverse consequences notwithstanding, the alliance reflected new and profound interdependencies between government and economic interests. On the one side, as the

Depression had starkly revealed, government was politically dependent on economic stability and growth, and dependent on stability and growth for its revenues as well. On the other side, capital had become increasingly dependent on the state as a source of investment and demand subsidies, and as a source of mechanisms to promote economic stabilisation.(3)

Over time, government also continued to be subject of popular demands. True, during the relative prosperity of the 1940s and 1950s, the benefit programmes established in the Depression remained relatively modest. In the absence of popular insurgency, very few people were admitted to the new categorical welfare programmes that had replaced the Federal Emergency Relief programme of the early years of the Depression, and Social Security payments kept the old who received them very poor. That began to change in the mid-1960s, in the wake of the black movement in the northern cities which was also very much a poverty movement. Its participants were the urban poor, and its demands were for jobs, income and housing. One response by Democratic administrations, which were extremely vulnerable to rising levels of conflict and alienation among blacks and whites in the urban strongholds of the party, was to launch the battery of 'Great Society' legislation. The resulting programmes provided services, information about entitlements, and some organising resources to the ghettos; they also provided a degree of legitimation of the grievances of the black poor. These resources combined with the smouldering anger of the ghetto to create enough political pressure to force more benefits from existing income-maintenance programmes and, at the same time, a variety of new programmes were enacted. In sum, the framework of benefit programmes created by popular insurgency in the 1930s was substantially elaborated by the insurgency of the 1960s.

THE MAGNITUDE OF THE AMERICAN SOCIAL WELFARE STATE

The welfare state, in other words, developed much later in the United States than in Western Europe, but it then expanded rapidly. The foundations were laid in 1935 with the enactment of Social Security pensions, unemployment insurance, and welfare payments for the blind, dependent children, and those of the aged poor not eligible for Social Security. Shortly afterwards, the federal programme for public housing was enacted. In 1951, the permanently and totally disabled were also granted aid. These programmes made up the initial income maintenance framework of the American welfare state.

Although the framework was built in the 1930s, the great expansion and elaboration of income-maintenance programmes did not occur until the 1960s and 1970s. From 1960 to the early 1970s, the number of people on the Aid to Families with Dependent Children (AFDC) rolls quadrupled. The food stamp programme and other programmes for nutritional

supplementation were enacted in these years; so was subsidised health care for the aged (Medicare) and for both
welfare recipients and the working poor (Medicaid); housing
subsidies, both for public housing and for rent supplementation, were also greatly enlarged. In 1973, the public
welfare categorical assistance programmes for the aged and
disabled (but not for dependent children and their mothers)
were absorbed into a few federal programmes called
Supplemental Security Income (SSI), and a sharp rise in the
disability rolls followed. Other disability programmes also
grew. Major new programmes were also enacted in the 1970s.
The Comprehensive Employment and Training Act (CETA) provided training and thousands of public service jobs for the
unemployed. The Trade Adjustment Assistance Act made payments available to workers displaced from their jobs by
foreign competition. And the Emergency Fuel Assistance Act
provided funds for low-income families who could not pay
rising fuel bills.

Federal expenditure in support of individual and family
incomes was projected by the out-going Carter administration
to reach ⊄25 billion in the fiscal year 1982, including
⊄25 billion in matching funds contributed by states and
localities for Medicaid and AFDC. These projected expenditures represented about 11.3 per cent of the ⊄3.3 trillion
1982 estimated Gross National Product (note that these
figures refer to income-maintenance expenditures, health
care, and housing, but do not include services such as
education).

Although American income-maintenance expenditure as a
percentage of GNP is only slightly less than the levels
prevailing in European social welfare states, the distribution of these benefits is quite different. American programmes are tilted more toward the bottom of the income
scale. A number of our programmes - such as unemployment
insurance, CETA, food stamps, AFDC, SSI and Medicaid - are
'means tested' or 'unemployment tested'. At the same time,
the United States has had higher levels of both unemployment and low-wage jobs, with the result that a larger flow
of funds is triggered through these means-tested programmes.
However, even Social Security pensions, though not means-
tested, are sharply redistributional, for half of the money
transferred goes to people who would otherwise fall below
the poverty line. Looked at another way, almost half of the
aggregate income of the bottom fifth of the population is
derived from social welfare benefits. The poorest people in
the country are now as much dependent on government for
their subsistence as they are dependent on the labour
market.

In fact, it is just this distributional tilt in the
American programmes that has attracted the Reagan budget
axe. The campaign promise to maintain a 'safety net for
needy Americans' has turned out to mean in practice that
the health and old age insurance programmes that are not
'means-tested' and 'unemployment-tested' will be left

intact, as well as a variety of veterans benefits. And so the cuts are falling mainly on the programmes directed to the poor and unemployed, including unemployment insurance, public service employment, Medicaid, public welfare, and the food stamp programme. Approximately $70 billion, or 20 per cent, will be taken from these particular programmes between 1982 and 1984, and at the time of writing (November 1981), the Reagan administration is pressing strenuously for still further reductions in the income-maintenance programmes. We will have more to say about the meaning of these cuts presently.

On the face of it, one would think this explosion of expenditure significant if only because it means that a significant portion of the total national income is being channelled through the public sector. More than that, important and well-organised business interests have declared this development to be significant to them by the intensity with which they have attacked social spending, an attack now reflected in the Reagan cuts. But analysts on the American Left have not paid much heed to this rapid and precipitous development, nor thought it very important when they have paid heed. Indeed, the opinion still seems to prevail among many that American social welfare expenditure consists in puny and largely symbolic concessions to the protestors of the 1960s, and in any case it is not thought that the concessions will be permanent, thus adding a fashionable despair with popular struggles to the despair of a particular systemic analysis.

Such judgements reflect a certain obliviousness to actual developments. The benefit programmes are anything but insignificant; they are now a factor of indisputable importance, for better or for worse, in the American political economy. Nor is it true that the concessions won in the 1960s did not last. To be sure, the AFDC rolls stopped expanding in the early 1970s, and benefit levels lagged behind inflation; but the Medicaid rolls continued to rise, the food stamp rolls ballooned after liberalising amendments in 1971, Social Security benefits climbed more quickly in the 1970s (by about 4 per cent a year in real terms), and a series of direct job creation programmes was legislated. It is time to take these developments more seriously. (4)

Even the serious appraisals made by left analysts have not led to an understanding of the central role played by welfare state programmes in strengthening the bargaining power of working people. The broad theme in neo-Marxist analysis is that social welfare programmes are 'functional' for capitalism (Miller, Devey and Devey). Some analysts see social welfare programmes as an instrument of economic stabilisation in advanced capitalist societies: the programmes serve to stimulate aggregate demand and to organise such essential requirements as transportation and housing, which can no longer, in a concentrated and complex economy, be left to the anarchy of the private market (Castells,

1977). Social welfare programmes, in other words, are dictated by the imperatives of the capitalist mode of production.

Other left critics argue that the welfare state arose in response to the imperatives of social control in capitalist society, to the need to pacify and depoliticise insurgent or potentially insurgent groups. (5) The yielding of social welfare programmes is thus seen as part of the strategy by which the ruling class rules, a strategy through which working people are induced to cash in their political capacities and political intelligence for a pittance in material benefits. With the expansion of these programmes, the body politic presumably grows more listless and enfeebled. And as popular politics weakens, the state bureaucracies - imagined as monoliths of far-seeing and cunning intelligence - rule America in collusion with their business allies (Wolin, 1981). This, in brief, is the left view of the corporate liberal state.

James O'Connor brought these diverse critiques together in a coherent and influential functionalist argument. He proposes (O'Connor, 1973) that social welfare programmes can be explained in terms of the basic imperatives that mould the activities of the state in a capitalist society. These imperatives, or 'functions', consist of the need to ensure profitability or 'accumulation' and the need to maintain sufficient social harmony to 'legitimate' a class society and a class state. Social welfare programmes presumably contribute to profitability by lowering the costs to employers of maintaining a healthy and skilled labour force. Without these programmes, employers would either have to pay for health and education services directly, or raise wages to permit workers to purchase them. Social welfare programmes also contribute to the legitimation function by quieting discontent, particularly the discontent generated by processes of economic concentration which create surplus or unemployed labour.

However, O'Connor's model differs from other left views because it is not ultimately functionalist in the sense of characterising a system in equilibrium. Rather, he points to the multiple crisis tendencies generated by the transposition of conflicts between labour and capital to the state sector, and particularly the fiscal crisis that results as state expenditures increase more rapidly than the revenues to finance them. In a similar vein, Gough claims that the scale of state expenditure on social welfare has become 'a fetter on the process of capital accumulation ... If capitalism more and more engenders a welfare state, it is also proving difficult for capitalism to cope with the problem of financing the requisite expenditures.' (Gough, 1979, p.14)

These qualifications aside, the major thrust of left views has been that welfare state programmes exist because their economic or their political effects are functional for

220

capitalism. We consider that this sort of perspective may no longer serve to account for the role of social welfare in the American political economy. Even if one thinks these programmes were originally inaugurated in order to 'regulate the poor', their effects have become perverse in the sense that as social welfare benefits expanded, their longer-run consequence in the labour market may not have been to regulate the poor, but to empower them.

LABOUR MARKETS, PRICE STABILITY AND INCOME SHARES

The connection between the social programmes and the labour market is indirect, but not complicated. To see the connection, it is necessary to consider the relationship between unemployment and worker bargaining power. Large numbers of unemployed exert a downward pressure on wages because people searching for work are forced to underbid the wages of those still working. A mass of unemployed also undercuts the ability of workers to make other workplace demands, since workers are less militant when there is a long line of job applicants outside the factory gates. Because the unemployed exert a downward pressure on wages and other labour costs, the existence of a large pool of unemployed tends to maintain and enlarge profits. (This effect is moderated by union contracts at one end of the wage scale and by minimum wage laws at the other end, but it is not eliminated.) By contrast, when the unemployed are absorbed and labour markets tighten, wage and workplace demands push against profits, as some analysts say happened in the late 1960s at the climax of the long post World War II boom (DuBoff, 1977).

The relationship between unemployment and wage levels was described by Marx when he claimed that the unemployed constitute an 'industrial reserve army of labour' used by capitalists to weaken and divide the proletariat. But most American analysts scoffed at the notion that large scale unemployment represented an advantage for capital, much less that this advantage was sometimes deliberately contrived. Instead, the fact that the United States has had consistently higher rates of unemployment than other western industrial countries, except during wartime, was attributed by more conservative analysts to 'frictional' unemployment, that is, to the exceptional mobility of the American workforce as people moved from job to job to take advantage of opportunities to improve their circumstances. Unemployment, in short, was taken to be a symptom of prosperity. High unemployment rates in the United States were also attributed to the composition of the labour force:

> The unemployed are an everchanging mass, on a kind of shuttle, moving and waiting, never fitting comfortably in any job, yet usually able to find another. This turbulence tracks back to shifts in the composition of the civilian labour force... The number of adult white men, who have a low rate of unemployment, has been

dwindling in relation to the total force. But teenagers, blacks, and women, who have high rates, have been joining in record numbers; surprisingly, they now make up half its total. (Guzzardi, quoted in Schlozman and Verba, 1979, p.31)

To make the point more clearly, the argument posits that prosperity enables many workers to circulate more freely from job to job as a means of improving their wages and working conditions. (7) Prosperity also brings to the labour market large numbers of people who presumably do not seriously need or want work (teenagers, women, blacks), and their consequent job instability also contributes to an artificial appearance of high unemployment. (8) Unemployment, in short, is caused by the unemployed themselves, an argument developed in purest form by Milton Friedman, who put forward the thesis that unemployment always settles at its 'natural' rate over the long term.

Liberal analysts following Keynes developed a very different interpretation of unemployment. They fastened on overall levels of economic activity as the cause of joblessness. Unemployment was seen as the consequence of sluggish business and consumer demand. Tighter labour markets in turn were the result of swelling business and consumer demand. The significance of this perspective, which acquired considerable legitimacy in the post World War II period, is that it defined unemployment levels as susceptible to government policy, for unemployment could be lowered by policies to stimulate aggregate demand.

But while high levels of aggregate demand are associated with lower unemployment rates, they are also associated with rising wage and price levels. And the very same formulation that led economists to think that unemployment levels could be controlled by government intervention to stimulate the economy also led them to think inflation could be controlled by government intervention to reduce aggregate demand. In other words, unemployment and inflation came to be seen as trade-offs, for the one could only be controlled at the expense of the other. This formulation was embodied in the well known Phillips curve (Phillips, 1958), which showed a correlation between levels of unemployment and wage levels. When unemployment falls, wages rise; when unemployment rises, wages fall. The Phillips curve was thus consistent with Marx's thesis regarding the industrial reserve army of labour, for it suggested that high levels of unemployment weaken the bargaining power of workers. However, economists did not define the trade-off between unemployment and wages as a reflection of conflicts over the distribution of wealth; they tended instead to see it as describing a relationship existing in nature, in economic nature.

Economists were even sometimes saddened by this 'natural' economic relationship. 'No one is happy with the prospect of unemployment', we are told by Fiedler (a former Assistant Secretary of the Treasury for Economic Policy in the Ford

222

administration), 'but in order to regain control over inflation, there is no other way ...' (Fiedler, 1979, p.175) Moreover the magnitude of unemployment must be considerable if economic laws are to do their work. Thus Fabricant (senior staff member of the Bureau of Economic Research): 'I do not mean to belittle the burden of unemployment, either on those who suffer it or on the consciences of the rest of us ...' Nevertheless, 'only when the rate of unemployment threatens to rise to intolerable levels, will it be time to consider (lowering it). This is not yet the prospect, in my view'. (Fabricant, 1975, p.165)

This conception of an unemployment-inflation trade-off was incorporated as an instrument of American public policy in the years after the Great Depression. Government planners tried to moderate the extremes of the business cycle with fiscal and monetary policies which regulated aggregate demand. Instead of business cycles that careened from trough to peak to trough again, relatively moderate recessions occurred every few years which increased unemployment without pushing it to staggering levels. In turn, higher unemployment rates produced lower wage and price levels. Government interventions to promote intervals of something less than depression levels of unemployment thus became major instruments of economic stabilisation, and the publication of the Phillips curve lent this strategy the legitimisation of science.

But these efforts at macro-economic stabilisation were not as neutral as they seemed. In the trade-off between unemployment and price inflation, American policy makers consistently elected to keep unemployment higher and price levels lower than other western countries. (9) This tilt in the trade-off benefited capital and weakened wage earners. To be sure, when the relationships underlying the trade-off are scrutinised, unemployment and price inflation can both be seen as strategies, although alternative ones, by which capital tries to maintain and enlarge profit shares, since price inflation is a way of attempting to erode wage increases won in tight labour markets. From the perspective of capital, however, inflation is the less successful strategy. Workers in the more unionised and less competitive sectors of the economy can keep pace with price increases, with the consequence that large numbers of working people gain relatively greater shares as the business cycle sweeps upward and the numbers of unemployed contract. Cost of living escalator clauses in union contracts (some of which also cover pensions) institutionalise this power, reducing the effectiveness of inflation as a strategy to maintain or enlarge profit shares. The indexing of Social Security benefits has also resulted in higher employer costs in the face of rising prices. Under these circumstances, price inflation is relatively less effective in eroding the wage and benefit gains won in tight labour markets.

Douglas Hibbs presents evidence which is persuasive in this regard. He reviews a series of studies which examine the distribution of income in western countries whose macro-economic policies emphasise holding down unemployment and letting inflation rise, compared with countries whose policies emphasise holding down inflation and letting unemployment rise. The evidence, he concludes, strongly indicates that policies of lower unemployment and higher inflation lead to substantial improvements in the economic well-being of the poor and, 'more generally, exert powerful equalising effects on the distribution of personal income'. Moreover, as one would expect, these redistributional effects follow the business cycle: shares of the national income going to business increase steadily after a trough in business activity and reach their peak about midway in the upward sweep of the cycle; thereafter the business share drops off markedly (Hibbs, 1977, pp.1468-9). These findings suggest that inflation does not entirely offset the gains labour is able to make when unemployment levels are low.

Furthermore, price inflation is an insecure and cumbersome solution to the profit squeeze produced by tight labour markets and rising wage levels in other ways. It greatly complicates corporate dealings with suppliers and customers, and interferes with long-term corporate investment and planning, because of the uncertainties it generates. Domestic inflation is also disadvantageous in marketing goods in a world economy. For all of these reasons, the better strategy to maintain profits is to drive labour costs down, and for that unemployment is the classic means. And it was just this strategy which was reflected in American post-war economic policy.

For two decades following World War II, all seemed well. The relationship embodied in the Phillips curve varied to order, as Haveman (1977) shows for the period from 1952-68, for cyclical increases in unemployment rates were matched by the expected fall-off in the rate of wage and price increases. (10) Then, toward the end of the 1960s, the relationship began to erode as prices spiralled upward despite high levels of unemployment. By the early 1970s, the relationship between unemployment and wage and price levels had disappeared. Barry Bosworth, head of Carter's Council on Wage and Price Stability in 1977-79, comments on this development when he says that an unemployment rate of 6 per cent failed to have an effect on inflation in the recession of 1969-71:

> Economists, at first, viewed the problem as one of lags in the response of prices and wage rates; they recommended patience and a continuation of restrictive policies. By the beginning of 1971, however, <u>wage rate increases had actually accelerated slightly despite the high unemployment</u>; and, once excess inventories had been disposed of, the rate of price increases also picked up. (Bosworth, 1980, pp.60-1, our emphasis)

Government economic stabilisation policies failed, in short, because price and wage levels could no longer be moderated by unemployment levels.

The spiralling of prices in the later 1960s and the 1970s had a variety of sources. An early stimulus was the spurt in aggregate demand generated by high military spending without offsetting tax increases during the Vietnam War. Another inflationary stimulus was the surge in imported energy prices followed by similar increases in domestic energy prices which pervaded an economy organised around low cost fuel consumption. Increasing speculation, declining rates of investment in productive capacity and monopoly pricing practices were still other factors which contributed to unprecedented inflation. Considering the magnitude of these inflationary forces, it is hardly surprising that price levels remained immune to the depressing effects of rising unemployment.

The surprise is that wage levels also remained immune. Given the history of business cycles, one would have expected that even in the context of an inflationary environment produced by exceptional forces, high levels of unemployment would at least have depressed wage demands, thus reducing this component of prices. And government planners strove to produce just that effect. Throughout the 1970s, unemployment rose and remained at the highest levels since the 1930s. But despite the weakening of the labour market, wages did not fall. Something had happened to disrupt the traditional relationship between unemployment and wage levels, between the supply of labour and the power of labour. Or, in another idiom, the reserve army of labour was no longer performing its historic function.

With these various points made, we come now to the bearing of the income-maintenance programmes on the bargaining power of workers in the labour market. The timing of the disruption of the unemployment/wage level trade-off coincided with the great expansion of income-maintenance benefits in the late 1960s and the 1970s, and that is suggestive. What it suggests is that welfare state benefits support wage levels despite high unemployment. The reason is not hard to see. If the desperation of the unemployed is moderated by the availability of various benefits, they will be less quick to take any job on any terms. (11) In other words, an industrial reserve army of labour with unemployment benefits and food stamps is a less effective instrument with which to deflate wage and workplace demands.

Many economists have recognised this. They now attribute the breakdown in the relationship between unemployment levels and wage levels to the great expansion of the income-maintenance programmes. As Haveman recently put it, the unemployed can now 'prolong job search ..., refuse to accept work except at higher offered wages or cease active labour market participation' (op. cit, p.46). Bosworth concurs:

> (Traditional policies to restrain inflation) are guided by the need to create a pool of unemployed sufficient for the threat of lost sales or jobs to

225

exert an adequate restraint on wages and prices.
Economists have been engaged in long technical debate
over the required size of the pool if price stability
is to be maintained. But if the unemployed refuse to
accept such a role, if they press for compensation
and will be satisfied only when there is no economic
penalty for not working, they will pose no threat to
the employed. (op.cit, pp.68-70)

And Fiedler reaches the same conclusion:

A change has taken place in the unemployment-inflation
trade-off since the mid 1950s. (One reason) is the
unemployed of today are subject to less economic pain
than used to be the case, because of the development
of more generous income-maintenance programmes ...
Consequently, most people who lose their jobs today
are under less pressure to accept the first offer they
get regardless of the pay and working conditions.
(op.cit, p.117)

This conclusion is exclusively about wage levels, which
are readily measured. But the effect of the income-
maintenance programmes in reducing economic insecurity and
increasing the power of workers is not restricted to wage
levels. Because insecurity makes workers vulnerable, it also
saps their strength to make other demands in the workplace.
When people fear for their subsistence, they accept onerous
and dangerous working conditions. They work harder, and
they work longer. They more readily submit to humiliation,
to orders and to discipline. An insecure labour force is
thus a more productive labour force and a cheaper one,
quite apart from wage levels. (The new regulations denying
food stamps to striking workers, and to entire welfare
families when a working member goes on strike, seem
intended to have exactly this effect.) Conversely, a labour
force which is made more secure by the possibility of
alternative means of subsistence is less docile, less
productive, and more costly.

In summary, there is a growing agreement that the income-
maintenance programmes have weakened capital's capacity to
depress wages and increase exploitation by means of economic insecurity, especially by means of manipulating the
relative numbers of people searching for work. In effect,
the income maintenance programmes of the welfare state have
altered the terms of the struggle between capital and
labour. As a result, unemployment has lost some of its
terrors - both for the unemployed and for those still
working. Despite unemployment rates in the 1970s ranging
between 6 and 10 per cent (not including one million
'discouraged' workers), there was no significant downward
pressure on wage levels. Economists now generally agree
that a reduction in the inflation rate by a single percentage point requires an increase in unemployment of at least
a million individuals for a two-year period. Because of the
social programmes, in short, the reserve army is no longer
quite so ready to be called up in defense of profits.

The Reagan administration's effort to slash the programmes that are intruding on the operation of the reserve army of labour may not, however, be so easy. The expansion of social welfare is itself evidence that the political leverage of American workers has enlarged. More than that, the broader process of state intervention in the economy of which social welfare programmes are only a part may be contributing to a widespread politicisation of economic issues - to the spread of beliefs in the political right to economic well-being. These beliefs are themselves at least a precondition of empowerment, and thus they add to the political leverage that the expansion of social welfare programmes signifies. We turn briefly, then, to a discussion of what might be called the emerging 'moral economy of the welfare state'.

THE NEW MORAL ECONOMY

If the constellation of the American political economy has been transformed as a consequence of developments outlined earlier, that transformation has not gone unnoticed by the American population. New institutional conditions ultimately give rise to new interpretations, to new understandings of social conditions and of what can be done about them. There is increasing evidence that laissez-faire ideology has eroded, Reagan's election notwithstanding, and that new ideas linking economic welfare to political rights are now deeply imprinted.

The expanded economic role of the state has been experienced by people as an institutional transformation. To be sure, government at all levels has always performed important functions for the American economy, beginning with its role in establishing and maintaining the legal framework of private and corporate property. But much has changed to make the role of government in the economy far more apparent. The scale of federal activity is vastly larger: as a percentage of the GNP, federal expenditure stood at 2.8 per cent in 1929; currently, all governmental expenditure, including state and local expenditure (which are much influenced by federal grants-in-aid), constitute about 40 per cent of the Nominal Net National Product (a measure roughly equivalent to GNP; cf. Reynolds and Smolensky, 1977, p.420).

If the role of the state has vastly enlarged, it is also more obvious for being regularly acknowledged. The role of government in maintaining economic growth and stability is continually emphasised, with the consequence that government activity is not only vastly larger, but more transparent than ever before. Every presidential campaign since 1932 has featured claims and counterclaims, promises and counter-promises, intended to appease popular economic discontents. Unemployment has been a key issue, a circumstance that has led political leaders to attempt to coordinate the business cycle with the election cycle: 'Unemployment levels twelve to eighteen months before presidential elections have exceeded unemployment levels at election time in six of the eight presidential elections' between 1948 and 1976 (Tufte, 1978, p.19). In the 1960s and 1970s, economic discrimination against minorities and women emerged as a source of contention, and inflation has recently been added to the litany of grievances.

Nor, as we have been at pains to point out, have presidents and legislatures been able to escape the implications of campaign rhetoric once in office. Over the course of the past half-century, programmes to deal with popular economic grievances have been initiated and then expanded. When possible, political leaders also coordinate the expansion of benefits with the election cycle: 'In four of the last seven election years, governmental transfer payments have reached their yearly peak in October or November' (ibid, p.39). And, in recent years, successive administrations have faltered and stumbled, paralysed by the choices between the tight money/high unemployment macroeconomic policies demanded by sectors of business and industry, and the expansionist policies demanded by working people.

This new vulnerability of the state may account for the continued expansion of the benefit programmes in the 1970s. If in 1946 the promises of the Employment Act of that year served the electoral political purposes of the national administration, in the 1970s rhetoric alone seemed insufficient. Although the national administration in its role as economic regulator created the recession of 1973-4, it also seemed to think it necessary to moderate the impact of this policy with the precipitous expansion of unemployment benefits. The Congress rapidly extended the period for which the jobless were eligible for benefits, and local unemployment insurance offices were kept open at night and on weekends. In 1974, without any fanfare, some $20 billion was funneled through the programme, up from 6.8 billion in 1972. If all of this happened without any visible protest by the unemployed, it nevertheless seems reasonable to think it reflected the vulnerability of government to the unemployed. Similarly, the steady increase in the flow of transfer payments throughout the 1970s may also reveal the vulnerability of government to the large numbers of citizens who increasingly view the state as responsible for their economic condition.

It is a further measure of the extent to which economic issues have become politicised that corporate mobilisations must now be based on rhetoric directed mainly to popular economic grievances. Big business has no votes; it cannot win elections by mobilising in its own name or in its own interests, and it never could. Corporate victories at the polls in the past were won by mobilising people around nationalism, nativism, racism, regionalism, and with the aid of the political machines. These themes still matter. But they are now overshadowed by straightforward economic grievances which must be addressed directly. That was certainly the case in the election of 1980: the state of the economy, which dominated the campaign debates, was not discussed from the business perspective of profits, but from the perspective of the problems of unemployment and inflation, which ordinary people perceive.

These public performances both reflect changing beliefs about the role of the state in economic life, and nurture these new beliefs by continually confirming them. As a consequence, the deeply imprinted understanding that characterised popular American thought at the time of the Great Depression - that economic well-being is determined by market forces which sort out and reward the talented and industrious but which are themselves beyond the reach of human intervention except at penalty of economic disaster - have slowly been fading. Thus one of the findings of the studies of the unemployed during the Depression was that most of the jobless felt they were somehow at fault, the scale of the calamity notwithstanding. Sherwood Anderson summed it up simply: 'There is in the average American a profound humbleness. People seem to blame themselves.' (in Garraty, 1978, p.181) However, in a survey conducted in 1976, Schlozman and Verba found that only 36 per cent of the unemployed, and only 46 per cent of the employed, believed that the jobless could find work if they looked hard enough. In follow-up interviews, they found:

> little evidence that people blame themselves for their unemployed state. Their descriptions of the circum-stances of job loss are quite matter-of-fact: the plant closed, business was slow; I didn't get along with my boss; I wanted to try something else; we lost a govern-ment contract. Sometimes the reports are tinged with bitterness ... but the unemployed do not appear to hold themselves at fault (op.cit, p.193).

This finding makes sense. It is what Garraty calls the internalisation of the Keynesian value system: 'If, in order to cool an overheated economy a government may deliberately cause workers to lose their jobs - and all governments claim and occasionally exercise this right, which is an essential weapon in the Keynesian arsenal - then those who lose their jobs are unlikely to feel either personally in-adequate or the helpless victims of an inscrutable fate.' (op.cit, p.251) But that the unemployed no longer feel so personally responsible is of itself important, for part of the power of market ideology was that it turned the victims of economic hardships against themselves, and by doing so helped to make them politically impotent.

It is just as significant that attitudes are changing toward government, and specifically toward government economic policies. In effect, people recognise government's enlarged economic role and increasingly charge government with responsibilities commensurate with that role. Thus a Harris poll in the summer of 1980 reported that people believe, by majorities of 69 to 27 per cent, that the President can make a real difference in avoiding inflation (ABC-Harris Survey II, 88 BSN 0163-4846 July 21, 1980). (12)

The market, with its mysterious and autonomous laws, has receded. In its place there are political leaders who are causing things to be the way they are. And if it is political leaders who are responsible, then political rights bear on economic well-being.

Viewed from the perspective of developed ideology, these may seem to be disarrayed opinions. After all, Americans have not changed their views about capitalism and socialism, they do not identify with 'the working class', demonstrate 'class consciousness' or profess a blueprint for future reconstruction. What they are expressing, however, is their recognition of the large role of the state in the economy and the large responsibility of the state in determining their economic well-being. But whether or not these beliefs satisfy one's particular criteria for a developed political ideology, they represent a profound transformation in popular understandings of the nature of the society we live in.

THE 'CRISIS' OF DEMOCRACY

There has been a great deal written of late about the contradictions or tensions within the democratic and capitalist state. For all of the new language and the form-idable new schemes, the issue was never more simply or eloquently put than at Putney, some three hundred years ago when democracy was only a vision, but a vision that had moved the men and women of England to revolution. How can it be, the Levellers asked, that the poor of England, who have fought the civil war, will be denied a say in govern-ment? The answer echoes through the ages: if the poor have a say in government, what safeguard is there then for property? Or, as the historian J.A. Froude warned in the aftermath of the Third Reform Bill some two hundred years later:

> It is one man one vote. And as the poor and the ignorant are the majority, I think it is perfectly certain - and it is only consistent with all one has ever heard or read of human nature - that those who have the power will use it to bring about what they consider to be a more equitable distribution of the good things of this world. (Quoted in Brittan, op.cit, p.146)

It was just this contradiction which Marx identified when he said that political democracy, which puts the proletar-iat, peasantry and petty bourgeoisie in possession of political power through universal suffrage, therefore jeopardises the foundations of bourgeois society.

As it turned out, capitalist democracies found ways to solve this fundamental problem, at least for a very long time. In the United States, where the franchise was ex-tended to white working class men very early (in most states in the 1820s), it was solved in part by the development of a

230

legal structure, enshrined in the Constitution and engraved
in judicial decisions, that prohibited many forms of state
intervention in the economy. It was as if the American
state-builders had learned from Schumpeter the lessons of
the importance of limiting the range of democratic decision-
making (Schumpeter, 1975, p.291). Of course, from the
beginning, and increasingly as industrial capitalism developed, the state did provide crucial services for the
capitalist economy. But as if following Schumpeter again,
these spheres of state activity were characteristically
ensconced in highly bureaucratic agencies insulated from
democratic processes, a form of structural differentiation
that became more pronounced as the state's role in the
economy expanded (Friedland, Piven and Alford, 1977).
Consistent with these structural arrangements were the main
precepts of a _laissez-faire_ political culture which argued
that politics and economics were necessarily separate
spheres, separate not as a consequence of the actions of
men and women who had shaped those institutional arrangements, but separate in nature. And people were more per-
suaded that this was so, that there was a kind of natural
law that had cleaved politics from economics, because a body
of belief known as classical economics, purporting to be a
science of human nature, said it was so.

Now the structural defenses against the long-standing
threat of democratic politics are collapsing, undermined by
the development of pervasive new linkages between state
and economy. One set of linkages is with capital, and has
resulted in the federal role in maintaining aggregate
demand, in the proliferation of federal subsidies to major
industries, and in federal measures which smooth the way
for overseas investment. The benefit programmes represent
another set of linkages, not with capital, but with the
working class. Each set of relationships can be broadly
understood as a reflection of the interdependence of the
state and the larger society as that took form at a particular historical juncture. Relations with capital reflect
the state's own need for a stable and growing economy, both
to maintain and enlarge its own revenue sources, and to
placate powerful economic interest groups. Relations with
working and poor people through the benefit programmes
reflect not only the demands of these groups, but reflect
another form of state dependence on the larger society. The
programmes came into being and were expanded at moments when
the legitimacy of the state was threatened by mass protest,
not merely in some abstract sense, but in the specific sense
that mass protest helped to throw electoral majorities into
jeopardy.

Once established, moreover, these programmes institutionalise the interdependence of state and society, and even
enlarge it. We recognise this process easily when we think
about relations between government and capital. The familiar
notion of the iron triangle, for example, refers to the
welding together in a pattern of mutual exchange and interdependence of economic interest groups, the public

bureaucracies to which they come to be oriented, and the specific legislative committees which exercise oversight over these bureaucracies and which are susceptible to influence by the economic interest groups. But this pattern of institutionalised interdependence may not, as we have usually thought, be restricted to the relations between government and capital. The benefit programmes may represent an analogous process through which government and larger groups in the population come to be welded together in a pattern of political interdependence. Once established, the benefit programmes generate legal and political rights for the population at risk, and an agency structure that is both mandated to implement those rights and more or less accessible to the population at risk. The result is not the articulated and well-organised interest groups that characterise capital, but the result nevertheless may be to articulate and focus popular demands, while creating state structures that are vulnerable to them. The result, in short, may be the re-emergence in contemporary forms of the old contradiction between the democratic and the capitalist state.

In sum, a century and a half after the achievement of formal democratic rights, the state has finally become the main arena of class conflict. Working people who once looked mainly to the marketplace as the sphere for action on their economic grievances and aspirations now look mainly to government and politics. The development confronts big business with a crisis of power whose dimensions are comparable to the earlier struggle by capital to win control of the state from an alliance of monarchy and landed classes. From this perspective, the Reagan administration's efforts to reverse the policies through which people were finally able to compel the state to protect them in marketplace relations is the surface manifestation of an evolving conflict of profound importance. The deeper expression of this conflict will take form over the ideological and structural developments which now make the state vulnerable to popular influence. Unless industry is able to restore the vitality of old doctrines, and more important, unless it is able to resurrect the institutional arrangements which once helped sustain those doctrines, its current successes in dismantling or reducing the array of twentieth century social programmes will be short-lived. Worsening economic conditions will once again bring to power national administrations committed to acting upon popular economic grievances by rebuilding the welfare state, and by giving it even greater power. These are, of course, the very developments that conservative intellectuals who are so alarmed by the 'crisis of democracy' have been pointing to. When they worry that the old institutional constraints on popular demands have collapsed, they are in effect worrying that democracy has emerged to challenge property. Their solution is familiar, for it is a very old solution. It is quite simply to limit democracy.

But what conservatives view with despair as the crisis of

democracy might also be viewed as an opportunity precisely because it is a challenge to unfettered capitalism. We are thus at a new juncture in the evolution of the institutional forms of the democratic and capitalist state, and the question is whether capitalism will be restrained, can be restrained, by democratic demands.

NOTES

(1) Vogel reports that major corporate advertisers are now spending about one third of their advertising budgets to influence people in their role as citizens rather than as consumers.

(2) American investment abroad has increased four-fold since 1960, mainly in Western Europe and Canada, and mainly in the form of foreign affiliates of US corporations that remain wholly or largely controlled by US capital. In a review of a series of studies on the much disputed question of how overseas investment affects the structure of US employment, Walton concludes: 'The loss of jobs resulting from production abroad tends to be concentrated in the ranks of blue collar, lower wage, skilled and semi-skilled workers. Conversely, the alleged job creation stemming from the exported production is among technical and managerial personnel' (Walton, 1978, p.32).

(3) There appears to be warrant for thinking that the thrust of most of these policies has been to support economic growth without economic redistribution. Indeed, there is reason to think that market processes have become more skewed in their distributional effects, perhaps as a consequence of federal subsidies to more capital intensive industries, subsidies for infrastructure that drain capital from the labour intensive industries of the older cities, and policies that promote the internationalisation of American capital and undercut the jobs and wages of American workers. All of these economic developments have depended crucially on government action, and it seems a reasonable surmise that they contribute to the increasingly regressive distribution of 'pre-tax' and 'pre-transfer' income. That tilt, in turn, has been offset by the expansion of the benefit programmes.

(4) Still another ground on which the Left dismisses the benefit programmes is that the distribution of income in the United States has remained relatively stable, the expansion of income support programmes notwithstanding. In fact, different analysts reach different conclusions about changes in the income distribution pattern, depending on definitions, data sets, and the measurement concepts used. See, for example, Sadka (1976), Reynolds and Smolensky (1977) and Smolensky, Stiefel, Schmundt and Plotnick (1977). These studies argue the distribution of income has remained relatively stable. Bowles and Gintis argue otherwise. But whichever position one accepts on this issue, it is

clear that the impact of tax and transfer programmes on the distribution of income is progressive.

(5) In _Regulating the Poor_, which was concerned only with poor relief or public welfare, we also argued that the expansion of public welfare was forced from below by protests of the poor which welled-up during periods of great hardship. We attributed an economic function to public welfare as well, but the economic function was not served by the expansion of welfare. It was served by a restrictive, punitive and minimalist relief system which forced most of the poor to offer themselves in the labour market on any terms, and which held up the pauper for public ridicule. However, as this paper makes evident, we now think the cyclical relief pattern may represent a better characterisation of the past than of the future.

(6) Only recently have Left analysts begun to argue that the welfare state has not turned out to be functional for capitalism at all. Juliet Schor proposes that social welfare programmes, 'by providing extra-market means of subsistence ... disrupt the functioning of the structures which currently reproduce the domination of labour by capital'. Bowles and Gintis go further when they claim that the social programmes have had the consequence of shifting wage and profit shares in the United States. And we ourselves wrote several years ago that: 'The expanding role of government in the distribution of income is evidence of a major transformation in the American political economy. It is a transformation that clearly enlarges the market leverage of American workers, particularly lower stratum workers, who are more likely to find themselves unemployed, and who are more susceptible to competition from the unemployed' (Piven and Cloward, 1979).

(7) In fact, only 11.8 per cent of those who were unemployed in April 1976 had quit their jobs. The vast majority had lost their jobs, and the remainder were new entrants to the labour market (_Employment and Earnings_, May 1976, pp.43-4). Nor had most of these people been working for pocket money; two-thirds of the unemployed were the main wage earners of their families. Finally, in a survey designed to probe the experience of the unemployed themselves, Schlozman and Verba conclude: 'When given an opportunity to express their feelings, most of those with whom we talked discussed at some length and with considerable intensity the difficulties they had endured: the struggle to make ends meet, the self-doubt, the family tension, the anxiety, the sleeplessness. What we learned from these more spontaneous utterances amplifies our understanding of the consistent pattern in the survey responses and makes clear that the dissatisfaction expressed by the unemployed is evidence of hardship, not petulance.' (_Op.cit_, p.84)

(8) The incidence of unemployment is of course not random. Simply put, it hits those groups who are most economically vulnerable the hardest, and those unequal

effects seem to be deepening. Unemployment rates are highest among low status workers, those least able to cushion the blow, and these class differentials in turn are distributed along gender and racial lines, so that more women are out of work than men, and many more blacks are out of work than whites. Thus when the overall unemployment rate was 7.5 per cent in April 1976 (a rate which was exceeded in October 1981), unemployment stayed low at only 2.8 per cent among managers and administrators, and only 3.4 per cent among professional and technical workers. But the numbers out of work reached 13.2 per cent among labourers, 9.3 per cent among operatives, 8.1 per cent among service workers generally. And unemployment among female workers reached 8.5 per cent, while black unemployment soared to 13 per cent. Ominously, the ratio of black unemployment to white unemployment has been rising recently from 1.8 jobless blacks to each jobless white in 1975 to a 2.4 ratio in April 1979, when white unemployment sank below 5 per cent, but black rates stayed up, reaching nearly 12 per cent (Dollars and Sense, July-August, 1979). Youth unemployment rates are the most staggering of all, and they are much worse for black teenagers, whose unemployment rate reached 38 per cent in 1977. It is widely agreed that if the large numbers of black youth dropping out of the labour market were included, the rate would be much higher, and perhaps as high as 60 per cent. There are other reasons to think official statistics sharply understate black teenage unemployment. In the spring of 1979, when black teenage unemployment had dropped to 28 per cent according to the Bureau of Labour Statistics' official count, another unpublished government study concluded that the rate was actually 39 per cent, a conclusion derived from interviewing the teenagers directly instead of asking the head of household, as is the practice in the BLS surveys (New York Times, February 29, 1980).

(9) Since the end of the boom that followed the Second World War, unemployment has only fallen below 4 per cent under the stimulus of large increases in military spending. By contrast, unemployment in Western European countries during this period hovered between 1 and 3 per cent (Haveman, 1977, p.45). In the Netherlands, for example, unemployment averaged 2 per cent in the 1950s, sank below 1 per cent in the early 1960s, and then rose to 1.4 per cent in the late 1960s. In Sweden, unemployment averaged 2 per cent in the 1950s, and sank to 1.5 per cent in the 1960s. In England unemployment remained below 2 per cent in the 1950s and rose to a little over 2 per cent in the 1960s. Of course, in the 1970s unemployment in Western Europe began to climb, although even then rates generally remained below the United States. Rates have been adjusted to conform to United States measurements (Bureau of Labour Statistics).

(10) But each decade drove the peaks and troughs of the

cyclical pattern of US employment higher. Rates averaged 4.5 per cent in the 1950s, 4.8 per cent in the 1960s and 6.2 per cent in the 1970s (DuBoff, 1977, p.1).

(11) To appreciate the extensiveness of this effect of the benefit programmes, it should be understood that unemployment rates for any group at any moment conceal the actual scope and depth of economic hardship and insecurity that ensue from unemployment. One way to get some sense of this is to consider the actual numbers who become unemployed at some time during any given year. In 1976, when unemployment averaged 7.7 per cent, 7.2 million people were jobless at any given time. But over the course of the year, 19.1 per cent of the labour force, or about 20 million people, were unemployed at some time or other. In a study designed to assess the true scale of unemployment in the city of New Brunswick, New Jersey during 1975, Leggett and Gioglio concluded that 44 per cent of blue collar males were unemployed at least once during the year, and that 57 per cent of blue collar females were unemployed at least once (Leggett and Gioglio, 1977). Nor are these periods of joblessness typically brief. The mean length of unemployment in 1976 was nearly 16 weeks, and fully 20 per cent of the jobless remained out of work for more than six months (Employment and Earnings, May 1976, pp.43-4).

(12) The Harris Survey also reports that by a majority of 78 to 20 per cent Americans feel 'the rich get richer and the poor get poorer'; by 68 to 29 per cent they think 'most people with power try to take advantage of people like yourself'; by 50 to 45 per cent they think 'the people running the country don't really care what happens to you'. These percentages were almost double the percentages who held such views in the mid-1960s (ABC News-Harris Survey, Vol. II, no.67, ISSN 0163-4846, June 2, 1980). Harris and other surveys also report enormous and precipitous drops in the percentages of people who report confidence in major institutions, down to 18 per cent who have confidence in the White House, and to 11 per cent who report confidence in the Congress (ABC News-Harris Survey, Vol. II, no.88, ISSN 0163-4846, July 21, 1980).

REFERENCES

Bell, Daniel, (1978) The Cultural Contradictions of
Capitalism, Basic Books/Harper Colophone Books, New York.

Bosworth, Barry, (1980) 'Re-establishing and Economic
Consensus: An Impossible Agenda?' Daedulus, Vol.109,
no.3, pp.59-70.

Bowles, Samuel and Gintis, Herbert, 'The Crisis of Liberal
Capitalism: The Case of the United States', unpublished
manuscript.

Brittan, Samuel, (1975) 'The Economic Contradictions of
Democracy', British Journal of Political Science, Vol.5,
pp.129-59.

Bureau of Labour Statistics, US Department of Labour, (1975)
'Unemployment in Nine Industrial Countries', Monthly
Labour Review, June.

Castells, Manuel, (1977) The Urban Question, Edward Arnold,
London.

Crozier, Michael, (1975) 'Chapter II - Western Europe',
pp.11-58, in Michael Crozier, Samuel P. Huntington and
Joji Watanuki, The Crisis of Democracy: Report on the
Governability of Democracies to the Trilateral Commission,
New York University Press, New York.

Dickson, David and Noble, David, (1981) 'By Force or Reason:
The Politics of Science and Technology Policy', pp.260-312
in Thomas Ferguson and Joel Rogers (eds.), The Hidden
Election: Politics and Economics in the 1980 Presidential
Campaign, Pantheon Books, New York.

DuBoff, Richard B, (1977) 'Full Employment: The History of
a Receding Target', Politics and Society, Vol.7, no.1,
pp.2-25.

Fabricant, Solomon, (1975) 'The Problem of Controlling
Inflation', in C. Lowell Harriss, Inflation: Long-term
Problems. Proceedings of the Academy of Political Science,
Vol.31, no.4, pp.156-68.

Ferguson, Thomas and Rogers, Joel, (1979) 'How Business
Saved the New Deal', The Nation, December 8.

Fiedler, Edgar R, (1975) 'Economic Policies to Control
Stagflation', in C. Lowell Harriss, op.cit, pp.169-78.

Fiedler, Edgar R, (1979) 'Inflation and Economic Policy', in
Clarence C. Walton (ed.), Inflation and National Survival.
Proceedings of the Academy of Political Science, Vol.33,
no.3, pp.113-21.

Friedland, Roger, Piven, Frances Fox and Alford, Robert J,
(1977) 'Political Conflict, Urban Structure and the Fiscal
Crisis', International Journal of Urban and Regional
Research, Vol.1, no.3, pp.447-71.

Garraty, John A, (1978) Unemployment in History, Harper and
Row, New York.

Gold, David A. and Wolpe, Alan, (1979) 'Counter-Keynesian:
Postwar Economic Policy in the United States', Institute
for the Study of Social Change, University of California,
Berkeley, unpublished manuscript.

Gough, Ian, (1979) The Political Economy of the Welfare
State, Macmillan, London.

Haveman, Robert H, (1977) 'Unemployment in Western Europe
and The United States: A Problem of Demand, Structure, or

Measurement', The American Economic Review, Vol.71, no.4, December, pp.1467-87.

Hibbs, Douglas A, (1977) 'Political Parties and Macro-economic Policy', American Economic Review, Vol.71, no.4, December, pp.1467-87.

Huntington, Samuel P, (1975) 'Chapter III - The United States', in Michael Crozier, Samuel P. Huntington and Joji Watanuki, The Crisis of Democracy: Report on the Governability of Democracies to the Trilateral Commission, New York University Press, New York, pp.59-118.

Leggett, John C. and Gioglio, Jerry, (1977) Break Out the Double Digit: Mass Unemployment in the City of New Brunswick, pamphlet available from John C. Leggett, Department of Sociology, Livingston College, Rutgers University, New Brunswick, New Jersey, 08903.

Miller, S.M, Tomaskovic-Devey, Barbara and Tomaskovic-Devey, Donald, 'Neo-Marxists and the Welfare State', unpublished manuscript.

O'Connor, James, (1973) The Fiscal Crisis of the State, St. Martin's Press, New York.

Phillips, A.W, (1958) 'The Relation between Unemployment and the Rate of Change of Money Wage Rates in the United Kingdom, 1861-1957', Economica, Vol.25, pp.283-99.

Piven, Frances Fox and Cloward, Richard A, (1971) Regulating the Poor, Pantheon Books, New York.

Piven, Frances Fox and Cloward, Richard A, (1979) 'The Politics of Unemployment in the 1980s', paper prepared for the Institute of Policy Studies, Washington, DC, unpublished.

Polanyi, Karl, (1957) The Great Transformation, Beacon Press, Boston.

Reynolds, Morgan and Smolensky, Eugene, (1977), 'Post-FISC Distributions of Income in 1950, 1961 and 1970', Public Finance Quarterly, Vol.5, no.4, October, pp.419-38.

Sadka, Efraim, (1976) 'Social Welfare and Income Distribu-tion', Econometrica, Vol.44, no.6, November, pp.1239-51.

Schlozman, Kay Lehman and Verba, Sydney, (1979) Injury to Insult: Unemployment, Class and Political Response, Harvard University Press, Cambridge, Massachusetts.

Schor, Juliet B, 'The Citizen's Wage: An Analysis of the Influence of Social Welfare Expenditures on the Wage Inflation-Unemployment Tradeoff', unpublished manuscript.

Schumpeter, Joseph, (1975) Capitalism, Socialism and Democracy, Harper and Row, Publishers, Harper/Colophone Books, Third Edition, New York.

Smolensky, Eugene, Stiefel, Leanna, Schmundt, Maria and Plotnick, Robert, (1977) 'Adding In-Kind Transfers to the Personal Income and Outlay Account: Implications for the Size Distribution of Income', from 'The Distribution of Economic Well-Being', F. Thomas Juster (ed.), Vol.41, in Studies of Income and Wealth, National Bureau of Economic Research.

Tufte, Edward R, (1978) Political Control of the Economy, Princeton University Press, Princeton, New Jersey.

Vogel, David, (1979) 'Business's "New Class" Struggle', The Nation, December 15.

Walton, John, (1978) 'The Internationalisation of Capital

and Class Structures in the Advanced Countries: The US
Case', paper presented at the annual meeting of the
Society for the Study of Social Problems, San Francisco.
Wolin, Sheldon, (1981) 'Why Democracy?' _Democracy_, January,
pp.3-5

10 Towards a Celebration of Difference(s): Notes for a Sociology of a Possible Everyday Future

PHILIP CORRIGAN

The so-called contemplation from the standpoint of society means nothing more than the overlooking of the differences which express the social relation (relation of bourgeois society). Society does not consist of individuals, but expresses the sum of interrelations, the relations within which these individuals stand.

Karl Marx, Grundrisse (1)

What the cultural revolution is then really proposing is a radical recasting of the old problem between special interests and the general interest. It has of course to find means of negotiating such relations, but it starts from the position that all existing institutions and procedures of the 'general interest' are in fact falsifications, either in the arbitrary definitions of a dominant class, or in those more complex procedures of representation in which the 'general interest' is a negative appropriation deployed against each 'special interest' in turn, the only means of ascertaining the true general interest in relation to any actual special interest, by direct consultation and specific popular decision, having been systematically excluded ... human emancipation is intrinsically, and as a matter of principle, more diverse than any philosophical definition of emancipatory transformation.

Raymond Williams, Problems in Materialism and Culture. (2)

Sexuality is the name that may be given to a set of interlocking historical mechanisms, not some reality below the surface on which it is difficult to get a hold, but a great surface network on which the stimulation of bodies, the intensification of pleasures, the incitement to discourse, the formation of sciences, the strengthening of controls and resistances are linked together in accordance with a few great strategies of knowledge and power.

Michel Foucault, History of Sexuality. (3)

INTRODUCTION

These 'Notes' (a typical authorial strategy to safeguard against questions or accusations of completeness, certainty and so on) are part of some preliminary thoughts about the need, specifically in 1981, to consider the project of and for a _scientific utopia_. Or a romantic realism. In other words, to try to hold together, as I have argued with others before, (4) the double militancy required to understand _and_ transform the social relations that currently define (but not completely) 'our' situation: _both_ a measured assessment of the objective constraints (force) _and_ a radical engagement with a 'going beyond', a subjective construction (will) for alternatives, for better, fuller, more conscious, more happy forms of life. (5) Mao Tsetung paradigmatically spelled out the 'deviations' which result from collapsing this project into either of its poles: an adventurist voluntarism (quite congenially linked to dogmatic authoritarianism as I would self-critically now see in the Great Proletarian Cultural Revolution) where _will_ (and correlatively consciousness) becomes the crucial causal variable, and failure results from individual defects. _Or_ an opportunist pragmatism ('realism') where _the facts_ (and correlatively 'what is possible') becomes the crucial determinant of correct action, and failure results from prematurity ('before the circumstances are ready') or a lack of preparedness ('the will of the people was not sufficiently energised or agonised').

But the project of a scientific utopianism is also about the ways we are represented to ourselves. It has to start from the work of the last, say, fifteen years which stresses (although the word is not without its problems) _mediations_, as against older theories of reflection. The ambiguity of the concept of representation ably captures this problem, containing the dual dangers of (a) a reductionism (forgetting the materiality of the ways that actual relations of power and domination are represented and arguing for a kind of transparency) and (b) an idealism (representations being floated free of the specific conditions of existence of particular social formations and the modes of production which define them, and located in, and only in, their discourses of elaboration). Nevertheless while it is true that ideological relations establish imaginary representations of ourselves to the social (including to ourselves) there is both a patterning (systematic quality) in the representations of identity in different clusters of social relations and a recurrent similarity in the mode of establishing, reinforcing, applying and using such representations. Despite problems, I think conceptions of _coding_ and _classification_ (6) remain helpful 'ways into' this area. Above all, they, and the term _representations_, remind us that we are always dealing with historical-materialist constructions, i.e. with relative rather than absolute conceptions, discourses and practices: _with what is changeable_ (although the

242

features of that change need the most careful attention).

Whatever is 'the social' (7) it is (also) the site of battles around the sign, a field of struggles around what is to signify _properly_ and what enjoys (at best) an underground, shadowy, oppositional semi-reality half in and half out of the permitted codes of representational practices. Some practices consistently work on such an edge - humour, artistic devices, scientific theories - but often only to confirm the boundary, to reinforce the normal-naturalness of the Obvious. (8) I think that _this_ social is regulated in three determining ways (not reducible to each other, not networked causally) but one establishes the possibility of any form of life (although always in specific ways): by production and reproduction of material life, by the state, and by moral regulation (the terrain of cultural production and ideological relations). 'Social control' (in the sense I intend) begins but does not end with the requirements of production. This is not to be read as 'the economic' nor as 'forces of production' since although we may analyse it abstractly (we know it involves human-natural relations, for example) we encounter it and try to explain it always historically and find there a range of relations which enable production to persist in the ways that it does. This is why, as Jameson says, there is a quality of the tautological in historical materialist explanations. (9) That is how and why it happened! An immediate problem, and the reason why the richest descriptions may be unhelpful, is _first_ finding out what indeed happened, or, more important, is happening.

State formation takes place under the conditions of existence of production-in-general and the specific moment and location of particular modes of production. But although it is clear that without production (of specific kinds of surplus, for example) state forms cannot exist, both the normal periodising of specific kinds of state and the base/superstructure metaphor read as a social law seem to me wrong. I do not want to go into that here as I have, with others, done so previously (10) and anyway that sort of point is far less relevant to my concerns than what follows. Modern democratic nation state forms have far more to do with (social) identities than is normally allowed. First, states determine the representations of official politics ('the political') and employ other discourses and practices to deal with the challenges to such definitions. These are, broadly, pathological: to declare non-official politics to be criminal, or sickness: to declare some areas no-go areas for politics ('let us not bring politics into this'); or to originate the 'disturbance' outside the permitted: the rhetoric of the 'outside agitator'. But there is more here than this nonetheless overlooked (until recently) emphasis. The state regulates forms of social identity through homogeneous categories (such as citizen-voters, for example) which mobilise and inflect the repertoires of a more general moral regulation and gear with relations of production more narrowly conceived. Thirdly, or as a specific class-related

example, state formation and the nationalism it signifies
have far more to do with bourgeois class formation (of whose
'making' we lack resources for a proper comprehension).
Marx's few asides about how the bourgeois necessarily adopts
particular forms for its expression as a class (thereby
overcoming the fissiparous tendencies in the enterprise
and sectoral competition of capitalism) - externally as
nation, internally as state - seem to me highly relevant.
Now, to avoid misreading, none of this implies rigidity -
indeed it is the 'sensitive' flexibility (within and between) which seems striking about state institutions - but,
at a certain risk (metaphoricality posing as understanding)
I am trying to talk about how states state. By which I do
not only mean official discourse as such, but the grammar
and rules which allow discourse, and enforce some effects.

Moral regulation - although the term is not much used -
has been the subject of much work within cultural production, ideological relations and 'the social' in the past
few years as part of a welcome anti-reductionist, anti-
expressionist approach to social formations. Out of this
has come a recognition of both the materiality (in actuality
and effects) of just those realms and relations which had
been given such a 'weak' place in the topology of social
formations and the difficulty of continuing to depict the
social as if it consisted of unitary social individuals
(normally aggregated into groups and classes). For some this
dissolves the whole structuration of the social formation as
such, dissolving thereby 'the social'; for others it is the
precise materiality of the moral and its regulation by the
state and 'elective affinity' with the changing and complicated 'requirements' of production which has been centred.
There are still many and massive problems (for me at least)
with work on this kind of area, for example, the tendency
still to explain away what one begins with, or the using of
'texts' as pre-texts for very abstract theorising, and there
are many central features of most human lives which remain
systematically understudied - for example, the fine texture
of familial forms. There is also a quite crippling dichoto-
misation between what one speaker in the television debate
'Them and Us' (11) called living differences and theories
allegedly explaining such experiences. (12) All of that
said, however, I think the recent work of the greatest
importance for scientific utopianism, for a sociology
neither dedicated to order nor control, but to human
emancipation.

DIFFERENTIATING DIFFERENTLY

The preliminary sketch above is dangerously like those
familiar layer-cake images of social formations (sequential-
ised like the courses of a meal in 'the economic', 'the
political' and the light delicacy of 'the ideological' in
more recent accounts). Not only are there evidential contradictions in all the relations within and between the forms
specified - which often makes the 'gearing' rasp and stutter

244

(one of our tasks is to make such noises clearly heard) like hesitation phenomena in the discourses - but they provide a series of contradictory relations which define the social individuals producing and produced by. Holding to both of the latter practices - that people produce their own history but not in circumstances of their own choosing - is essential if the polarities of essential active humanism or abstract passive systemism are to be avoided.

It seems to me that a lot of sociology amd Marxist or socialist elaborations ignore the persistent reality of living differences in two ways. First, the way that social contradictions entail contradictory rather than unitary individuals; second, how differences are to be depicted. However much the relations of regulation in societies are contradictory within their field of operation it seems to me clear that in the long history of capitalist formations there is a tendency to the creation of homogeneous categories - indeed a whole grammar of social classification in which the rather 'soft' adjectives have enormous materiality - little words like 'good' and 'proper' may in the end have been more violent than the big words of exploitation and oppression (to which, of course, they are intimately connected). Some of this I sketched above. The evaluative nature of these classifications entails a 'figure' against which the gradings can be made, this is the specifically gendered, raced, located, 'religioused' individual. This is the writing-point, or, to change the metaphor, camera rather than point-of-view, of the social classificatory discourses. I will return to these emphases drawn from the work in cultural production of the last few years in a moment. There is a little more to be said at the general level first.

Difference(s) are, as it were, indexed against the figure-in-dominance, it is portrayed (whether there or not) in all social depictions and in the living differences by the evaluative schema applied in the cognitive appropriation of what is seen/lived. As a non-trivial aside I should stress how curious it is that we offer social analyses based upon lives lived cognitively (as in some Marxisms, lives lived textually) in which, in particular, the specific visuality of a social context is erased. Or: Why do sociology texts carry no photographs - except when they are discussing the sociology of culture? For over a hundred years (in England) the intensity of the constructed and elaborated environment (streets and their signs; houses and their decoration; institutions and their messages) has been an ingredient of knowledge and identity. Equally (relatedly?) the degree to which the evaluative and emotional are pervasive, seems to evade sociological and much Marxist theorising.

Now although I believe that each social form of life (= mode of production) has one defining feature - which for feudalism would be Land: Service, for capitalism, Capital: Labour - the forms of expression of such a fundamental constituent are always to be empirically specified. Class

245

dominates _through_ other public and semi-public expressions but it does not determine either the form or the salience of the latter. Some versions of theorising class (which I want to call positional) effect a minimisation if not erasure of other differences. Others (which I want to call relational) understand how class relations are themselves contradict-ory (no class is understabdable apart from the others) and empirically diverse. Different analyses of social differ-ences begin with the material social classifications of race, gender, location, religion, age, occupation, 'grading' and so on. But these and much more (i.e. the historical genesis and trajectory of each alone and in combination) are never salient and totally determining alone. They are doubly combined - specific social individuals have to construct and live through 'making sense' (or not) of the overlapping definitions - and the contradictions between public de-pictions and lived experiences within the latter. But they are also combined _in_ the social, both in the unsaid of class, and the oversaid of individualising homogeneous categories such as consumers, viewers, 'the public'.

Now, the project of sovereign individualism at the heart of the ideology of bourgeois society (which bears the dominant figure I mentioned earlier, a figure subject to different depiction in different societies and in the same society at different times) has had determinate consequences within sociology and Marxism-socialism. In the former the notion of the unitary individual reigns in most of the 'applied' investigative work. There is no completely satis-factory account, in theory, of classifications and com-binations which does not slip into emphasising how history makes people or that people make history, leaving aside the dialectical contradiction between constraint and construc-tion, and how the former unevenly decreases (at least in the nature-people realms, at the price, within capitalism, of an increase in the society-people spheres) in the long cultural revolution coextensive with the history of human-ity. Radical objectivism and radical subjectivism solve the problem by erasing the 'reality' of the other side of the relation.

I mainly want to take up the points about Marxism and socialism in my third section (Overcoming the Obvious) below, but some points are relevant here. Differences within bourgeois societies (and within socialist societies also) are indexed against the figure of dominance understood through both the unsaid of class and the oversaid of supreme individualism (in which the worth of the human being is displayed in the possession of his goods, such possessions being the very apex of freedom as such). Difference(s) are lived as disadvantage in a double sense. First, whole groups (the majority) cannot ever become (assume) the qualities of the figure of dominance because they are incapable of speaking its 'language'. Indeed the languages available for the public expression of the majority so operate as to establish this impossible dream as the said but unobtainable texture of much public discussion. Secondly, and I do not

want to say 'more materially', difference(s) result in disadvantage because, as it happens, social formations consist
of massive structural differences. Capitalism reproduces
disadvantage not as a minor quirk of its early forms - the
progressivist thesis in brief, (13) but as a central part of
its operation in its most mature forms. Capitalism, to use
an older language, establishes the path of achievement (and
self-responsibility) as the ideal whilst ensuring that the
slow death of ascription (fixing by disadvantage) is the
normal experience.

Now, it seems to me, that much Marxism and socialism takes
over (and it is part-and-parcel of a wider willingness to
'take' rather than 'transform' of course) the hidden message
of bourgeois ideologies of difference(s). This is clear in
the rhetoric and practices established within all the disadvantaged groups who have attempted to 'fight back'. The first
step in such a 'fight back' is to elaborate a language of
struggle that turns or weakens the power of public expressions that repeat the difference = disadvantage equations
endlessly, whilst - and again, with some anger, I do want to
insist on the massive quality of violence entailed here -
individualising those who 'fail' to overcome such disadvantage. Those who affirm they are 'Glad to be Gay', that
'Sisterhood is Powerful' or 'Black is Beautiful' are holding
back the normal ways they are depicted. But frequently behind and beyond such initial moments or organisation (and is
it not the history of all such movements that there is
nothing short of a festival of exploding consciousness, a
true, genuine and poetic celebration of strength at the start
followed by a splintering, a diffusion, a hesitation, a
pausing, a slowing in the face of the question 'how now to
move forward while staying together'?) beyond that moment
comes an elaboration, a discourse and practices of analysis
and struggle that again and again entails a set of equival-
ences to the figure of dominance. Historically, as examples,
working class people (predominantly men) are 'as good as'
their middle and ruling class equivalents - look at them
being respectable, going to university, entering Parliament
and other signifying institutions and, rather differently
because more complex, forming their 'own' institutions.
Women can do things that men do, are as good as men; children are really like adults; the aged remain as good as those
aged less; black people are really as good as white people;
and so on. 'As good as' here can, of course, be increased to
'better than' without altering the algebra at all.

What this leaves though is the algebra intact. The ways of
conceptualising difference(s) as disadvantage remain. We
have to find ways of conceptualising, practising and cele-
brating difference(s) in new ways. To recall my favourite
slogan of 1968: our task is not to portray or live what the
old ways do not permit (or permit only in damaged forms)
but to live and portray difference(s) differently. I shall
return to this at the end - it is the purpose of all of
these Notes - but first I want to indicate some of the ways
in which I think the languages of difference operate under

247

present social arrangements since until we understand that we shall not know how to alter those arrangements through finding new modes of representation and understanding that facilitate human emancipation.

Barbara Taylor (14) has recently drawn attention to the totality of the critique of the obvious offered by socialist feminists in the 1830s, when one woman (in The Pioneer) argued that 'nothing short of a total revolution in all present modes of acting and thinking among all mankind, will be productive of the great change so loudly called for by (women's) miserable state ...' That is as precise a statement of scientific utopianism as I need for the present purposes. But the 'story' of what happened is well known - the repeated brushing aside of such strategies as utopian (along with, recently, a huffing and puffing off the stage of much other working class socialism as 'pre-Marxist') and the repeated declarations that those who struggle for such positions are 'weakening our great movement'. But that this happens is not a causal result of the monstrous regiment of men who rise, like grease, to the top of the socialist and other hierarchies of struggle. Their rise and the subordination of the non-male, non-white, non-respectable humans is itself caused by the determinations I sketched in my introduction. Which is not to say, which would be incorrect, that patriarchy, racism, elitism, ageism and so on, do not have forms and features which pre-date capitalism and which the latter does not finally encapsulate. But it is to repeat, in Ros Coward's words, that:

> Consciousness raising and a variety of feminist writings demonstrated how oppression was not exclusively the effect of economic and legal discrimination. Oppression is also something which exists in personal relationships, in the relationships in the home, between 'maleness' and 'femaleness' (whether this occurs between men and women, or two people of the same sex), between parents and children. And the fight around these 'ideological' relations is a fight which is of enormous importance for feminists. But it is a fight which cannot be waged by an appeal to the common experience of womankind. People are always crossed by a multitude of other interpellations, involving definite forms of recognition. Class background, racial difference and educational differences all are sources of different experience. None of these factors is sufficient to generate a politics which corresponds to these experiences. (15)

What I am trying to say (and the fact of saying is itself a difficulty hence a certain metaphoricality, a playing with words, the neologisms and so on!) is that the 'trick' accomplished by reality (or rather the dominant regime of representation) is to seem to individualise around equivalence thus simultaneously denying class structuration and relations and the material differences which inform (i,e. in-form) class. There is thus a curious truth in all the

248

heavy structuralism which reduces human beings to <u>bearers</u> or the weighty psychoanalytic analyses which create nothing but a <u>space</u> for 'the subject'. But it is a truth which reproduces in seemingly oppositional theory the trick it sets out to expose. For, what then would be the resources to restructure the world? Or is that (too) an effect of the structure, a restructuration of the psychic subject, a trick of the light?

By chance, a recent issue of <u>Sociological Review</u> contains two articles which offer indications of what I am trying to talk about: S. Prendergast and A. Prout's 'What will I do ...? Teenage girls and the construction of motherhood' and C. Hakim's 'Census reports as documentary evidence: the census commentaries 1801-1951'. (16) The latter provides ingredients (from official discourses and the knowledge/power they entail) for the former contemporary views. The censal accounts simultaneously summate (one-sidedly) and display-and-enforce certain definitions of work, gender, home and family. We are also here reminded that one way in which states crystallise knowledge/power relations is through their insistence on (and often sole right to) collecting 'facts' in certain forms and the way that we tend to see these forms (and the 'facts' they make available) as neutral techniques. The other article shows the contemporary forms <u>and a number of signifying contradictions</u>. The authors point to four of these which, in my terms, perfectly illustrate the difference between public encouraged expressions and the difficult-to-say, lived experiences of the areas which the public expressions are supposed to accurately signify. Thus the authors found a domination in the girls' accounts of the negative image of motherhood (in the midst of accounts which were far richer, more detailed and certainly less normative than expected). Secondly, depression was seen as endemic and chronic and yet also occasional and relatively minor. Third and fourth, the actual language of the accounts was both marked by 'pauses, silences, hesitancy, as well as persistent modification and qualification which seemed to undercut the explicit meaning of the actual words spoken' <u>and</u> (in my terms) the girls switched modes of expression:

> The interview appeared to follow a rather paradoxical pattern. Children would seem to be exploring experience and knowledge in one framework and direction, when we asked them to <u>formalise that knowledge</u> around a proposition, as described earlier, they often made a complete switch in direction. (17)

It is this central area of experience/expressions which I am trying to suggest is crucial to theorising a present which contains a history without closing down a range of futures. Culturalism, to return to an earlier point, characteristically raises active experience as its banner, whilst structuralism points up its pacification by regulated expressions. Articles like the one just described (and, once said, do we now recognise how general those negotiations are?) show that both positions fail to represent the social as a terrain of struggle. Public regimes and rituals of representation (regulated in non-unitary ways by the state and having, in the end, to gear, for the majority, with the requirements of production, that, for instance, wants can be supplied in commodity forms) do not sufficiently register historical and material experiences. The 'left over' and 'left out' (and the results of combining different public languages and seeing how they contradict) may enjoy a shadowy existence - all too often reduced to the terror of private worries, anxieties, or, ironically, 'not being oneself today' - but it nevertheless has material effects.

The problem is then to both recognise the resources of resistance and new forms of resistance leading to a new, different regime of representation. Thus, to take two important recent areas of work, that 'men' (usually particular kinds of academic, intellectual or artist) speak (18) differently and write (19) differently (and are these sets of differences the same?) from 'women' (the comparison group is usually similar to that of the 'men') does not mean that any solution is to be found in repositioning or demonstration effects - that 'women' could occupy such voices and styles (and here is evidence that they have done so) but, that the relations which establish those kinds of voices and styles as dominant have to be exposed and transformed, simultaneously weakening the domination of 'men' and the regulated subordination of 'women'. This is what I mean by the celebration of differences differently. But, as the qualifications I indicated for 'women' and 'men' above attempt to show, the voices and the styles being compared occur within particular contexts; the academic world of quite violent individualism and competition embodying the division between mental and manual labour, for example, and these have to be transformed before differences can be celebrated in a truly oppositional manner rather than simply pluralising alternative forms of those same contexts.

Finally, in this highly sketchy middle section of my Notes, what of those accounts that establish difference differently. I mean the socio-biological discourses which fix difference(s) as disadvantage and assign naturalness to such fixity. Reading history as evolution, the fitness of the fix is seen as invariant properties of human beingness. Although sociology, as it were, epistemologically sets itself against any biologism (and, with rather more qualifications, most Marxisms) there is much slippage here which enables the return of the 'natural' in other guises. I myself disagree with any language of representation which includes both positioning (preferring relating) and constituting (preferring regulating) as one, as it were, externally and the other inwardly registers in too definite a manner some final content-and-form of what for me is the ever-opening project of human potential. But it is another, rather dominant, discourse I want briefly to engage with at this point - that of the Lacanian reading of Freud (not, I hasten to add in its pure form, but in the profane forms

250

of understanding subjectivity as a sign). As is now common
in the critique of Lacan, if the unconscious is structured
like a language: which language, and how? The structuring
moments pointed up have to be regularly and consistently
stated (known). As Stephen Heath has pointed out, of
Lacan's enunciation:

> the topic is often sexual difference but the treatment
> of that topic has no incidence and the possibility of
> a problem of sexual difference across the enunciation
> and the pattern of address of a discourse ... (20)

Further such silent assurance (The Master, no less, our
Jacques!) repeats the dominant code, in

> a discourse that is finally masculine, not because of
> some conception of theory as male but because in the
> last resort any discourse which fails to take account
> of the problem of sexual difference in its enunciation
> and address will be, within a patriarchal order,
> precisely indifferent, a reflection of male domination.
> (20)

Heath's careful summation of the varied alternations within
and beyond the Lacanian problematic has the advantage of
showing both the limits and dangers of an incipient
biologism - making signification as such result from a
sexuality founded upon biology, dehistoricising the hence
naturalised difference - and the implications of such work
for politics and for what the obvious is: that which we
might begin to joyfully overcome differently.

> The joining-disjoining overlap of the biological by
> the mental as the turn of the subject allows a quite
> radical conception of sexuality, allows the
> possibility of a quite other posing of difference...
> Sexuality is not given in nature but produced: the
> individual subject is not constructed from sexuality,
> sexuality is constructed in the history of the
> subject, with difference a function of that con-
> struction, not its cause, a function which is not
> necessarily single (on the contrary) and which,
> a fortiori, is not necessarily the holding of that
> difference to anatomical difference (phallic
> singularity). Production, construction in the history
> of the subject, sexuality engages also from the
> beginning, and thereby, the social relations of
> production, classes, sexes - an engagement which
> cannot be, the lesson of psychoanalysis, a reduction
> but which equally, the lesson of the limiting
> certainties of psychoanalysis against the effective
> implications of its theory, cannot be left aside,
> for later, beyond the enclosure of an analytically
> defined area... the need is constantly to push and
> rework analysis and theory into the richness and
> variety of experience, in order to understand and
> extend its transforming possibilities. (21)

OVERCOMING THE OBVIOUS

I have been arguing against any residual social understandings which retain some conceptions of the natural/
universal, rather than the social/specific, qualities of
the social. But I am also arguing against versions of a
denaturalising (good) structuralism which too completely
fix, determine and limit (bad) human potential. In overcoming the Obvious we first have to make ourselves aware
of it. The best outcome of the ethnomethodology 'moment'
for me was the strong recall of the pervasiveness of the
'taken-for-granted' as ground rules which make other
activities and productions possible. As Jameson expresses
it 'the simple is in reality only a simplification ... the
self-evident draws its force from hosts of buried presuppositions'. (22) I once polemically suggested, in 1978,
that as we had had a decade of Marxism = Science, we
should perhaps try one of Marxism = Poetry! What I meant
(as social analysis) is also indicated by Jameson:

> faced with obscure poetry, the naive reader attempts
> at once to interpret, to resolve the immediate
> difficulties back into the transparency of rational
> thought; whereas for the dialectically trained
> reader, it is the obscurity itself which is the
> object of his (n.b.) reading, and its specific
> quality and structure which he (n.b.) attempts to
> define and compare with other forms of verbal
> opacity. Thus our thought no longer takes official
> problems at face value... (23)

I think much sociological and socialist analyses deal
with difference(s) as naive readers deal with obscurity,
trying to efface and erase the materiality in favour of
some (for me, thoroughly bourgeois) rationalism. This takes
two forms, one, that of supreme individualism and its discourses centring on the figure of dominance I have sketched
above; the other is to aim (more or less) to complete the
'project' of bourgeois revolution. The latter carries
forward (takes rather than transforms) such slogans as
equality, freedom and (even) property to 'realise' them in
the world of 'the social' for everyone. Here the contradiction 'general interest'/'special interest' of Bahro
(taken up by Williams in the quotation I gave at the start)
is highly relevant. I am arguing against those interpretations of Marx who see the project to be one of the
realisation of so many rational kernels (or real essences)
in the philosophies of bourgeois emancipation. I am
arguing for the degree to which such equality, freedom and
properties can only be realised through accomplishment by
social individuals grouped by difference(s). That is what
I understand to be the celebration of difference(s), freed
from any indexing to disadvantage, but not parcellised
and patronised from above through social policies of provision, so much as emancipated (practices which reveal new
tasks in a constant delimiting and transformation of constraint in favour of increasing areas of construction)

specifically and particularistically from below. Politics, in this scenario, loses its demarcation as a separate realm and becomes _different_ (24) in the deconstruction of the state as regulator of expressions, as the police force of denial of difference.

Such understandings (and very hard work!) cannot be relegated to some convenient 'future' (after The Revolution, for example) but is a constituent of socialist construction now. (25) If by socialism we understand (as I do) the more conscious, more collective, more egalitarian application of human energies (26) this cannot be read either serially (at the moment, comrades, the main task is ... everything else can wait) or sequentially (first, comrades, the national system of accounting, then ... the moon), but it should not be read as a general submerging within a general interest (with its bearers, the working class, and _its_ agents, THE PARTY) nor as correlatively expressed through certain institutions (THE PLAN). Because it begins now – in conceptualisations of the specificity of difference(s) and the forms of their struggles – it also effects a new 'reading' of politics within capitalism. Power and Politics shows this in, for example, Nik Rose's discussion of _equality_ in issue two, where, again, the general interest/ special interest contradiction is evidentially a singularly obdurate problem (solvable, historically and violently, by 'our' state acting as guarantor of the 'socialism' of policies). But Fran Bennett, Rosa Heys and Ros Coward's general review, from a socialist feminist perspective, of taxation and social security (in Power and Politics, 1) taken with some points drawn out by Ros Coward at a later seminar, (27) is exactly the kind (i.e. there is no unanimity here – and what on earth would that mean in terms of my own analysis!) of work that I am pointing to. The text explicitly argues that state social policies are neither homogeneous in their gearing with relations of production nor uniform in their identifying and stereotyping (or, better, reinforcing of stereotypes). But the text implicitly also shows how the common argument about the difference between struggles 'now' and struggles 'later' (under socialism, after the Revolution) is fundamentally mistaken.

I think this is a quite general point. Victories depend on means as much as ends (with means that begin to illuminate, and show some ways of overcoming, the Obvious, then defeats, mistakes, errors are all highly fruitful) because socialist construction is, above all, about _form_ and _representations_. Given the endemic contradictory features of the contents of capitalist relations, the central problem is that of recognising and deconstructing the regime of forms and representations around uniformity (and its dark side of disadvantages linked to difference(s)). It is often argued that the 'new' politics is essentially a cultural politics but this carries the danger that back at the last instance, in the hearty world of 'the economic' there is a more solid, more important, yes, more real politics to be attended to. As though production relations

253

were not, in fact, all those relations which make possible
the making of things (commodities) in particular ways in
forms and through representations which (under capitalism)
systematically (i,e, not accidentally or contingently)
deny specific and general human emancipation. It is a
cultural revolution that I am discussing, but one which,
through its forms and representations alone, (I am quite
insistent here) makes possible a socialism worth the name.
To do this, it seems to me, we have to find _either_ (I am
not clear) the ways which the central analysis of commodity
forms, especially the wage-form, in fact illuminates all
social relations, _or_ some conceptual equivalents of wage-
form and commodity analysis for those realms heretofore
relegated to the superstructure. If capitalism entails a
particular regime of money, does not the state entail a
regime of power/knowledge (Foucault) and if money is
available in units of cash-time and rituals of exchange,
are there not forms, inscriptions and rituals within the
state?

But this is not really an argument for such separations
strategically since the one set of social relations that
has been so consistently taken and not transformed is that
of production narrowly conceived. It was, if I may be
forgiven, no accident that Lenin's infamous texts welcoming
the joys of Taylorism were published in China within weeks
of the death of Mao Tse-tung (Mao Zedong) but, even there,
the first signs of such a major reversal were found in the
wider 'social'. No, the argument is that recognitions of
the sort I am arguing as _initial_ ingredients of/for
socialist construction have the most material effects and
outcomes in the comprehension and, of necessity, transformation of work in all its forms. But look at the
glissades in some of Marx's best scientific-utopian
passages from the first volume of _Capital_:

> Let us picture (n.b.) to ourselves, by way of change,
> a community of free individuals, carrying on their work
> with the means of production in common, in which the
> labour-power of _all_ the different individuals is
> consciously applied as the combined labour power of
> the community...

> The religious reflex of the real world can, in any
> case, only then finally vanish, when the practical
> relations of everyday life offer to _man_ none but the
> perfectly intelligible and reasonable relations with
> regard to _his fellowmen_ and to Nature.

> The life-process of society, which is based on the
> process of material production, does not strip off
> its mystical veil until it is treated as production
> by freely associated _men_, and is consciously regulated
> by them in accordance with a settled plan... (28)

Now the point is not simply the one about exclusion
(although why it should not seem important to make this
puzzles me) but that mobilised here are as many questions

as there are (good) answers. Read with what we might call
the 'Late' writings of Marx (1871 onwards) we have the
possibility of seeing methodologies of socialist construction that do not smother difference(s) but celebrate
them in a recognition of the more complex, more rich, more
dense features that demarcate socialist construction from
other forms of sociation.

Against such feelings (if repressed) amongst the male
scions of the left, I am arguing for the benefits of
difference(s) in the organisational forms of resistance,
which often takes cultural forms precisely because the
terrain of politics is dominated by both 'official politics'
(with its rituals of systematic exclusion) and organisational forms of subordination of difference(s). These are
not a weakening of 'our (whose?) great movement' but a
practical critique of how far that movement had become
formed through homologies with bourgeois social relations,
and unfit to take part in founding society anew. But there
seem to me dangers in some ways in which terms like
'alliance' and 'broad front' are being practised. I have
always made a contrast between Popular Frontism and United
Frontism, whilst the former characteristically submerges
differences in a focussed struggle (one main enemy, lowest
common denominator programmes) the latter points to the
making explicit of the differences between allied groups
and the recognition of such differences in organisations
and programmes (complex nature of enemies, differentiated
programmes) and affords maximum spaces for the declaration
of divergences. Parties paradigmatically reduce their
organisations to the singularly uniform category of member
and characteristically have exhibited strong resistances
to understanding themselves as representing collectivities
(aside from that of some general uniform interest). What
the different forms of struggle, and their accomplishment
(however fragile) of new regimes of representation,
represent for me is the range of resources for - and, to
be sure, problems to overcome in - socialist construction.

Central here are all those issues around 'the personal'
which socialist construction (and 'actually existing
socialism') leaves aside. But, as others have argued, (29)
these are actually central to any new forms of 'the social'
since they concern needs. Fears, anxieties, despair,
chronic loneliness, as negativities (of a sort), and desires
for intimacy, pleasure, passion, as positivities (of a
sort!) are not going to disappear or be attended to by the
fifty-eighth subsection of the 12th Five Year Plan. If ever
there was a first instance of socialism, needs must be
somewhere in it.

All of these Notes turn on (turn to) the theory of the
subject, of the relations and the regulation of social
individuals. How sense is made or the limitations on its
making, (30) leads to the 'space' of the subject, who/what
does the making - whilst, of course, being made. Osgood's

255

two articles offer another metaphor - words may be
conservative, sentences radical (31) - meaningless elements
(in and of themselves) conventionalised into the symbolic
structures of the rules and grammar of the Obvious are
never finally closed. But those rules and that grammar has
first to be denaturalised and denied easy universality
(itself a giant labour one of whose facets is imperialism,
others can be seen as patriarchy, racism) before it can
be challenged. Structuralism or semiology are progressive
if, and only if, they are historical and materialist -
recognising, first, that the structures and codes are
historical products (whose origins in struggle are traceable
in their contemporary forms), and, second, that they are
material. The world is lived/experiened this or that
sidedly: reality (re)presents itself conformably with the
dominant material powers.

The mistake of much radical critique is to transfer the
truly revolutionary theories and practices of modernist
culture (denaturalising and deconstructing the regime of
representations) to the group of practitioners in and of
themselves, so that the avant garde artist (along with
others of los marginiladados, unincorporated, so it is
claimed) is the truly revolutionary figure. The cage is
closed too finally - Weberian despair can be found in such
otherwise contrasting thinkers as Marcuse and Foucault. This
revival of the artist (and/or the mad person) as the truly
revolutionary figure is an echo of the moment when
categories of special persons were made out of recognising
precisely the diversity of capacities and skills, the
artist as special kind of worker became a special kind of
person. It is the unpacking of that 'second nature' which
is now so necessary.

CONCLUSION

So the cultural revolution is about production in at least
three ways. It is about transforming production relations
(which begins by 'blowing up' the distinctions 'economic',
'political' and 'cultural' and recognising the necessary
inconclusiveness of production to human emancipation in its
specifically differentiated forms). It is about the
production and reproduction of social identities which
break from a regime of representations which establish a
difference(s) = disadvantage algebra. It is, thirdly, about
the materiality of culture: its absolutely basic qualities,
rather than its regional location as caused and secondary.
Capitalism is as much a regime of representations as it is
a set of (more real?) material relations - however much
language (hence the metaphors) and lives (a kind of
desperate silence of the unsayable or the endless average-
ness of discourse, as Barthes noted) (32) struggle to
represent and 'be' these distinctively. This is why (for
me, even before I knew anything at all, as it were) (33)
Marx's project is about the long cultural revolution of
humanity - that minimisation of constraint and extension of

human capacities for construction - which only seems sayable in the excess of utopianism or the viciously deforming and denying terms of some current (whenever that might be) depiction, such as the religious or the technological fixes. A reductionism which is always a matter of actually reducing human capacities, as much as a feature to be pinioned through the choloroforms and and formaldehydes (like butterflies) of theoretical analysis.

Raymond Williams' historical materialism has always striven to hold to this. It is well displayed in his 1978 essay 'Means of communication as means of production' in which

> perspective ... we can reasonably and practically achieve Marx's sense of communism as 'the production of the very form of communication'... Socialism is then not only the general 'recovery' of specifically alienated human capacities but is also, and much more decisively, the necessary institution of new and very complex communicative capacities and relationships. (34)

For that reason, as I argued previously, (35) cultural studies has to be strategically romantic (subjecting all that exists to a withering and rigorous critique) and tactically formalist. Yes, historically and materially, the regime of representations do indeed fix people as if these categories were all that they are or can become, but yes, equally, or with more force, not only could everyone be more alive and happy, but look (a second time, and with some care and compassion) they can generate a regime which would celebrate their differences differently. Imagine. (36)

ACKNOWLEDGEMENTS

Despite the single name attached to these Notes, there is clearly no sense - in my own epistemology - that they can be considered other than personally styled or shaped, both their energy and their content-and-form come from sustained collective work. Apart from various individuals, I would like to select a number of working collectives whose discussions have been significant in my work: the Socialism Discussion Group, the Representation/Education Workshop, the Adult Education Workshops and the Cultural Studies Network.

NOTES AND REFERENCES

(1) K. Marx, Grundrisse, Penguin, (1973), pp.264-5.
(2) R. Williams, 'Beyond actually existing socialism', Problems in Materialism and Culture, New Left Books, (1980), pp.261, 267.
(3) Michel Foucault, The History of Sexuality, vol.1, pp.105-6, quoted in Alan Sheridan, Michel Foucault:

The Will to Power, Tavistock, (1980), p.187, whose gloss about the 'machinery of alliance' is extremely relevant.

(4) Initial formulations by myself can be found in 'China: Thought reform for intellectuals', *Journal of Contemporary Asia*, (1974); 'Dichotomy is contradiction' and 'On Moral Regulation' in *Sociological Review*, (1975) and (1981) respectively. My work with others can be seen in (with Derek Sayer) 'Moral relations, class struggle, political economy', *Radical Philosophy*, 12, (1975); 'Hindess and Hirst', *Socialist Register*, (1978); 'How the law rules' in A. Hunt et al. (eds), *Law, Society, State*, Croom Helm, (1981); (with Harvie Ramsay and Derek Sayer) *Socialist Construction and Marxist Theory*, Macmillan/Monthly Review, (1978); *For Mao*, Macmillan/Humanities, (1979); 'The state as a relation of production', in P.R.D. Corrigan (ed), *Capitalism, State Formation and Marxist Theory*, Quartet/Urizen, (1980); 'Bolshevism and the USSR', *New Left Review*, 125, (1981); (with Paul Willis), 'Cultural form and class mediations', *Media, Culture and Society*, 2, 3 (1980); 'The orders of experience', *Social Text*, 3/4, (1981).

(5) This argument - summarised by the need for the simultaneous transformation of circumstances and selves - is one which runs throughout Marx's writings and received added emphasis in the 'Late Writings' from the late 1860s, which led to specific revisions in earlier texts, e.g. the *Manifesto of the Communist Party*. For one facet of this see Teodor Shanin's important introductory essay (as well as the text itself) to Haruki Wada, 'Karl Marx and Revolutionary Russia', *History Workshop Journal*, 12, (1981).

(6) On codes and coding see B. Bernstein, *Class, Codes and Control*, vols. 1-3, Routledge, and 'Codes, modalities and the process of cultural reproduction: a model' (1980, forthcoming); on classification see, for example, R.F. Allen and D. Reason (eds), *Classifications in their Social Context*, Academic Press, (1979) and generally E. Leach, *Culture and Communication*, Cambridge University Press, (1976). For some criticisms, see J. Corner, 'Codes and cultural analysis', *Media, Culture and Society*, 2, 1 (1980).

(7) For some preliminary thoughts on the 'curiousness' of 'the social' see P. and V. Corrigan, 'State formation and social policy before 1871' in N. Parry and others (eds), *Social Work, Welfare and the State*, Edward Arnold, (1979) and G. Deleuze 'The Rise of the Social', Foreword to J. Donzelot, *The Policing of Families*, Hutchinson/Random House, (1979), originally published in France (1977).

(8) I am drawing here from V.N. Volosinov, *Marxism and the Philosophy of Language*, Ink Links, (1979), and R. Williams, *Marxism and Literature*, Oxford University Press, (1977). For an excellent account of the 'literate code' see G. Steiner, 'The future of the book, I', *Times Literary Supplement*, 2 October, 1970,

reprinted as 'In a post-culture' in his book Extra-territorial, Penguin, (1975). Recent materials are analysed usefully by R. Fowler et al, Language and Control, (1979) and G. Kress and R. Hodge, Language as Ideology, Routledge, (1979).

(9)   F. Jameson, Marxism and Form, Princeton University Press, (1971), pp.343f. which draws upon T. Adorno, 'Society', Salmagundi, 10-11, (1969-70).

(10) For example, several of the texts in (4) above - especially the first two chapters of Capitalism, State Formation and Marxist Theory, and in State Formation and Moral Regulation in nineteenth century Britain: Sociological Investigations, Ph.D. thesis, University of Durham, (1977). Derek Sayer and I hope to produce a preliminary statement on the English State 1066 to 1966 shortly.

(11) Panorama, 21 January 1980. The speaker was one 'born into' one social class and now self-defined as 'living in' another.

(12) Preliminary discussions of this theme can be followed through the following: Richard Johnson, 'Edward Thompson, Eugene Genovese and Socialist-Humanist History', History Workshop Journal, no.6, (1978), and subsequent debate in that journal; 'Theories of Ideology/Histories of Culture' in M. Barrett and others, (eds), Ideology and Cultural Production, Croom Helm, (1979); contributions to J. Clarke and others (eds), Working Class Culture, Hutchinson, (1979). E.P. Thompson, 'The Poverty of Theory' in his book The Poverty of Theory, Merlin Press, (1978); chapters 47-9 in R. Samuel (ed), People's History and Socialist Theory, Routledge, (1980); P. Anderson, Arguments within English Marxism, NL Books, (1980); P. Corrigan, 'Against rabid idealism/For historical materialism' in B. Swai (ed), Towards Socialist Historiography, (forthcoming).

(13) I have argued against this progressivist illusion in 'Feudal relics or capitalist monuments?', Sociology, 11, (1977). The illusion has rather less effectivity in 1981 than 1971, I suspect.

(14) B. Taylor, (1980), 'Socialist feminism: Utopian or scientific', in R. Samuel (ed), People's History and Socialist Theory, Routledge.

(15) '"This Novel changes lives"...', Feminist Review, 5, (1980), p.63. This is an area of extensive debate; see for example, issues of the journals m/f and Feminist Review; L. Vogel, 'Questions on the women question' Monthly Review, 31, 2 (1979); H. Hartmann, 'The unhappy marriage of marxism and feminism', Capital and Class, no.8 (1979); M. Molyneux, 'Beyond the domestic labour debate', New Left Review, 116, (1979); and C. von Werhof, 'Notes on the relation between sexuality and economy', Review, 4, 1 (1980). Two recent books provide the complementary overviews: E. Wilson, Only Halfway to Paradise: Women in postwar Britain 1945-1968, Tavistock, (1980); M. Barrett, Women's Oppression Today: Problems in Marxist Feminist Analysis, NL Books,

(1980).

(16) Both in Sociological Review, 28, 3 (1980), August. The Prendergast and Prout article is very central for my own argument; see their conclusions.

(17) S. Prendergast and A. Prout, (1980), 'What will I do...? Teenage girls and the construction of motherhood', Sociological Review, 3, August, p.519. This and earlier quotes, my emphasis here.

(18) For example, D. Spender, Man Made Language, Routledge, (1980). See, especially, A. Coote, 'The nature of mantalk'; B. Page's reply, 'Sense and sensibility'; and A. Coote's response, all New Statesman, 2, 9 and 16 January, 1981.

(19) For example, Red Letters, 9 (1979); M. Jacobus (ed), Women, Writing and Writing about Women, Croom Helm, (1979); A. Kolodny, 'Some notes on defining a "feminist literary criticism"', and P. Schwenger, 'The masculine mode', both Critical Inquiry, 2, 1 (1975) and 5, 4 (1979) respectively. For film, see Camera Obscura, 1978 onwards, and, for example, C. Johnston, 'The subject of feminist film theory/practice', Screen, 21, 2 (1980) and references there.

(20) S. Heath, 'Difference', Screen, 19, 3 (1978), the quotations come from pp.52-3 and p.53 respectively. This article is really quite central to my argument here, but see also S. Heath, 'The turn of the subject', Cine Tracts, 2, 3/4 (1979) and E. Lyon 'Discourse and difference', Camera Obscura, 3/4 (1979).

(21) Heath, 'Difference', pp.65-6, and Heath, 'Turn of the Subject', p.45 respectively.

(22) Jameson, op.cit, 7, p.308.

(23) Jameson, op.cit, 7, p.341, his emphasis. The occasion of my own polemical excess was a seminar presentation with Derek Sayer at the Centre for Contemporary Cultural Studies on 'Overcoming the obvious', 19 May, 1978.

(24) This is a general discussion in the texts cited in (4) above; see, for example, Part I of For Mao.

(25) Ditto. See for example, the conclusions of both For Mao and Socialist Construction and Marxist Theory.

(26) Ditto again, see the text 'Bolshevism and the USSR', New Left Review, 125, (1981), especially the concluding section.

(27) Seminar on Feminism and Social Policy, Institute of Education, London, 25 November 1980.

(28) K. Marx, (1967), Capital, vol.1, Progress Publishers, Moscow, pp.78, 79-80, my emphases. The passages in the Penguin/NLR edition on pages 171, 173, have different words but they emphasise my point - e.g. in the first quotation 'a community of free individuals' becomes 'an association of free men'.

(29) For example, Stephan Feuchtwang, 'Socialist, feminist and anti-racial struggles', m/f, 4, (1980), esp. p.55.

(30) See Marx, op.cit, ch.1, section 4. I am very grateful to John Hayes for the benefit of his 'reading' of this and other parts of Capital, vol.1. I am also drawing here on the insights provided in Derek Sayer's Marx's

260

Method, Harvester, (1979), a useful critique of the now fashionable revival of orthodoxy enshrined in Gerry Cohen's work and its endorsement by, for example, NLR.

(31) C. Osgood, (1967), 'The words of power' and 'Radical sentences', *Listener*, 5 and 19, October. Cf. M. Cohen, *Sensible Words: Linguistic Practice in England 1640-1785*, Johns Hopkins, (1977); N. Bisseret, *Education, Class Language and Ideology*, Routledge, (1979).

(32) It is probably true (the cautious qualification is interesting, the fear of excessive affirmation?) that Barthes has 'reached' me more than any other writer (with the possible and different exception of Mao) and of Barthes' texts, *Roland Barthes by Roland Barthes*, Macmillan (1979), from which I could have provided quotations the length of this paper. Here I am thinking of his statements on *Jubilatory Discourse*:

> 'I love you, I love you', welling up from the body, irrepressible, repeated, does not this whole paroxysm of love's declaration conceal some *lack*? We would not need to speak this word, if it were not to obscure, as the squid with his ink, the failure of desire under the excess of its affirmation.

> Then are we forever doomed to the grim return of an *average* discourse?...

> There's no help for it: *I love you* is a demand: hence it can only embarrass anyone who receives it, except the Mother - and except God!

> Unless I should be justified in flinging out the phrase in the (improbable but ever-hoped-for) case when two *I love yous*, emitted in a single flash, would form a pure coincidence annihilating by this simultaneously the blackmail effects of one subject over the other: the demand would proceed to *levitate*. (*op.cit*, p.112)

(33) Aside from the excesses of poetry and fictive writing from 1959, I am thinking here of my (significantly all unpublished) attempts to grapple with this from 1970 onwards: *Concerning Consciousness* (1970), *Regarding Rationality* (1972) and *Illuminating Imagination* (1973) - all papers produced for/at the University of Durham; and, more recently, *Capitalism's Cultural Revolution* (1979), 'On not writing on the back of the new issue of postage stamps', (1979), circulated with the papers for the 13th History Workshop Conference, and 'mentioned' in the volume, *People's History and Socialist Theory*, *op.cit*, 10, p.407; and *For the Love of Theory*, (1980). From Barthes, *op.cit*, p.102, 'The image-system of solitude', I see these as attempts to work through/ beyond the 'great systems' and as he suggests (*op.cit*, p.110, 'The writing-machine') I now see very clearly how my 'work proceeds by conceptual infatuations, successive enthusiasms, perishable manias. Discourse advances by little fates, by amorous fits'.

(34) In R. Williams, *Problems in Materialism and Culture*, NL Books, (1980), ch.3. The quotations come from pp.57 and 63 respectively. I try to argue for Williams' historical materialism in my review of his *Politics and Letters*, in *Media, Culture and Society*, 2, (1980), pp.87-91.

(35) 'Cultural studies: some perspectives, or a look round the talent in the room', paper to the founding meeting of the Cultural Studies Network, 7 July, 1979, p.2. More accessible texts include those with Paul Willis, *ops.cit*, (4) above, and Michèle Barrett, Philip Corrigan, Annette Kuhn, Janet Wolff, *Ideology and Cultural Production*, Croom Helm, (1979), ch.1. Cf. M. Barrett, *op.cit*, (15) above, and review essay, *New Left Review*, 126, (1981); J. Wolff, *The Social Production of Art*, Macmillan, (1981) and A. Kuhn's forthcoming book on feminism and film (Routledge, 1982).

(36) I hope to focus the arguments here (and in all my other work) in *Capitalism's Cultural Production*, a book to be published by Macmillan. See also review essays on socialist construction and the audience in the text in *Sociological Review*, (1982); D. Sayer and P. Corrigan, 'Revolution against the State', *History Workshop Journal* (forthcoming) and P. Corrigan and D. Sayer, 'Marxist Theory and Socialist Construction in Historical Perspective', *Utafiti*, Dar Es Salaam (forthcoming).